WRIGHTSLAW

IDEA 2004
Parts A & B

With Commentary, Strategies, Cross-References

Peter W. D. Wright

Pamela Darr Wright

Harbor House Law Press, Inc.
Hartfield, Virginia 23071

Wrightslaw: IDEA 2004
By Peter W. D. Wright and Pamela Darr Wright

Wright, Peter W. D. and Pamela Darr Wright
Wrightslaw: IDEA 2004 / 1ˢᵗ ed.
p. cm.
13 Digit ISBN 978-1-892320-05-6
10 Digit ISBN 1-892320-05-3
1. Law — special education — United States. I. Title
2. Special education — parent participation — United States.

10 9 8 7 6 5 4 3 2 1

Printing History
Harbor House Law Press, Inc. issues new printings and new editions to keep our publications current. New printings include technical corrections and minor changes. New editions include major revisions of text and/or changes.
First Edition   September 2005.

Disclaimer
The purpose of this book is to educate and inform. While every effort has been made to make this book as accurate as possible, there may be mistakes, both typographical and in content. The authors and Harbor House Law Press, Inc. shall have neither liability nor responsibility to any person or entity with respect to and loss or damage caused, or alleged to be caused, directly or indirectly, by the information contained in this book. If you do not wish to be bound by the above, you may return the book to the publisher for a full refund. Every effort has been made to ensure that no copyrighted material has been used without permission. The authors regret any oversights that may have occurred and are happy to rectify them in future printings of this book.

When You Use a Self-Help Law Book
Law is always changing. The information contained in this book is general information and may or may not reflect current legal developments. This book is designed to provide general information in regard to the subject matter covered. It is sold with the understanding that the publisher and authors are not engaged in rendering legal or other professional services. For legal advice about a specific set of facts, you should consult with an attorney.

Bulk Purchases
Harbor House Law Press books are available at half price discounts for bulk purchases, academic sales or textbook adoptions.

For information, contact Harbor House Law Press, P. O. Box 480, Hartfield VA 23071. Please provide the title of the book, ISBN number, quantity, how the book will be used, and date needed.
Toll Free Phone Orders: (877) LAW IDEA or (877) 529-4332.
Toll Free Fax Orders: (800) 863-5348.
Internet Orders: http://www.harborhouselaw.com

ACKNOWLEDGEMENTS

This book is dedicated to the advocates and attorneys who represent children with disabilities and their families and who believe the promise made by the Individuals with Disabilities Education Act IDEA 30 years ago:

> ...that all children with disabilities have available to them a free appropriate public education that emphasizes special education and related services designed to meet their unique needs and prepare them for further education, employment, and independent living... (Section 1400(d)(1)(A))

We are grateful to members of the Council of Parent Attorneys and Advocates (COPAA) for their dedication, support, and determination to secure quality educational services for children with disabilities. (www.copaa.org)

We thank Wayne Steedman of the Baltimore law firm of Callegary and Steedman. Wayne shared his exceptional knowledge about special education law and practice as we wrote drafts of *Wrightslaw: IDEA 2004*. His recommendations about changes and clarifications led to a vastly improved publication.

We thank Meredith Warshaw, a special needs educational advisor for families with twice-exceptional children and Contributing Editor to the publication *2e: Twice-Exceptional Newsletter*. Meredith edited the manuscript and offered valuable suggestions about how to present information so it is more easily understood. Thanks to Meredith, *Wrightslaw: IDEA 2004* includes Appendices on topics that are of interest to readers.

We owe a special debt of gratitude to Sue Heath, research editor at Wrightslaw. Sue collected resources that will help readers use IDEA 2004 and No Child Left Behind to get quality services for children with disabilities.

WRIGHTSLAW: IDEA 2004

Wrightslaw: IDEA 2004 is an interim publication that includes the full text of Part A (General Provisions) and Part B (Assistance for Education of All Children with Disabilities) of the Individuals with Disabilities Education Act, with commentary, cross-references, and strategies. *Wrightslaw: IDEA 2004* includes several appendices and a bibliography of resources.

We expect to publish *Wrightslaw: Special Education Law, 2nd Edition* in 2006, after the U. S. Department of Education issues the final special education regulations and the U. S. Supreme Court issues a decision in *Schaffer v. Weast* during the 2005-2006 term. The proposed special education regulations were published in the Federal Register on June 21, 2005. The final regulations are expected to be issued in January or February, 2006, and will be included in *Wrightslaw: Special Education Law, 2nd Edition*.

When *Wrightslaw: Special Education Law, 2nd Edition* is published, *Wrightslaw: IDEA 2004* will go out of print.

Updates on IDEA: http://www.wrightslaw.com/idea/

Updates on *Schaffer v. Weast*: http://www.wrightslaw.com/news/05/schaffer.weast.htm

TABLE OF CONTENTS

Part B – Assistance for Education for All Children with Disabilities   48

Appendices   131

Glossary of Acronyms, Abbreviations and Terms   149

**THIS PAGE LEFT BLANK
FOR YOUR NOTES
AND
QUICK INDEX**

1 | INTRODUCTION

The reauthorized Individuals with Disabilities Education Act of 2004 is confusing to most parents, educators, and even to many attorneys. Ignorance of the law can be as damaging as the child's disability.

What are the requirements for highly qualified special education teachers? When do these requirements go into effect? How can special education teachers meet the highly qualified teacher requirements?

What does the Individuals with Disabilities Education Act say about child find? Special education services to children who attend private schools and charter schools? What does the law say about least restrictive environment, mainstreaming and inclusion?

What does the law say about evaluations, reevaluations and parental consent? What does the law say the use of discrepancy formulas and response to intervention to identify children with specific learning disabilities?

What does the law say about Individualized Education Programs (IEPs) and IEP teams? Transition plans? What does the law say about reviewing and revising IEPs? Who may be excused from IEP meetings and under what circumstances? What are "multi-year IEPs"?

What are early intervening services? Who is eligible for early intervening services? What does the law say about who must be tested on state and district assessments? Who is entitled to accommodations? Alternate assessments? Who makes these decisions?

What does the law say about independent educational evaluations? Parent access to educational records? Mediation? Parent notice? Prior written notice? Due process complaint notice? What are the new requirements and timelines for due process hearings? Resolution sessions? Qualifications for hearing officers? Attorneys' fees?

What does the law say about discipline? Manifestation Review Hearings? Who decides whether a child will be placed into an interim alternative educational setting, why, and for how long? What does the law say about Functional Behavioral Assessments and Behavior Intervention Plans?

Wrightslaw: IDEA 2004 will help you find answers to your questions in the reauthorized statute.

Wrightslaw: IDEA 2004 includes the full text of Part A (General Provisions) and Part B (Assistance for Education of All Children with Disabilities) of the Individuals with Disabilities Education Act, with commentary, cross-references, strategies, and tips. Part C (Infants and Toddlers with Disabilities), Part D (National Activities to Improve Education of Children with Disabilities) and Part E (National Center for Special Education Research) were omitted from *Wrightslaw: IDEA 2004*, but will be included in *Wrightslaw: Special Education Law, 2nd Edition.* [1]

---

[1] *Wrightslaw: Special Education Law, 2nd Edition,* is scheduled for publication in the winter of 2006.

WHO SHOULD READ THIS BOOK?

If you are the parent of a child with a disability, you represent your child's interests. To effectively advocate for your child, you need to learn about your child's rights, your rights and responsibilities under the Individuals with Disabilities Education Act and how the law will affect your child's education.

If you work as a teacher, related services provider, or administrator, the Individuals with Disabilities Education Act of 2004 will have a profound impact on you and your job. You may receive conflicting information and advice about this law. You need to know what the law actually says.

If you teach special education, school psychology, school administration, or education law courses, your students need to know how to find answers to their questions about what the law requires of them. If you are an employee of a state department of education, you may be responsible for investigating complaints, collecting data, or other activities to improve educational results. You need to know about the new requirements in IDEA 2004 that will affect your work.

If you are an attorney or advocate who represents children with disabilities, you need to have the Individuals with Disabilities Education Act of 2004 on your desk, in your briefcase and in your computer.

HOW THE BOOK IS ORGANIZED

The first chapter introduces you to the law, regulations, and caselaw. You learn about legal citations and how to do legal research. The next chapter is an Overview of IDEA 2004 that describes how the law is organized, highlights, and new requirements in IDEA 2004. The Table of Sections is in Chapter 4. Chapter 5 includes the complete text of Part A and Part B of the Individuals with Disabilities Education Act of 2004 with commentary, strategies, and cross-references.

Wrightslaw: IDEA 2004 includes appendices on several topics: Section 504 and IDEA; tuition reimbursement for private programs; discrepancy models and response to intervention to identify children with specific learning disabilities; a roadmap to the IEP; due process procedures and timelines; reading and research based instruction, including the federal definitions of reading, scientifically based reading research, diagnostic reading assessments, and the essential components of reading programs. A Glossary of Acronyms, Abbreviations and Terms and a bibliographic list of resources is at the end.

This book is set in Minion font. The authors used **bold type** to emphasize key words and phrases in the statute. Commentary and cross-references are in footnotes.

UPDATES

We expect to publish *Wrightslaw: Special Education Law, 2ⁿᵈ Edition* in 2006, after the U. S. Department of Education issues the federal special education regulations and the U. S. Supreme Court issues a decision in *Schaffer v. Weast* during the 2005-2006 term. When *Wrightslaw: Special Education Law, 2ⁿᵈ Edition* is published, *Wrightslaw: IDEA 2004* will go out of print.

Updates on IDEA: http://www.wrightslaw.com/idea/

Updates on *Schaffer v. Weast*: http://www.wrightslaw.com/news/05/schaffer.weast.htm

2 | LAW, REGULATIONS AND CASELAW

In this chapter, you will learn about law, regulations and caselaw. You will learn about legal research, legislative intent, and how law evolves through judicial interpretations.

Congress enacted the Individuals with Disabilities Education Improvement Act of 2004 (IDEA 2004) on November 17, 2004. The President signed the Act into law on December 3, 2004. The law went into effect on July 1, 2005.

When Congress reauthorized the Individuals with Disabilities Education Act in 2004, they made many significant changes to the law. **Purposes** is the mission statement of IDEA and the most important statute:

> ...to ensure that all children with disabilities have available to them a free appropriate public education that emphasizes special education and related services **designed to meet their unique needs** and prepare them for **further education**, employment and independent living . . . [and] to ensure that the rights of children with disabilities and parents of such children are protected... (Section 1400(d))

The authorization of any new law brings about a spate of interpretations and questions. Self-styled experts may spread wrong interpretations, misinformation and disinformation. Do not rely on the opinions of others or advice you may find in articles or at training programs.

To find answers to your questions about the Individuals with Disabilities Education Act, you need to do your own legal research. The intention of this book is to bridge the gap between the law and one's understanding of the legal language within it, in an accurate, objective manner and through direct reference to the law itself.

In this book, you will read the law. In the beginning, this is more difficult than reading articles about the law or having the law explained to you. As you continue to read, the law will begin to fit together in your mind. When you learn how the law is organized, you can find sections or regulations that are relevant to your questions.

STATUTES

Statutes are laws passed by federal, state and local legislatures. The original federal special education law was "The Education of All Handicapped Children Act of 1975." When Congress amended the law in 1990, they gave it a new name, "The Individuals with Disabilities Education Act." When Congress reauthorized the law in 2004, they renamed it again as "The Individuals with Disabilities Education Improvement Act of 2004." (IDEA 2004 is Public Law 108-446 and is cited as Pub. L. 108-446.)

Congress first publishes laws an "Act" in the *Statutes at Large,* then organizes laws by subject in the *United States Code* (U.S.C.) The Individuals with Disabilities Education Act is printed in the *Statutes at Large* and in the *United States Code.* The numbering system used to categorize an *Act* in the *Statutes at Large* is different from the system used in the *United States Code.*

The *United States Code* has fifty subject classifications called Titles. For example, Title 20 is about education, Title 26 is the Internal Revenue Code, and Title 42 is about public health and welfare. In each title, laws are indexed and assigned section numbers. The Individuals with Disabilities Education Act is cited as 20 U.S.C. § 1400, *et. seq.* Statutes published in the *Statutes at Large* have sections (section 1, 2, 3, 4, etc.) and may have subsections ((a), (b), (c), (d), etc.).

The "Act" begins with Section 600. When the Act is published in the *United States Code* (U.S.C.), the numbers change. IDEA 2004 is in Title 20 of the *United States Code,* beginning with Section 1400. For example, "Definitions" are in Section 1401 of the *United States Code* (cited as 20 U.S.C. § 1401) and are in Section 602 of "the Act."

Legal Citations

References to law are called legal citations. Legal citations are standardized formats that explain where you will find a particular statute, regulation, or case. When you see a legal citation such as 20 U. S. C. § 1400 *et. seq.*, the term "*et. seq.*" means beginning at Section 1400 and continuing thereafter.

In the *United States Code*, "Findings and Purposes" are in Section 1400 of Title 20. The legal citation for Findings and Purposes is 20 U.S.C. § 1400. You may refer to Findings and Purposes as "20 U. S. C. § 1400" or "Section 1400."

In *Wrightslaw: IDEA 2004*, legal citations will not include the Title. For example, the full legal citation for the law about IEPs is 20 U.S.C. § 1414(d). In most cases, the authors will use a simpler format for citations, such as Section 1414 and Section 1414(d).

Purposes

"Purposes" at Section 1400(d) is the most important section in the law is because it describes the overall purpose of the law. If you have questions about a specific section in the Individuals with Disabilities Education Act, re-read Purposes to see how the particular section fits into the overall purpose of the law.

Other Federal Statutes

Other important federal acts and statutes that affect educational issues are:

- The No Child Left Behind Act of 2001 begins at 20 U. S. C. § 6301, *et. seq.*
- Section 504 of the Rehabilitation Act of 1973, begins at 29 U. S. C. §794, *et. seq.*
- The Family Educational and Rights and Privacy Act, begins at 20 U. S. C. § 1232, *et. seq.*

States must ensure that their statutes and regulations are consistent with the *United States Code* (U. S. C.) and the *Code of Federal Regulations* (C. F. R.). While state statutes and regulations may provide more rights than federal laws, they cannot provide fewer rights than guaranteed by federal law. If a state law or regulation is in direct conflict with a federal law, the federal law controls, pursuant to the "Supremacy Clause" of the U. S. Constitution.

REGULATIONS

Regulations clarify and explain the United States Code. A regulation must be consistent with the United States Code and has the same force of law.

The U. S. Department of Education develops and publishes the federal special education regulations. Before the Department publishes these regulations, the agency must publish the proposed regulations in the Federal Register (F. R.) and solicit comments from citizens about the proposed regulations. The final special education regulations will be published in Volume 34, Part 300 of the Code of Federal Regulations. For example, the legal citation for the IDEA regulations is 34 C. F. R. § 300.

On June 11, 2005, the Department of Education issued the proposed regulations for public comment. The final regulations are expected to be issued in January or February 2006, and will be included in *Wrightslaw: Special Education Law, 2nd Edition*.

JUDICIAL INTERPRETATIONS AND CASELAW

Evolving Caselaw

Caselaw is always changing and evolving. The Individuals with Disabilities Education Act will continue to evolve and be re-defined by caselaw.

Special education litigation usually starts with a special education due process hearing. A party that loses at the due process / review hearing level, can appeal to state court or federal court. State courts and federal courts are different judicial systems. Once a case is filed in state or federal court, it remains within that system (i.e., cases filed in state court remain within the state court system while cases filed in U. S. District Courts generally remain in the federal court system.)

When a state court issues a decision, the decision may be appealed to a higher state court. For example, a Virginia trial judge's interpretation of a statute is governed by earlier rulings from the highest state court in Virginia. The highest state court is usually the state Supreme Court. A losing party in state court cannot appeal to the federal court, but must follow the appellate process outlined in that state's judicial system.

Federal judges are bound by rulings of their Circuit Court of Appeals. Since Virginia, Maryland, North Carolina, South Carolina, and West Virginia are in the Fourth Circuit, a U. S. District Court judge in any of those states must follow rulings from the United States Court of Appeals for the Fourth Circuit. The judge is not required to follow legal rulings from other circuits although these opinions may be cited as persuasive authority.

All state and federal courts must follow rulings by the U. S. Supreme Court. If the U. S. Supreme Court issues a ruling with which Congress disagrees, Congress may enact a new law to change the impact of a decision of the Supreme Court.

Judicial Interpretations

Compelling facts may cause a judge to want to rule in one direction, even if the ruling is contrary to current caselaw. The decision-maker who faces this situation often finds and uses unique facts in the case to create an exception to general caselaw. These "exceptions to the rule" decisions cause the body of law to change and grow.

How a court interprets a law or regulation may be dictated by a single word (e.g., "may " instead of "shall"). When Congress wants to pass a bill but cannot agree on the wording of a statute, they often use vague compromise language. Confusing words or phrases often lead to litigation. For example, in special education law, the term "appropriate education" has been litigated for more than twenty-five years.

Over time, when courts agree on the same interpretation, a majority rule evolves. A minority rule may also develop. If a majority rule does not develop, the legal issue becomes more confusing. U. S. Courts of Appeal in different circuits around the country often issue conflicting rulings. This leads to a "split among circuits." When there is a split among circuits, the U. S. Supreme Court may agree to hear the case to clarify the issue and resolve the split among the circuits.

In *Schaffer v. Weast*, the issue is who has the "burden of proof" in a special education case – the parents or the school?[2] The U. S. Courts of Appeal were split. The U. S. Supreme Court will probably issue a decision in *Schaffer v. Weast* in November or December 2006.

Legislative Intent

Judges look at legislative intent when analyzing the meaning of a statute. When you read decisions by the United States Supreme Court, you will see that the Justices often discuss legislative history and legislative intent in their decisions. Legislative intent is usually based on Committee Reports, transcripts of debate in the *Congressional*

---

[2] For Updates on *Schaffer v. Weast*, go to www.wrightslaw.com/news/05/schaffer.weast.htm

Record and other sources. You can find many of these documents and other legislative information at http://thomas.loc.gov/

Legal Interpretations

Law is subject to different interpretations. Attorneys and judges will interpret a section of the law differently, depending on their perspectives. If you read an article about special education law, the interpretations and conclusions are likely to represent the author's opinions. If you read the law and regulations on your own, you will form your own interpretations and conclusions about the law and impact it is likely to have on you.

LEGAL RESEARCH

When you research a legal issue, you should study three types of law:

- United States Code
- State and Federal Regulations
- Judicial decisions and case law

If you have questions about a legal issue, read the United States Code section related to your issue. Next, read the proposed regulation[3] that discusses or clarifies your issue. Expect to read the Code and regulation several times. Then find out if there are any cases about your legal issue.[4]

If you find cases about your issue, read the earlier decisions first, then tackle the recent decisions. If you know a case was appealed, read the decision that was appealed and reversed (or appealed and affirmed). When you read earlier decisions, you will learn how law in that area is evolving.

For every position taken by one court that the law is clear, another court is likely to have interpreted the law differently and arrived at a different opinion. This is the nature of law.

IN SUMMATION

In this chapter, you learned about law, regulations and caselaw. You learned about legal research, legislative intent, judicial interpretations and how law evolves. The next chapter, ***An Overview of IDEA 2004,*** describes how the law is organized, highlights, and new requirements in the law.

---

[3] On June 21, 2005, the U.S. Department of Education issued proposed regulations for a 75-day public comment period. After the comments are reviewed and proposed regulations revised, Final Regulations will be issued. The final regulations are expected in January or February, 2006 and will be included in ***Wrightslaw: Special Education Law, 2nd Edition***, which will replace this book.

[4] Selected special education cases are in the Wrightslaw Caselaw Library at http://www.wrightslaw.com/caselaw.htm

Other good sources of legal information are Findlaw.com and Versuslaw.com. Many cases are not available online and must be located in a court or academic law library.

3 | AN OVERVIEW OF IDEA 2004

The Individuals with Disabilities Education Act of 2004 includes significant changes from the previous authorization, IDEA 97. This chapter will provide you with an overview of the law, how the law is organized, and new requirements in the law.

The Individuals with Disabilities Education Act of 2004 is divided into five parts:

> Part A – General Provisions (Sections 1400 – 1409)
>
> Part B – Assistance for Education of All Children with Disabilities (Sections 1411 – 1419)
>
> Part C – Infants and Toddlers with Disabilities (Sections 1431 – 1444)
>
> Part D – National Activities to Improve Education of Children with Disabilities (Sections 1450-1482)
>
> Part E – National Center for Special Education Research

Parents, advocates, attorneys, and educators will refer most often to the following sections:

> Section 1400 – Findings and Purposes
>
> Section 1401 – Definitions
>
> Section 1412 – State Responsibility (the Catch-all Statute)
>
> Section 1414 – Evaluations, Eligibility, Individual Education Programs, Educational Placements
>
> Section 1415 – Procedural Safeguards

PART A – GENERAL PROVISIONS

Part A of the Individuals with Disabilities Education Act of 2004 includes Sections 1400 through Section 1409 of Title 20 of the United States Code (U.S.C.). The most important section in the law is Section 1400(d) that describes the Purposes of the law. Section 1401 includes the legal definitions in alphabetical order. Section 1403 advises that states are not immune from suit if they violate IDEA. Section 1406 describes the requirements and timelines for the federal special education regulations. Section 1408 is a new section about paperwork reduction. (Note: There is no Section 1410.)

SECTION 1400: FINDINGS & PURPOSES

Findings in Section 1400(c) describe the events and findings that led Congress to pass the Education for All Handicapped Children Act of 1975 (Public Law 94-142) which is now the Individuals with Disabilities Education Improvement Act of 2004.

In Findings, Congress described obstacles to implementation of the law:

> …implementation of this title has been impeded by low expectations, and an insufficient focus on applying replicable research on proven methods of teaching and learning for children with disabilities. (Section 1400(c)(4))

Congress reported that "over 30 years of research and experience" demonstrates that special education would be more effective by:

> …having high expectations for such children and ensuring their access to the general education curriculum in regular classrooms, to the maximum extent possible…to meet the challenging expectations that have been established for all children; and be prepared to lead productive and independent lives to the maximum extent possible. (Section 1400(c)(5))

The language in Findings about meeting the "developmental goals" and "challenging expectations that have been established for nondisabled children" so children will "be prepared to lead productive and independent adult lives" is new.

Purposes is the most important statute in the law:

> to ensure that all children with disabilities have available to them a free appropriate public education that emphasizes special education and related services designed to meet their **unique needs and prepare them for further education, employment and independent living**" and "to ensure that the rights of children with disabilities and parents of such children are protected… (Section 1400(d))

The phrase "further education" is new, as is the increased emphasis on "effective transition services to promote successful post-school employment or education."

When you have questions about a term or section in the law, re-read Section 1400, especially Purposes in Section 1400(d). This will help you understand how the term or the section fits into the overall purpose of the law. When the U.S. Supreme Court issues a ruling, they discuss the purpose of the law.

SECTION 1401: DEFINITIONS

Six new definitions were added to IDEA 2004: core academic subjects, highly qualified teacher, homeless children, limited English proficient, universal design, and ward of the state. Read the definitions carefully, especially the definitions of child with a disability, free appropriate public education, highly qualified teacher, least restrictive environment, IEP, related services, special education, and specific learning disability.

Highly Qualified

The requirements for highly qualified special educators are new and bring IDEA into conformity with the No Child Left Behind Act. A "highly qualified teacher" has full State certification (no waivers), holds a license to teach, and meets the State's requirements. The requirements are somewhat different for new and veteran teachers, for elementary, middle school, and high school teachers, for teachers of multiple subjects, and for teachers who teach to alternate standards. (Section 1401(10)(B))

Special educators who teach core academic subjects must meet the highly qualified teacher requirements in NCLB and must demonstrate competence in the core academic subjects they teach. Special educators who do not provide instruction in core academic subjects do not have to meet the highly qualified teacher requirements.

States can develop a method by which teachers can demonstrate competence in the subjects they teach. This method must be based on a "high objective uniform state standard of evaluation" (HOUSSE) and must provide an objective way to determine if teachers have subject matter knowledge in the core academic subjects they teach. (Section 1401(10)(D))

Transition Services

The definition of transition services was changed to a "results-oriented process" that improves "the academic and functional achievement of the child with a disability" and facilitates the child's transition from school to employment and further education. Transition services must be based on the individual child's needs, including the child's strengths. (Section 1401(34)) The IEP requirements for transition also changed.

Paperwork Reduction

The section about "paperwork reduction" is new in IDEA 2004. The Department of Education may grants waivers to 15 States for pilot programs to reduce paperwork and other "non-instructional burdens." These pilot programs may not waive procedural requirements under Section 1415. Two years after IDEA is enacted, the Secretary must report to Congress on the effectiveness of these waivers. (Section 1408)

PART B – ASSISTANCE FOR EDUCATION OF ALL CHILDREN WITH DISABILITIES

Part B governs special education and related services for children between the ages of 3 and 21 and includes Section 1411 through Section 1419 of Title 20 of the United States Code.

For most readers, the most important statutes in Part B are Section 1412, Section 1414, and Section 1415. Section 1412 includes child find, least restrictive environment, unilateral placements, reimbursement, and state and district assessments. Section 1414 describes requirements for initial evaluations, reevaluations, parental consent, eligibility, IEPs, and educational placements.

Section 1415 describes the procedural safeguards designed to protect the rights of children and their parents. These safeguards include the right to examine educational records and obtain an independent educational evaluation, and the legal requirements for prior written notice, procedural safeguard notice, due process complaint notice, due process hearings, resolution sessions, mediation, attorney's fees, and discipline.

Risk Pools for High-Need Children

IDEA 2004 includes a new optional Local Educational Agency (LEA) Risk Pool. (Section 1411(e)(3)) To help school districts meet the "needs of high need children with disabilities," states may reserve funds for "risk pools." States must define a "high need child with a disability" and create a State Plan for the high cost funds. These funds may not be used for litigation expenses and may not limit the child's right to a free appropriate public education or authorize the state or school district to "establish a limit on what may be spent" to educate a child with a disability.

SECTION 1412: STATE ELIGIBILITY ("CATCH-ALL STATUTE")

Section 1412 is called the "Catch-All" statute because it includes diverse topics: child find, least restrictive environment, transition to preschool programs, equitable services for children in private schools, unilateral placements, tuition reimbursement, and assessments.

All children who are eligible for special education services under IDEA are entitled to a free, appropriate public education (FAPE), including children who have been suspended or expelled. (Section 1412(a)(1)(A)) To remedy evaluations that have led to over-representation of minority children in special education, the law requires that evaluations be administered in the child's native language or mode of communication and that "no single procedure shall be the sole criterion." (Section 1412(a)(6)(B))

Child Find

Child find requires school districts to identify, locate, and evaluate **all** children with disabilities and determine which children are and are not receiving special education and related services. IDEA 2004 was amended to include children who are homeless, wards of the state, and children who attend private schools. School districts must report data about the number of children who are evaluated, found eligible and provided services. These requirements apply to children who attend private schools in the district. (Section 1412(a)(10)(A)(ii))

Children Who Attend Private Schools

The law includes new requirements about equitable participation of children who attend private schools and consultation between public and private school officials. The consultation process includes written affirmation, compliance, and complaints by private schools to the state. Children who attend private schools are entitled to equitable services. Special education and related services may be provided on the premises of private religious schools. (Section 1412(a)(10))

Under "Child Find," it appears that school districts are responsible for locating and identifying children with disabilities who attend private schools in the district, even if the child's parents do not live in the district. However, existing caselaw may lead to rulings that do not require school districts to accept responsibility for special education services to out-of-district children who attend private schools in the district. The child's parents and original school district may be responsible.

Tuition Reimbursement

The law about reimbursement for parental placements in private schools is unchanged. If the parent removes the child from a public school program and places the child into a private program, the parent may be reimbursed for the costs of the private program if a hearing officer or court determines that the public school did not offer a free, appropriate public education (FAPE) "in a timely manner." (Section 1412(a)(10)(C))

Personnel Qualifications

The No Child Left Behind Act describes the requirements for highly qualified teachers and provides timelines so teachers of core academic subjects meet these requirements by the end of the 2005-2006 school year. When Congress reauthorized the Individuals with Disabilities Education Act, they clarified that the highly qualified teacher requirements apply to special education teachers.

All teachers of core academic subjects, including special educators, must be highly qualified. Core academic subjects are "English, reading or language arts, mathematics, science, foreign languages, civics and government, economics, arts, history, and geography." The definition of "core academic subjects" is in Section 1401(4).

IDEA 2004 requires states to take measurable steps "to recruit, hire, train, and retain highly qualified personnel to provide special education and related services." (Section 1412(c)(14))

Participation in State and District Assessments

The No Child Left Behind Act requires that schools teach **all children**, including children with disabilities, to proficiency in reading, math and science by 2014. All students in grades 3 through 8 will participate in the annual proficiency testing of reading and math. Annual science assessments are required by 2007.

In IDEA 2004, the language about who will participate in assessments was changed to "**All** children with disabilities are included in **all** general State and districtwide assessment programs…with appropriate accommodations, where necessary and as indicated in their respective individualized education programs." (Section 1412(c)(16)(A))

For the child with a disability who has an Individualized Education Plan (IEP), the IEP **shall** include:

a statement of any individual appropriate accommodations that are necessary to measure the academic achievement and functional performance of the child on State and districtwide assessments… [and]

if the IEP Team determines that the child shall take an **alternate assessment** on a particular State or districtwide assessment of student achievement, a statement of why…the child cannot participate in the regular assessment; and… [why] the particular alternate assessment selected is appropriate for the child… (Section 1414(d)(1)(A)(i)(VI))

IDEA 2004 includes new requirements for **accommodation guidelines** and **alternate assessments**. (Section 1412(a)(16)) States and districts must issue reports to the public about state and district assessments, alternate assessments, and the performance of children with disabilities on assessments. (Section 1412(a)(16)(D))

Over-Identification of Minority Children

"Overidentification and Disproportionality" is new in IDEA 2004. Congress found that African-American children are identified with mental retardation and emotional disturbances at far greater rates than white children. Schools with predominately white students and teachers place disproportionately high numbers of minority students into special education. (Section 1400(c)(12)(C)) States must develop policies and procedures to correct these problems. (Section 1412(c)(24))

Mandatory Medication Prohibited

School personnel are prohibited from requiring a child to obtain a prescription for a controlled substance (i.e., Ritalin, Adderal) to:

- attend school

- receive an evaluation

- receive special education services

SECTION 1413: LOCAL EDUCATIONAL AGENCY ELIGIBILITY

Section 1413 includes requirements for local school districts and charter schools about:
- instructional materials
- records of migratory children
- early intervening services
- services to charter school students
- access to instructional materials

Early Intervening Services

Early intervening services are new in IDEA 2004. Early intervening services focus on "proven methods of teaching and learning" based on "replicable research." (Section 1413(f)) School districts may use early intervening funds for:
- Academic and behavioral assistance for students who are not identified as needing special education services

- Professional development so teachers have the knowledge and skills to deliver scientifically based academic instruction and literacy instruction

- Educational evaluations, services and supports, scientifically based literacy instruction for students

SECTION 1414: EVALUATIONS, ELIGIBILITY, INDIVIDUALIZED EDUCATION PROGRAMS, EDUCATIONAL PLACEMENTS

Section 1414 includes requirements for initial evaluations; reevaluations; eligibility; Individualized Education Programs; IEP team members; developing, reviewing and revising IEPs; and educational placements.

Initial Evaluations

Parents, departments of education, state agencies, and school staff may request an initial evaluation. The school must obtain parental consent before conducting the initial evaluation. If the parent does not consent to an evaluation, the district may pursue a due process hearing against the parent.

The initial evaluation and eligibility must be completed within **60 days** of receiving parental consent. (Section 1414(a)(1))

Parental consent for an evaluation is not consent for the child to receive special education services. The school must obtain informed parental consent before providing special education services. If the parent does not consent to special education services, the district may **not** pursue a due process hearing against the parent. If the parent refuses consent for services, the district has not violated the IDEA, and is not required to convene an IEP meeting or develop an IEP for the child. (Section 1414(a)(1)(D))

Reevaluations

The school is not required to reevaluate a child more often than once a year, unless the parent and school agree to more frequent evaluations. The school shall evaluate at least every three years, unless the parent and school agree that a reevaluation is unnecessary. The school must reevaluate if changing educational needs warrant a reevaluation **or** if the child's parent or teacher request a reevaluation. (Section 1414(a)(2))

Requirements for Assessments

The school must ensure that assessments "are provided and administered in the language and form most likely to yield accurate information on what the child knows and can do academically, developmentally, and functionally…" (Section 1414(b))

When a child transfers to a new school, the receiving school must complete assessments "as expeditiously as possible to ensure prompt completion of full evaluations." The language about assessing children "in all areas of suspected disability" and that assessments shall provide relevant information to determine the child's educational needs did not change. (Section 1414(b)(3))

Eligibility and Educational Needs

"Determination of Eligibility" was changed to "Determination of Eligibility and Educational Need." A team of qualified professionals and the parent will determine "whether the child is a child with a disability . . . **and the educational needs of the child …**" The child may not be found eligible if the child's problems are caused by "lack of appropriate instruction in reading, including in the essential components of reading instruction" and/or "lack of instruction in math." (Section 1414(b)(5))

The school shall give the parents copies of the evaluation report and documentation of eligibility. (Section 1414(b)(4))

Specific Learning Disabilities

The law has moved away from using discrepancy models to identify children with specific learning disabilities. The school is not required to determine if the child has a severe discrepancy between achievement and intellectual ability to find that the child has a specific learning disability and needs special education services. The school may use **response to intervention** to determine if the child responds to scientific, research-based intervention as part of the evaluation process. (Section 1414(b)(6))

Additional Requirements for Evaluations and Reevaluations

Information from evaluations and reevaluations will be used to determine "the educational needs of the child" and "the present levels of academic achievement and related developmental needs of the child." The school must review evaluations and information provided by the parents. (Section 1414(c)(1))

IDEA 2004 changed the "Additional Requirements for Evaluations and Reevaluations" so they conflict with the requirement that schools "shall evaluate at least every three years." If the IEP team and other qualified professionals decide they do not need additional data to determine if the child is eligible or the child's educational needs, the school can notify the parents that they do not intend to reevaluate. The school must provide the reasons for their decision. Under these circumstances, the parent must specifically request a reevaluation. (Section 1414(c)(4))

The school must evaluate the child before terminating eligibility. The school is not required to evaluate when the child graduates from high school with a regular diploma or "ages out" of special education. (Section 1414(c)(5)) If the child graduates with a regular diploma or is no longer eligible because of age, the school must provide the child with a summary of "academic and functional performance" and recommendations about how to help the child meet postsecondary goals. (Section 1414(c)(5)(B))

Individualized Education Programs (IEPs)

Congress made changes to Individualized Education Programs (IEPs) in several areas, including:

- content of IEPs
- IEP team members
- IEP meeting attendance
- consolidated meetings
- review and revision of IEPs
- alternate means of participating in meetings

Content of IEPs

Some requirements for the contents of IEPs changed. Others remained the same.[5]

Present Levels of Performance. Previously, IEPs were required to include "a statement of the child's present levels of educational performance…" Now, the child's IEP must include "a statement of the child's present levels of academic achievement and functional performance…" Present levels of academic achievement and functional performance are objective data from assessments.

Annual Goals. Previously, IEPs were required to include a "statement of measurable annual goals, including benchmarks or short-term objectives." IDEA 2004 eliminated the requirements for "benchmarks and short-term objectives" in IEPs, except that the IEPs of children who take alternate assessments must include "a description of benchmarks or short-term objectives." IDEA 2004 added new language about "academic and functional goals." IEPs must now include "a statement of measurable annual goals, including academic and functional goals…"

Educational Progress. Previously, the law required IEPs to include a statement about how the child's progress toward the annual goals would be measured, how the child's parents would be regularly informed about "their child's progress toward the annual goals," and whether the child's progress was sufficient. Now, the child's IEP must include "a description of how the child's progress toward meeting the annual goals…will be measured and when periodic reports on the progress the child is making toward meeting the annual goals (such as through the use of quarterly or other periodic reports, concurrent with the issuance of report cards) will be provided."

Special Education and Related Services. IDEA 2004 includes important new language about research-based instruction. The child's IEP must include "a statement of the special education and related services and supplementary aids and services, based on **peer-reviewed research**[6] to the extent practicable, to be provided to the child…and a statement of the program modifications or supports for school personnel…"

Accommodations and Alternate Assessments. IDEA 2004 contains new language about "individual appropriate accommodations" on state and district testing and new requirements for alternate assessments. The child's IEP must include:

> …a statement of any individual appropriate accommodations that are necessary to measure the academic achievement and functional performance of the child on State and districtwide assessments…

---

[5] See **Appendix D: A Roadmap to the Individualized Education Program (IEP)**.

[6] See **Appendix F: Reading and Research Based Instruction**.

...if the IEP Team determines that the child shall take an alternate assessment on a particular State or districtwide assessment of student achievement, a statement of why (AA) the child cannot participate in the regular assessment; and (BB) the particular alternate assessment selected is appropriate for the child...

Transition. Congress made extensive changes to the legal requirements for transition. Previously, the law required "a statement of transition services needs" (beginning at age 14) and "a statement of needed transition services for the child" (beginning at age 16). The statement of transition services needs at age 14 was eliminated. Now the first IEP after the child is 16 (and updated annually) must include:

...appropriate measurable postsecondary goals based upon age appropriate transition assessments related to training, education, employment, and, where appropriate, independent living skills...and the transition services (including courses of study) needed to assist the child in reaching these goals. (Section 1414(d)(1)(A))

IEP Meeting Attendance

A member of the IEP team may be excused from attending an IEP meeting if the member's area of curriculum or service will not be discussed or modified and if the parent and school agree. A member of the IEP team may also be excused if the member's area of curriculum or service will be discussed or modified, if the member submits a written report to the parent and the IEP team in advance, and if the parent provides written consent. (Section 1414(d)(1)(C))

In State and Out-of State Transfers

If a child transfers to a district in the same state, the receiving school must provide comparable services to those in the sending district's IEP until they develop and implement a new IEP. If a child transfers to another state, the receiving district must provide comparable services to those in the sending district's IEP until they complete an evaluation and create a new IEP. (Section 1414(d)(2)(C))

Developing the IEP

In developing the IEP, the IEP team **shall** consider:

- the child's strengths
- the parent's concerns for enhancing the child's education
- the results of the initial evaluation or most recent evaluation
- the child's academic, developmental, and functional needs (Section 1414(d)(3)(A))

The IEP team shall consider special factors for children:

- whose behavior impedes learning
- who have limited English proficiency
- who are blind or visually impaired
- who are deaf or hard of hearing (Section 1414(d)(3)(B))

Reviewing and Revising the IEP

The IEP must be reviewed at least once a year to determine if the child is achieving the annual goals. The IEP team must revise the IEP to address:

- any lack of expected progress
- results of any reevaluation
- information provided by the parents
- anticipated needs (Section 1414(d)(4)(A))

IDEA 2004 changed the process by which IEPs can be amended or modified. If the parent and school agree to amend or modify the IEP, they may revise the IEP by agreement without convening an IEP meeting. The team must create a written document that describes the changes or modifications in the IEP and note that, by agreement of the parties, an IEP meeting was not held. (Section 1414(d)(3)(D))

Multi-Year IEPs

Fifteen states may request approval to implement optional "comprehensive, multi-year IEPs" for periods of no longer than three years. IEP review dates must be based on "natural transition points." Parents have the right to opt-out of this program. The parent of a child served under a multi-year IEP can request a review of the IEP without waiting for the "natural transition point." (Section 1414(d)(5))

Educational Placements

The law about educational placements is in Section 1414(e). Parents are members of the team that decides the child's placement. The decision about the child's placement cannot be made until after the IEP team, which includes the parent, reaches consensus about the child's needs, program, and goals.

Although the law is clear on this issue, the child's "label" often drives decisions about services and placement, leading school personnel to determine the child's placement before the IEP meeting. These unilateral actions prevent parents from "meaningful participation" in educational decision-making for their child. When Congress added this provision to the law in 1997, they sent a message to school officials that unilateral placement decisions are illegal.

Alternative Ways to Participate in Meetings

School meetings do not have to be face-to-face. IEP and placement meetings, mediation meetings, and due process (IEP) resolution sessions may be convened by conference calls or videoconferences. (Section 1414(f))

SECTION 1415: PROCEDURAL SAFEGUARDS

Section 1415 describes the safeguards designed to protect the rights of children with disabilities and their parents including the right to:

- participate in all meetings about their child
- examine all educational records
- obtain an independent educational evaluation (IEE) of the child
- written notice when school proposes to change or refuses to change program
- mediation
- due process hearing

The Procedural Safeguards also describe legal requirements for notices and timelines that apply to parents and school districts:

- Prior Written Notice
- Due Process Complaint Notice
- Amended Complaint Notice
- Mediation
- Due Process Hearings
- Appeals

Procedural Safeguards Notice

The Procedural Safeguards Notice provides parents with specific information about their rights and protections under the law, including the right to an independent educational evaluation (IEE), prior written notice, consent, access to educational records, notice of the time period (**statute of limitations**) within which "**to make a**

complaint," mediation, due process, current educational placement / stay put, discipline, reimbursement for private placements, and attorneys' fees. (Section 1415(d))

Prior Written Notice (PWN)

If the school proposes to change or refuses to change the child's identification, evaluation, educational placement, or other matters related to providing FAPE, the school is required to provide the parent with detailed Prior Written Notice (PWN). (Section 1415(c)(1)) This Notice must:

- describe the action proposed or refused
- explain why the school proposed or refused to take action
- describe each evaluation procedure, assessment, record, or report used as a basis for the proposed or refused action
- provide sources the parent can contact to obtain assistance
- describe other options considered and why these options were rejected
- describe the factors that were relevant to the school's proposal or refusal

Mediation

Mediation is a confidential process that allows parties to resolve disputes without litigation. The mediator helps each party express their views and positions, and helps the other party understand these views and positions. A successful mediation requires both parties to discuss their views and differences frankly, without the presence of lawyers. Before entering into mediation, both parties should understand their rights and the law. A due process hearing does not have to be pending to request mediation. (Section 1415 (e))

Legally Binding Written Settlement Agreements

Legally binding written settlement agreements are new. Previously, when a party breached a mediation agreement, the other party had to enforce the agreement by filing suit under a breach of contract theory, usually in state court. Now the power of federal courts can be used to ensure that settlement agreements are honored. (Section 1415(e)(2)(F))

DUE PROCESS

Most pre-trial procedures and timelines for due process hearings are new. Section 1415(c)(2) includes the requirements and timelines for the Due Process Complaint Notice and the Amended Complaint Notice.[7]

Due Process Complaint Notice

If the parent or school requests a special education due process hearing, the party that requests the hearing must provide the other party with a "**Due Process Complaint Notice**." (Section 1415(b)(7)) The Due Process Complaint Notice must include identifying information about the child, the nature of the problem, facts, and proposed resolution. The party that requests the due process hearing may not have a hearing until they provide this notice. (Section 1415(c)(2))

Pre-Trial Procedures and Timelines

If the school did not provide the parents with Prior Written Notice previously, the school must provide the Notice within 10 days. The non-complaining party must send a response to the complaint that addresses the issues within 10 days.

---

[7] See **Appendix E: Due Process Procedures and Timelines** for specific information about these issues.

If the notice is insufficient, the receiving party must complain to the Hearing Officer within 15 days. (Section 1415(c)(2)(C)) This requirement is similar to the "12(b)(6)" Motion to Dismiss proceeding in the Federal Rules of Civil Procedure (FRCP). (Section 1415(c)(2))

Statute of Limitations

IDEA 2004 includes a new two-year Statute of Limitations (Section 1415(b)(6)(B)). If your state does not have a statute of limitations, you must request a due process hearing within two years.

Resolution Session

The school district is required to convene the Resolution Session within 15 days of receiving the parent's Due Process Complaint Notice. The purpose of the Resolution Session is to provide the parties with an opportunity to resolve their complaint before a due process hearing. The Resolution Session is not an IEP meeting or a mediation session. The school district must send "relevant member or members of the IEP team" who have knowledge of the facts in the parent's complaint and a district representative who has decision-making authority (settlement authority). (Section 1415(f))

Minimum Standards for Hearing Officers

The law now requires hearing officers to be knowledgeable about the law, federal and state regulations, and caselaw. Hearing officers must also have the knowledge and ability to "conduct hearings and write decisions in accordance with appropriate standard legal practice." (Section 1415(f)(3)(A))

Attorneys' Fees from Parents and their Attorneys

While parents can recover attorneys' fees from school districts if they prevail, in some very limited circumstances, school districts may recover attorneys' fees from the parent's attorney or the parent. This can occur if the complaint is frivolous, unreasonable, or for an improper purpose, i.e., to harass, cause unnecessary delay, or needlessly increase the cost of litigation. (Section 1415(i)(3))

DISCIPLINE

The discipline statute in Section 1415(k) authorizes school personnel to place children in interim alternative educational settings. IDEA 2004 includes new requirements for placing children in interim alternative settings if they violate a "code of student conduct." This section includes requirements for manifestation determinations, placements, appeals, authority of the hearing officer, and transfer of rights at the age of majority. (Section 1415 (k))

Suspensions & Placements in Interim Alternative Educational Settings

If a child with a disability violates a code of student conduct, school officials may suspend the child for **up to 10 days**. If the school determines that the child's behavior was **not** a manifestation of the child's disability and suspends the child for **more than 10 days,** they may utilize the same procedures as with non-disabled children, but they must continue to provide the child with a free appropriate public education (FAPE). (Section 1415(k)(1))

If the school district suspends a child with a disability for **more than 10 days,** regardless of severity of the child's misconduct (i.e. violation of a code of conduct v. possession of a weapon), the school must continue to provide the child with FAPE. The child will participate in the general education curriculum, make progress on the IEP goals, and receive a functional behavioral assessment, behavioral intervention services and modifications to prevent the behavior from reoccurring. (Section 1415(k)(1)(D)) The decision to place a child into an interim alternative educational setting is determined by the IEP Team, not the principal, superintendent or school board.

Functional Behavioral Assessments and Behavior Intervention Plans

If the child's behavior was a manifestation of the disability, the IEP Team shall conduct a Functional Behavioral Assessment (assuming one has not been completed previously) and implement a Behavioral Intervention Plan

(BIP). If a Behavior Intervention Plan was developed previously, it should be modified to address the child's behavior. (Section 1415(k)(1)(F))

45 Day-Suspension: Dangerous Weapon, Drugs, And Serious Bodily Injury

If the child engages in behavior that involves a dangerous weapon, illegal drugs, or serious bodily injury, the child may be suspended for 45 school days even if the behavior was a manifestation of the disability. The child is still entitled to FAPE. (Section 1415(k)(1)(G))

IN SUMMATION

In this chapter, you learned how the Individuals with Disabilities Education Act is organized. You learned about important changes Congress made when the law was reauthorized. The next chapter is the Table of Contents for the Sections of IDEA 2004, which is followed by the full text of Part A and Part B of the Individuals with Disabilities Education Act of 2004.

4 | SECTION HEADINGS

Chapter 4

(d) Procedural Safeguards Notice.

(e) Mediation.

(f) Impartial Due Process Hearing.

(g) Appeal.

(h) Safeguards.

(i) Administrative Procedures.

(j) Maintenance of Current Educational Placement.

(k) Placement in Alternative Educational Setting .

(l) Rule of Construction.

(m) Transfer of Parental Rights at Age of Majority.

(n) Electronic Mail.

(o) Separate Complaint.

(a) Federal and State Monitoring.

(b) State Performance Plans.

(c) Approval Process.

(d) Secretary's Review and Determination.

(e) Enforcement.

(f) State Enforcement.

(g) Rule of Construction.

(h) Divided State Agency Responsibility.

(i) Data Capacity and Technical Assistance Review.

(a) Responsibilities of Secretary.

(b) Prohibition Against Federal Mandates, Direction, or Control.

(c) Confidentiality.

(d) Personnel.

(e) Model Forms.

(a) In General.

(b) Data Reporting.

(c) Technical Assistance.

(d) Disproportionality.

(a) In General.

(b) Eligibility.

(c) Allocations to States.

(d) Reservation for State Activities.

(e) State Administration.

(f) Other State-Level Activities.

(g) Subgrants to Local Educational Agencies.

FOR YOUR NOTES

5 | THE INDIVIDUALS WITH DISABILITIES EDUCATION IMPROVEMENT ACT OF 2004

PART A — GENERAL PROVISIONS

➔ **OVERVIEW:** Part A of the Individuals with Disabilities Education Improvement Act, General Provisions, includes Sections 1400 through Section 1409 of Title 20 of the United States Code (U.S.C.):

20 U.S.C. § 1400 - Congressional Findings and Purposes

20 U.S.C. § 1401 - Definitions

20 U.S.C. § 1402 - Office of Special Education Programs

20 U.S.C. § 1403 - Abrogation of State Sovereign Immunity

20 U.S.C. § 1404 - Acquisition of Equipment; Construction or Alteration of Facilities

20 U.S.C. § 1405 - Employment of Individuals with Disabilities

20 U.S.C. § 1406 - Requirements for Prescribing Regulations

20 U.S.C. § 1407 - State Administration

20 U.S.C. § 1408 - Paperwork Reduction

20 U.S.C. § 1409 - Freely Associated States

The most important statute in IDEA is Section 1400(d) that describes the purposes of the law. Section 1401 includes the legal definitions in alphabetical order. Section 1403 advises that states are not immune from suit if they violate IDEA. Section 1406 describes the requirements and timelines for the federal special education regulations. Section 1408 is a new section about paperwork reduction.

20 U.S.C. § 1400. Short Title; Table of Contents; Findings; Purposes.

➔ **OVERVIEW:** Section 1400 is Findings and Purposes. Section 1400(c) describes the history and findings that led Congress to pass the Education for All Handicapped Children Act of 1975 (Public Law 94-142) which is now the Individuals with Disabilities Education Improvement Act of 2004. The most important statute is Purposes in Section 1400(d): "to ensure that all children with disabilities have available to them a free appropriate public education that emphasizes special education and related services designed to meet their **unique needs** and prepare them for **further education, employment and independent living**" and "to ensure that the rights of children with disabilities and parents of such children are protected . . ."

When you have questions about a confusing term or section in the law, re-read Section 1400, especially Purposes in Section 1400(d). This will help you understand how the confusing portion fits into the overall purpose of the law.

(a) **Short Title.** This title may be cited as the 'Individuals with Disabilities Education Act'.

(b) **Table of Contents.** [8] [9]

---

[8] The footnotes in this book are comments by the authors and are not a part of the statute.

[9] Section 1400(b) lists the sections and subsections of Parts A, B, C, D, and E of the Individuals with Disabilities Education Act in a table of contents format. This Table of Contents is in Chapter 4.

(c) Findings. Congress finds the following:

(1) Disability is a natural part of the human experience and in no way diminishes the right of individuals to participate in or contribute to society. Improving educational results for children with disabilities is an essential element of our national policy of ensuring **equality of opportunity, full participation, independent living, and economic self-sufficiency for individuals with disabilities**,

(2) Before the date of enactment of the Education for All Handicapped Children Act of 1975 (Public Law 94-142), the educational needs of millions of children with disabilities were not being fully met because--

(A) the children did not receive appropriate educational services;

(B) the children **were excluded entirely from the public school system** and from being educated with their peers;

(C) **undiagnosed disabilities** prevented the children from having a successful educational experience; or

(D) a **lack of adequate resources** within the public school system forced families to find services outside the public school system.[10]

(3) Since the enactment and implementation of the Education for All Handicapped Children Act of 1975, this title has been successful in ensuring children with disabilities and the families of such children access to a free appropriate public education and in improving educational results for children with disabilities.

(4) However, the implementation of this title has been impeded by **low expectations, and an insufficient focus on applying replicable research on proven methods** of teaching and learning for children with disabilities.[1112]

5. Almost 30 years of research and experience has demonstrated that the education of children w/ disabilities can be made more effective by:

(A) having **high expectations** for such children and ensuring their **access to the general education curriculum** in the regular classroom, to the maximum extent possible, in order to -

(i) **meet developmental goals** and, to the maximum extent possible, the **challenging expectations that have been established for all children**; and

(ii) be **prepared to lead productive and independent adult lives**, to the **maximum extent possible;**[13]

---

[10] Before Congress passed the Education for All Handicapped Children Act (Public Law 94-142) in 1975, more than one million handicapped children were excluded from school. Initially, the law focused on ensuring that children had access to an education and due process of law. When Congress reauthorized the law in 1997, they emphasized accountability and improved outcomes while maintaining the goals of access and due process. IDEA 2004 increased the focus on accountability and improved outcomes by bringing IDEA into conformity with the No Child Left Behind Act, and adding requirements for early intervening services, research-based instruction, and highly qualified special education teachers.

[11] IDEA 2004 addresses poor educational outcomes for children with disabilities by requiring "proven methods of teaching and learning" based on "replicable research." These terms are important. Many school districts continue to use educational methods that are not research-based. Pressure from litigation, legal rulings requiring schools to use research-based methods, and No Child Left Behind are forcing school districts to adopt research based methods of teaching.

[12] *The Road to Nowhere: The Illusion and Broken Promises of Special Education in the Baltimore City and Other Public School Systems* by Kalman R. Hettleman and published by the Abell Foundation. www.abell.org/publications/detail.asp?ID=92

[13] The language about meeting the developmental goals and challenging expectations established for nondisabled children so children are "prepared to lead productive and independent adult lives to the maximum extent possible" is important. (Section 1400(c)(5)(E))

(B) strengthening the **role and responsibility of parents** and ensuring that families of such children have meaningful opportunities to participate in the education of their children at school and at home;[14]

(C) **coordinating** this title with other local, educational service agency, State, and Federal school improvement efforts, including improvement efforts under the **Elementary and Secondary Education Act of 1965**,[15] in order to ensure that such children benefit from such efforts and that special education can become a <u>service for such children rather than a place</u> where such children are sent;[16]

(D) providing appropriate special education and related services, and aids and supports in the regular classroom, to such children, whenever appropriate;

(E) supporting **high-quality, intensive preservice preparation and professional development** for all personnel who work with children with disabilities in order to ensure that such personnel have the skills and knowledge necessary to improve the academic achievement and functional performance of children with disabilities, including the use of **scientifically based instructional practices**, to the maximum extent possible;

(F) providing incentives for whole-school approaches, **scientifically based early reading programs**,[17] **positive behavioral interventions and supports**, and **early intervening services**[18] to reduce the need to label children as disabled in order to address the learning and behavioral needs of such children;[19]

(G) focusing resources on teaching and learning while reducing paperwork and requirements that do not assist in improving educational results; and

(H) supporting the development and use of technology, including assistive technology devices and assistive technology services, to maximize accessibility for children with disabilities.

(6) While States, local educational agencies, and educational service agencies are primarily responsible for providing an education for all children with disabilities, it is in the national interest that the Federal

---

[14] The language of Section 1400(c)(5)(B) changed from "strengthening the role of parents" to "strengthening the role and responsibility of parents."

[15] IDEA is the federal law that requires schools to provide special education and related services to qualifying children with disabilities. The Elementary and Secondary Education Act of 1965 (ESEA) is the federal law that was originally enacted to help schools educate disadvantaged children. When the ESEA was reauthorized in 2001, it was renamed "No Child Left Behind." The "improvement efforts under the ESEA" refers to No Child Left Behind (NCLB). NCLB and IDEA often use the same terms or incorporate the identical language, definitions and requirements of the other statute by reference.

[16] Special education is a service. Special education is not the classroom in the trailer, Ms. Jones' class, or the special education school across town. When school personnel view special education as a "place," they fail to evaluate the child's unique needs and how the school can meet these needs. Coordinating IDEA and NCLB will help to ensure that special education is "a service for such children rather than a place where such children are sent."

[17] See **Appendix F: Reading and Requirements for Research Based Instruction.**

[18] When children receive intensive, research-based early intervention (early intervening services), many will not need special education services. Parents and teachers must educate their school boards about the need to provide early intervention for all children who need these services. Remedial programs are in addition to special education services provided to children with disabilities.

[19] Many school districts refuse to evaluate or provide special education services until after a child fails. This "wait to fail" model has tragic results. The neurological "window of opportunity" for learning to read begins to close during elementary school. Late remediation is more difficult and carries a high price tag, emotionally and economically.

Government have a supporting role in assisting State and local efforts to educate children with disabilities in order to improve results for such children and to ensure equal protection of the law.

(7) A more equitable allocation of resources is essential for the Federal Government to meet its responsibility to provide an **equal educational opportunity** for all individuals.

(8) Parents and schools should be given **expanded opportunities to resolve their disagreements** in positive and constructive ways.

(9) Teachers, schools, local educational agencies, and States should be relieved of **irrelevant and unnecessary paperwork burdens** that do not lead to improved educational outcomes.

(10)
 (A) The Federal Government must be responsive to the growing needs of an **increasingly diverse society**.

 (B) America's **ethnic profile** is rapidly changing. In 2000, **1 of every 3 persons** in the United States was a member of a **minority group** or was limited English proficient.

 (C) Minority children comprise an increasing percentage of public school students.

 (D) With such changing demographics, recruitment efforts for special education personnel should focus on increasing the participation of **minorities in the teaching profession** in order to provide appropriate role models with sufficient knowledge to address the special education needs of these students.

(11)
 (A) The **limited English proficient** population is the fastest growing in our Nation, and the growth is occurring in many parts of our Nation.

 (B) Studies have documented apparent discrepancies in the levels of referral and placement of limited English proficient children in special education.

 (C) Such discrepancies pose a special challenge for special education in the referral of, assessment of, and provision of services for, our Nation's students from non-English language backgrounds.

(12)
 (A) Greater efforts are needed to **prevent** the intensification of problems connected with **mislabeling and high dropout rates among minority children with disabilities**.

 (B) More minority children continue to be served in special education than would be expected from the percentage of minority students in the general school population.

 (C) African-American children are **identified as having mental retardation and emotional disturbance** at rates greater than their White counterparts.

 (D) In the 1998-1999 school year, African-American children represented just 14.8 percent of the population aged 6 through 21, but comprised 20.2 percent of all children with disabilities.

 (E) Studies have found that schools with predominately White students and teachers have placed **disproportionately high numbers of their minority students into special education**.

(13)

    (A) As the number of minority students in special education **increases**, the number of minority teachers and related services personnel produced in colleges and universities continues to **decrease**.

    (B) The opportunity for **full participation by minority individuals**, minority organizations, and Historically Black Colleges and Universities in awards for grants and contracts, boards of organizations receiving assistance under this title, peer review panels, and training of professionals in the area of special education is essential to obtain greater success in the education of minority children with disabilities.

(14) As the graduation rates for children with disabilities continue to climb, providing **effective transition services** to promote **successful post-school employment or education is an important measure of accountability** for children with disabilities.

(d) Purposes. The purposes of this title are--

(1)

    (A) to ensure that all children with disabilities have available to them a free appropriate public education that emphasizes special education and related services designed to meet their **unique needs and prepare them for further education,**[20] **employment, and independent living;**[21]

    (B) to ensure that the **rights of children** with disabilities **and parents** of such children **are protected**; and

    (C) to assist States, localities, educational service agencies, and Federal agencies to provide for the education of all children with disabilities;

(2) to assist States in the implementation of a statewide, comprehensive, coordinated, multidisciplinary, interagency system of **early intervention services for infants and toddlers** with disabilities and their families;

(3) to ensure that educators and parents have the necessary **tools to improve educational results** for children with disabilities by supporting system improvement activities; coordinated research and personnel preparation; coordinated technical assistance, dissemination, and support; and technology development and media services; and

(4) to **assess, and ensure the effectiveness of, efforts to educate children with disabilities.**[22]

---

[20] The phrase "further education" is new in IDEA 2004, as is the emphasis on effective transition services. Section 1400(c)(14) describes "effective transition services to promote successful post-school employment or education." The definition of "Transition Services" was changed to a "results-oriented process that is focused on improving the academic and functional achievement of the child" to facilitate "movement from school to post-school activities, including post-secondary education . . ."

[21] Purposes in Section 1400(d) is the mission statement of IDEA. The purpose of special education is to prepare children with disabilities for **further education, employment, and independent living**. In developing IEPs, you can use this "mission statement" as a long-term goal.

[22] IDEA 2004 requires that all children with disabilities participate in all state and district assessments, with appropriate accommodations as determined by the IEP team. The law includes new requirements about accommodations guidelines and alternate assessments. (See Section 1412(c)(16))

20 U.S.C. § 1401. Definitions.

➔ **OVERVIEW: New Definitions in IDEA 2004.**

Six new definitions were added to IDEA 2004: core academic subjects, highly qualified teacher, homeless children, limited English proficient, universal design, and ward of the state. Read the definitions carefully, especially the definitions of child with a disability, free appropriate public education, highly qualified teacher, least restrictive environment, IEP, related services, special education, and specific learning disability. A definition will often take you to another section of the law that provides more information on that subject. The definitions are in alphabetical order.

Except as otherwise provided, in this title:

(1) Assistive Technology Device.

(A) In General. The term 'assistive technology device' means any item, piece of equipment, or product system, whether acquired commercially off the shelf, modified, or customized, that is used to increase, maintain, or improve functional capabilities of a child with a disability.

(B) Exception. The term does not include a medical device that is surgically implanted, or the replacement of such device.[23]

(2) Assistive Technology Service. The term 'assistive technology service' means any service that **directly assists a child** with a disability in the selection, acquisition, or **use of an assistive technology device**. Such term includes–

(A) the **evaluation of the needs** of such child, including a functional evaluation of the child in the child's customary environment;[24]

(B) purchasing, leasing, or otherwise **providing for the acquisition of assistive technology devices** by such child;

(C) selecting, designing, fitting, **customizing, adapting, applying, maintaining, repairing, or replacing** assistive technology devices;

(D) coordinating and using other therapies, interventions, or services with assistive technology devices, such as those associated with existing education and rehabilitation plans and programs;

(E) **training or technical assistance for such child, or,** where appropriate, **the family** of such child; and

(F) **training or technical assistance for professionals** (including individuals providing education and rehabilitation services), employers, or other individuals who provide services to, employ, or are otherwise substantially involved in the major life functions of such child.[25]

---

[23] Although schools are not responsible for providing or replacing surgically implanted medical devices (like cochlear implants) the term "assistive technology device" refers to equipment that increases, maintains or improves the functional capabilities of a child. When you read the definitions of "Assistive Technology Service" in Section 1401(2) and "Related Services" in Section 1401(26), you will see that these services include selecting, fitting, customizing, adapting, applying, maintaining, repairing or replacing assistive technology devices. Mapping a cochlear implant to ensure that it is working properly, may be necessary for the hearing impaired child to learn.

[24] An assistive technology evaluation may be conducted in the home, which is a customary environment for a child.

(3) Child With A Disability.

    (A) In General. The term '**child with a disability**' means a child–
    (i) **with** mental retardation, hearing impairments (including deafness), speech or language impairments, visual impairments (including blindness), serious emotional disturbance (referred to in this title as 'emotional disturbance'), orthopedic impairments, autism, traumatic brain injury, other health impairments, or specific learning disabilities; **and**
    (ii) **who, by reason thereof, needs special education and related services.**[26]

    (B) Child Aged 3 Through 9. The term 'child with a disability' for a child aged **3 through 9** (or any subset of that age range, including ages 3 through 5)[27], **may, at the discretion of the State** and the local educational agency, include a child–
    (i) experiencing **developmental delays**, as defined by the State and as measured by appropriate diagnostic instruments and procedures, in 1 or more of the following areas: physical development; cognitive development; communication development; social or emotional development; or adaptive development; and
    (ii) who, by reason thereof, needs special education and related services.[28]

(4) Core Academic Subjects. The term '**core academic subjects**'[29] has the meaning given the term in section 9101 of the Elementary and Secondary Education Act of 1965.[30] *Improvements 2001 No Child Left Behind*

(5) Educational Service Agency. The term 'educational service agency' means a regional public multiservice agency-authorized by State law to develop, manage, and provide services or programs to local educational agencies; and recognized as an administrative agency for purposes of the provision of special education and related services provided within public elementary schools and secondary schools of the State; and includes any other public institution or agency having administrative control and direction over a public elementary school or secondary school.

(6) Elementary School. The term 'elementary school' means a nonprofit institutional day or residential school, including a public elementary charter school, that provides elementary education, as determined under State law.

---

[25] Children with disabilities need to use technology devices and services to increase and improve their ability to function independently in and out of school. Technology devices include dictation software, text readers, and computerized speaking devices. Parents, teachers, and other professionals will need training before they can teach the child to use technology.

[26] A child with a disability is not automatically eligible for special education and related services under IDEA. The key phrase is "who, by reason thereof, needs special education and related services." Does the child's disability adversely affect educational performance? If a child has a disability but does not need special education services, the child is not eligible for special education under the IDEA. The child may be eligible for protections under Section 504 of the Rehabilitation Act. (See **Appendix A for a discussion of Section 504 and IDEA**)

[27] Part C describes special education for infants and toddlers with disabilities (birth to two years of age).

[28] School districts may provide special education services to children with developmental delays who have not been classified or "labeled." If a child between the ages of 3 and 9 has a developmental delay but has not been found eligible for services under Section 1401(3)(A)(i), this section may open the door to special education services. The requirement that schools provide services to young children with developmental delays is intended to address their needs for early intervention services.

[29] Core academic subjects are "English, reading or language arts, mathematics, science, foreign languages, civics and government, economics, arts, history, and geography." (20 U. S. C. § 7801)

[30] All No Child Left Behind definitions are in Appendix A of *Wrightslaw: No Child Left Behind*.

(7) **Equipment.** The term 'equipment' includes–

(A) machinery, utilities, and built-in equipment, and any necessary enclosures or structures to house such machinery, utilities, or equipment; and

(B) all other items necessary for the functioning of a particular facility as a facility for the provision of educational services, including items such as instructional equipment and necessary furniture; printed, published, and audio-visual instructional materials; telecommunications, sensory, and other technological aids and devices; and books, periodicals, documents, and other related materials.

(8) **Excess Costs.** The term 'excess costs' means those costs that are in excess of the average annual per-student expenditure in a local educational agency during the preceding school year for an elementary school or secondary school student, as may be appropriate, and which shall be computed after deducting--

(A) amounts received–
    (i) under part B;
    (ii) under part A of title I of the Elementary and Secondary Education Act of 1965; and
    (iii) under parts A and B of title III of that Act; and

(B) any State or local funds expended for programs that would qualify for assistance under any of those parts.

(9) **Free Appropriate Public Education.** The term 'free appropriate public education'[31] means special education and related services that–

(A) have been provided at public expense, under public supervision and direction, and without charge;

(B) meet the standards of the State educational agency;

(C) include an appropriate preschool, elementary school, or secondary school education in the State involved; and

(D) are provided in conformity with the individualized education program required under section 1414(d) of this title. [32] [33]

---

[31] The term "free appropriate public education" (FAPE) is not clearly defined in IDEA but has been defined in case law. In *Board of Education v. Rowley*, 458 U.S. 176 (1982), the U. S. Supreme Court concluded that FAPE is not the best program, nor is it a program designed to maximize a child's potential or learning. When courts analyze the changes in IDEA 2004, they may require a higher standard.

[32] In *Reexamining Rowley: A New Focus in Special Education Law*, attorney Scott Johnson argues that the "some educational benefit" standard in *Rowley* no longer reflects the requirements of the Individuals with Disabilities Education Act. www.harborhouselaw.com/articles/rowley.reexamine.johnson.htm

[33] Parents must never ask for what is "best" for a child or that they want a program that will maximize their child's potential. Evaluations and reports from experts in the private sector should never say, "The best program for Johnny is . . ." or "Ideally, Johnny should receive . . ." Courts have held that children with disabilities are entitled to an "appropriate" education, not the "best" education. Use the terms "appropriate" or "minimally appropriate."

✳ **(10) Highly Qualified.**

(A) In General. For any special education teacher, the term 'highly qualified' has the meaning given the term in section 9101 of the Elementary and Secondary Education Act of 1965[34], except that such term also-
(i) includes the requirements described in subparagraph (B); and
(ii) includes the option for teachers to meet the requirements of section 9101 of such Act by meeting the requirements of subparagraph (C) or (D).[35]

(B) Requirements For Special Education Teachers. When used with respect to any public elementary school or secondary school special education teacher teaching in a State, such term means that-
(i) the teacher has obtained **full State certification** as a special education teacher (including certification obtained through alternative routes to certification), **or passed** the State special education teacher **licensing examination, and holds a license to teach** in the State as a special education teacher, except that when used with respect to any teacher teaching in a public charter school, the term means that the teacher meets the requirements set forth in the State's public charter school law;
(ii) the teacher **has not had** special education certification or licensure requirements **waived** on an emergency, temporary, or provisional basis; **and**
(iii) the teacher holds **at least a bachelor's degree.**

(C) Special Education Teachers Teaching to Alternate Achievement Standards. When used with respect to a special education teacher who teaches **core academic subjects exclusively to children who are assessed against alternate achievement standards** established under the regulations promulgated under section 1111(b)(1) of the Elementary and Secondary Education Act of 1965, such term means the teacher, whether new or not new to the profession, may **either-**
(i) meet the applicable requirements of section 9101 of such Act for any **elementary, middle, or secondary school teacher** who is new or not new to the profession; **or**
(ii) meet the requirements of subparagraph (B) or (C) of section 9101(23) of such Act as applied to an **elementary school teacher, or,** in the case of instruction above the elementary level, **has subject matter knowledge appropriate to the level of instruction** being provided, as determined by the State, needed to effectively teach to those standards.[36]

(D) Special Education Teachers Teaching Multiple Subjects. When used with respect to a special education teacher who teaches **2 or more core academic subjects** exclusively to children with disabilities, such term means that the teacher may either-
(i) meet the applicable requirements of section 9101 of the Elementary and Secondary Education Act of 1965 for any **elementary, middle, or secondary school teacher** who is new or not new to the profession;

---

[34] The definition of "highly qualified teacher" is in Title IX of No Child Left Behind at 20 U. S. C. § 7801(23). See also 20 U.S.C. § 6311(b)(1). No Child Left Behind definitions are in the Glossary of Terms of *Wrightslaw: No Child Left Behind*.

[35] Special educators who teach core academic subjects must meet the highly qualified teacher requirements in NCLB and must demonstrate competence in the core academic subjects they teach. Special educators who do not provide instruction in core academic subjects do not have to meet the highly qualified teacher requirements. A "highly qualified teacher" has full State certification (no waivers), holds a license to teach, and meets the State's requirements. The requirements are somewhat different for new and veteran teachers, for elementary, middle school, and high school teachers, for teachers of multiple subjects, and for teachers who teach to alternate standards.

[36] For guidance on how No Child Left Behind applies to special educators and paraprofessionals read Chapter 6, "NCLB for Teachers, Principals and Paraprofessionals" in *Wrightslaw: No Child Left Behind*. Dozens of resources are in the NCLB CD-ROM in *Wrightslaw: No Child Left Behind*.

(ii) in the case of a teacher who is not new to the profession, **demonstrate competence in all the core academic subjects in which the teacher teaches** in the same manner as is required for an elementary, middle, or secondary school teacher who is not new to the profession under section 9101(23)(C)(ii) of such Act, which may include a **single, high objective uniform State standard of evaluation**[37] covering multiple subjects; or

(iii) in the case of a new special education teacher who **teaches multiple subjects and who is highly qualified** in mathematics, language arts, or science, **demonstrate competence in the other core academic subjects** in which the teacher teaches in the same manner as is required for an elementary, middle, or secondary school teacher under section 9101(23)(C)(ii) of such Act, which may include a single, **high objective uniform State standard of evaluation** covering multiple subjects, not later than 2 years after the date of employment.

(E) Rule of Construction. Notwithstanding any other individual right of action that a parent or student may maintain under this part, nothing in this section or part shall be construed to create a **right of action on behalf of an individual student or class of students** for the failure of a particular State educational agency or local educational agency employee to be highly qualified.[38]

(F) Definition For Purposes of the ESEA. A teacher who is highly qualified under this paragraph shall be considered highly qualified for purposes of the Elementary and Secondary Education Act of 1965.[39]

(11) Homeless Children. The term 'homeless children' has the meaning given the term 'homeless children and youths' in section 11434a of title 42.[40]

(12) Indian. The term 'Indian' means an individual who is a member of an Indian tribe.

(13) Indian Tribe. The term 'Indian tribe' means any Federal or State Indian tribe, band, rancheria, pueblo, colony, or community, including any Alaska Native village or regional village corporation (as defined in or established under the Alaska Native Claims Settlement Act (43 U.S.C. 1601 et seq.)).

(14) Individualized Education Program; IEP. The term 'individualized education program' or 'IEP' means a written statement for each child with a disability that is developed, reviewed, and revised in accordance with section 1414(d) of this title.[41]

(15) Individualized Family Service Plan. The term 'individualized family service plan' has the meaning given the term in section 1436 of this title.

---

[37] States have the option of developing a method by which teachers can demonstrate competence in the subjects they teach. The method must be based on a "high objective uniform state standard of evaluation" (HOUSSE) and must provide an objective way to determine if teachers have subject matter knowledge in the core academic subjects they teach.

[38] There is no right of action, i.e., right to sue a state or school district because a teacher is not highly qualified. However, parents may file complaints about inadequately trained teachers with the State Department of Education.

[39] The timelines for highly qualified teachers are in No Child Left Behind, 20 U. S. C. § 6319(a)(2). (See *Wrightslaw: No Child Left Behind*.) Teachers hired after the law was enacted in 2002 (new hires) must be highly qualified. Teachers of core academic subjects must be highly qualified by the end of the 2005-2006 school year.

[40] Homeless children "lack a fixed, regular, and adequate nighttime residence . . . [are] sharing the housing of other persons . . . living in motels, hotels, trailer parks, or camping grounds . . . [or are] living in cars, parks, public spaces, abandoned buildings, substandard housing, bus or train stations, or similar settings." (42 U.S.C. § 11434a)

[41] The legal requirements for IEPs, IEP teams, meeting attendance, when IEPs must be in effect, reviewing and revising IEPs, placements, and alternative ways to participate in IEP meetings are in Section 1414(d).

(16) Infant or Toddler With A Disability. The term 'infant or toddler with a disability' has the meaning given the term in section 1432 of this title.[42]

(17) Institution of Higher Education. The term 'institution of higher education'—

(A) has the meaning given the term in section 1001 of this Title; and

(B) also includes any community college receiving funding from the Secretary of the Interior under the Tribally Controlled College or University Assistance Act of 1978.

(18) Limited English Proficient. The term 'limited English proficient' has the meaning given the term in section 9101 of the Elementary and Secondary Education Act of 1965.[43]

(19) Local Educational Agency.

(A) In General. The term 'local educational agency' means a public board of education or other public authority legally constituted within a State for either administrative control or direction of, or to perform a service function for, public elementary schools or secondary schools in a city, county, township, school district, or other political subdivision of a State, or for such combination of school districts or counties as are recognized in a State as an administrative agency for its public elementary schools or secondary schools.

(B) Educational Service Agencies and Other Public Institutions or Agencies. The term includes –
    (i) an educational service agency; and
    (ii) any other public institution or agency having administrative control and direction of a public elementary school or secondary school.

(C) BIA Funded Schools. The term includes an elementary school or secondary school funded by the Bureau of Indian Affairs, but only to the extent that such inclusion makes the school eligible for programs for which specific eligibility is not provided to the school in another provision of law and the school does not have a student population that is smaller than the student population of the local educational agency receiving assistance under this title with the smallest student population, except that the school shall not be subject to the jurisdiction of any State educational agency other than the Bureau of Indian Affairs.

(20) Native Language. The term 'native language', when used with respect to an individual who is limited English proficient, means the language normally used by the individual or, in the case of a child, the language normally used by the parents of the child.

(21) Nonprofit. The term 'nonprofit', as applied to a school, agency, organization, or institution, means a school, agency, organization, or institution owned and operated by 1 or more nonprofit corporations or

---

[42] "An individual under 3 years of age who needs early intervention services because the individual (i) is experiencing developmental delays, as measured by appropriate diagnostic instruments and procedures in 1 or more of the areas of cognitive development, physical development, communication development, social or emotional development, and adaptive development; or (ii) has a diagnosed physical or mental condition that has a high probability of resulting in developmental delay; and . . ." (See 20 U.S.C. §1432 in Part C for the full definition.)

[43] "An individual between the ages of 3 and 21 who attends an elementary school or secondary school, who was not born in the United States or whose native language is not English, who may be a Native American, Alaska Native, or a resident of the outlying areas, or a migratory child whose native language is not English. The individual's difficulties in speaking, reading, writing, or understanding English may not permit the individual to be proficient on state assessments." (20 U.S.C. § 7801) For all NCLB definitions, see Appendix A of *Wrightslaw: No Child Left Behind*.

associations no part of the net earnings of which inures, or may lawfully inure, to the benefit of any private shareholder or individual.

(22) Outlying Area. The term 'outlying area' means the United States Virgin Islands, Guam, American Samoa, and the Commonwealth of the Northern Mariana Islands.

(23) Parent. The term 'parent' means–

(A) a **natural, adoptive, or foster parent** of a child (unless a foster parent is prohibited by State law from serving as a parent);

(B) a **guardian** (but not the State if the child is a ward of the State);

(C) an **individual acting in the place of a natural or adoptive parent** (including a grandparent, stepparent, or **other relative**) with whom the child lives, **or an individual who is legally responsible** for the child's welfare; or

(D) except as used in sections 1415(b)(2) and 1439(a)(5), an individual assigned under either of those sections to be a **surrogate parent.**[44]

(24) Parent Organization. The term 'parent organization' has the meaning given the term in section 1471(g) of this title.

(25) Parent Training and Information Center. The term 'parent training and information center' means a center assisted under section 1471 or 1472 of this title.

(26) Related Services.

for Special Education

(A) **In General.** The term 'related services' means **transportation**, and such **developmental, corrective, and other supportive services** (including speech-language pathology and audiology services, interpreting services, psychological services, physical and occupational therapy, recreation, including therapeutic recreation, social work services, **school nurse services**[45] designed to enable a child with a disability to receive a free appropriate public education as described in the individualized education program of the child, counseling services, including rehabilitation counseling, orientation and mobility services, and medical services, except that such medical services shall be for diagnostic and evaluation purposes only) as **may be required to assist a child with a disability to benefit from special education**, and **includes the early identification and assessment** of disabling conditions in children.[46]

---

[44] IDEA 2004 expanded the definition of "parent" to include natural, adoptive, and foster parents, guardians, individuals who act in the place of a parent, individuals who are legally responsible for the child, and surrogate parents.

[45] "School nurse services" is a new related service and replaces "school health services" in IDEA 97.

[46] Related services are services the child needs to benefit from special education. Compare the definitions of "related services" with "supplementary aids and services" (at Section 1401(33)). Related services and supplementary services may include one-on-one tutoring or remediation of reading, writing, spelling and arithmetic skills. The law does not require that a child be placed in a special education class in order to receive tutoring or academic remediation.

(B) Exception. The term does **not include a medical device that is surgically implanted**, or the replacement of such device.[47]

(27) Secondary School. The term 'secondary school' means a nonprofit institutional day or residential school, including a public secondary charter school, that provides secondary education, as determined under State law, except that it does not include any education beyond grade 12.

(28) Secretary. The term 'Secretary' means the Secretary of Education.

(29) Special Education. The term 'special education' means **specially designed instruction**, at no cost to parents, **to meet the unique needs of a child** with a disability[48], including--

(A) instruction conducted in the **classroom**, in the **home**, in **hospitals and institutions**, and in **other settings**[49]; and

(B) instruction in **physical education**.

(30) Specific Learning Disability.

(A) In General. The term 'specific learning disability' means a disorder in 1 or more of the basic psychological processes involved in understanding or in using language, spoken or written, which disorder may manifest itself in the imperfect ability to listen, think, speak, read, write, spell, or do mathematical calculations.[50][51]

(B) Disorders Included. Such term includes such conditions as perceptual disabilities, brain injury, minimal brain dysfunction, **dyslexia**, and developmental aphasia.[52]

(C) Disorders Not Included. Such term does not include a learning problem that is primarily the result of visual, hearing, or motor disabilities, of mental retardation, of emotional disturbance, or of environmental, cultural, or economic disadvantage.

(31) State. The term 'State' means each of the 50 States, the District of Columbia, the Commonwealth of Puerto Rico, and each of the outlying areas.

---

[47] The exclusion of surgically implanted medical devices tracks the exception in the definitions of "Assistive Technology Device" and "Assistive Technology Service." While school districts are not responsible for surgically implanting devices, they may be responsible for corrective and supportive services. For example, schools may have to provide audiology services to operate, adjust and map cochlear implant devices.

[48] Special education is defined as "specially designed instruction, at no cost to the parents, to meet the unique needs of a child with a disability . . ."

[49] Special education encompasses a range of services and may include one-on-one tutoring, intensive academic remediation, and 40-hour Applied Behavioral Analysis (ABA) programs. Special education is provided in a variety of settings, including the child's home.

[50] The definition of "specific learning disability" did not change.

[51] For more about specific learning disabilities and discrepancy models, read Section 1414(b)(6) and see **Appendix C: Discrepancy Models and Specific Learning Disabilities** in the back of this book.

[52] The terms used to describe disabilities in IDEA are those used during the 1970's when Congress enacted Public Law 94-142. The term "minimal brain dysfunction" is "Attention Deficit Disorder." "Dyslexia" is a language learning disability in reading, writing, spelling, and/or math. From a legal perspective, dyslexia is a learning disability that adversely affects educational performance. For further discussion of specific learning disabilities and discrepancy formula, see **Appendix C: Discrepancy Models and Specific Learning Disabilities** in the back of this book.

(32) **State Educational Agency.** The term 'State educational agency' means the State board of education or other agency or officer primarily responsible for the State supervision of public elementary schools and secondary schools, or, if there is no such officer or agency, an officer or agency designated by the Governor or by State law.

[handwritten: for Regular Education]

(33) **Supplementary Aids and Services.** The term 'supplementary aids and services' means aids, services, and other supports that are provided in **regular education classes** or other education-related settings to enable children with disabilities to be educated with nondisabled children to the maximum extent appropriate in accordance with section 1412(a)(5) of this title.[53]

(34) **Transition Services.** The term 'transition services'[54] means a **coordinated set of activities** for a child with a disability that–

[handwritten: ✶]

(A) is designed to be within a **results-oriented process**, that is **focused on improving the academic and functional achievement of the child with a disability to facilitate the child's movement from school to post-school activities,** including **post-secondary education,** vocational education, integrated employment (including supported employment), continuing and adult education, adult services, independent living, or community participation;
(B) is based on the **individual child's needs**, taking into account the **child's strengths, preferences, and interests**; and
(C) includes instruction, related services, community experiences, the development of employment and other post-school adult living objectives, and, when appropriate, acquisition of daily living skills and functional vocational evaluation.[55]

(35) **Universal Design.** The term 'universal design' has the meaning given the term in section 3002 in title 29.[56]

(36) **Ward of the State.**
(A) **In General.** The term 'ward of the State' means a child who, as determined by the State where the child resides, is a foster child, is a ward of the State, or is in the custody of a public child welfare agency.[57]

(B) **Exception.** The term **does not include a foster child who has a foster parent** who meets the definition of a parent in paragraph (23).

---

[53] Supplementary aids and services are provided in general education classes so children with disabilities can be educated with their non-disabled peers. Compare "supplementary aids and services" with "related services" in Section 1401(26).

[54] Remember the language in the "Purposes" about preparing disabled children for "further education." See also the new language about IEPs in Sections 1414(d)(1)(A)(i)(VIII)(aa) and (bb) that describes "measurable postsecondary goals" and "courses of study" to reach those goals and Section 1400(c)(14) that describes "effective transition services to promote successful post-school . . . education."

[55] The definition of transition services changed to a "results-oriented process" that improves "the academic and functional achievement of the child with a disability" and facilitates the child's transition from school to employment and further education. Transition services are based on the individual child's needs and strengths.

[56] The definition of universal design in the Assistive Technology Act designing and delivering products and services that may be used by people with a range of functional capabilities. (29 U.S.C. § 3002(19))

[57] "Ward of the State" is a new term in IDEA 2004. See also Section 1401(23) for the expanded definition of "parent" and Section 1414(a)(1)(D)(iii) about parental consent for children who are wards of the state.

20 U.S.C. § 1402 - Office of Special Education Programs.

➔ **OVERVIEW:** This section authorizes the Office of Special Education Programs as the principal agency to administer the IDEA. The Secretary selects the Director who reports directly to the Assistant Secretary for Special Education and Rehabilitative Services.

(a) Establishment. There shall be, within the Office of Special Education and Rehabilitative Services in the Department of Education, an Office of Special Education Programs, which shall be the principal agency in the Department for administering and carrying out this title and other programs and activities concerning the education of children with disabilities.

(b) Director. The Office established under subsection (a) shall be headed by a Director who shall be selected by the Secretary and shall report directly to the Assistant Secretary for Special Education and Rehabilitative Services.

(c) Voluntary and Uncompensated Services. Notwithstanding section 1342 of title 31, United States Code, the Secretary is authorized to accept voluntary and uncompensated services in furtherance of the purposes of this title.

20 U.S.C. § 1403 - Abrogation of State Sovereign Immunity.

➔ **OVERVIEW:** States are not immune from suit in Federal court if they violate the IDEA.

(a) In General. A State **shall not be immune under the 11th amendment** to the Constitution of the United States from suit in Federal court for a violation of this title.

(b) Remedies. In a suit against a State for a violation of this title, remedies (including remedies both at law and in equity) are available for such a violation to the same extent as those remedies are available for such a violation in the suit against any public entity other than a State.

(c) Effective Date. Subsections (a) and (b) apply with respect to violations that occur in whole or part after October 30, 1990.

20 U.S.C. § 1404 - Acquisition of Equipment; Construction or Alteration of Facilities.

➔ **OVERVIEW:** The U.S. Department of Education may authorize funds to acquire equipment, construct new facilities, or alter existing facilities.

(a) In General. If the Secretary determines that a program authorized under this title will be improved by permitting program funds to be used to acquire appropriate equipment, or to construct new facilities or alter existing facilities, the Secretary is authorized to allow the use of those funds for those purposes.

(b) Compliance With Certain Regulations. Any construction of new facilities or alteration of existing facilities under subsection (a) shall comply with the requirements of–

(1) appendix A of part 36 of title 28, Code of Federal Regulations (commonly known as the Americans with Disabilities Accessibility Guidelines for Buildings and Facilities'); or

(2) appendix A of subpart 101-19.6 of title 41, Code of Federal Regulations (commonly known as the Uniform Federal Accessibility Standards').

20 U.S.C. § 1405 - Employment of Individuals with Disabilities.

➜ **OVERVIEW:** Recipients of funds must make positive efforts to employ individuals with disabilities.

The Secretary shall ensure that each recipient of assistance under this title makes positive efforts to employ and advance in employment qualified individuals with disabilities in programs assisted under this title.

20 U.S.C. § 1406 - Requirements for Prescribing Regulations.

➜ **OVERVIEW:** The U.S. Department of Education is responsible for developing the federal special education regulations. After the Department publishes the proposed regulations, there will be a 75-day public comment period. The Department will review these public comments, which can be made in writing or at public meetings, then publish the Final Regulations. The federal special education regulations will be published in the Federal Register (FR) and the Code of Federal Regulations (C.F.R.) beginning at 34 C.F.R. Part 300. The new special education regulations may not lessen the protections in effect on July 20, 1983.

(a) In General. In carrying out the provisions of this title, the Secretary shall issue regulations under this title only to the extent that such regulations are necessary to ensure that there is compliance with the specific requirements of this title.

(b) Protections Provided to Children. The Secretary **may not implement**, or publish in final form, **any regulation** prescribed pursuant to this title **that**–

(1) **violates or contradicts** any provision of this title; or

(2) **procedurally or substantively lessens the protections** provided to children with disabilities under this title, **as embodied in regulations in effect on July 20, 1983** (particularly as such protections related to parental consent to initial evaluation or initial placement in special education, least restrictive environment, related services, **timelines,** attendance of evaluation personnel at individualized education program meetings, or qualifications of personnel), except to the extent that such regulation reflects the **clear and unequivocal intent of Congress** in legislation.[58]

(c) Public Comment Period. The Secretary shall provide **a public comment period of not less than 75 days on any regulation** proposed under part B or part C on which an opportunity for public comment is otherwise required by law.

(d) Policy Letters and Statements. The Secretary **may not issue policy letters** or other statements (including letters or statements regarding issues of national significance) that–

(1) violate or contradict any provision of this title; or

(2) establish a rule that is required for compliance with, and eligibility under, this title **without following the requirements of section 553 of title 5**, United States Code.

(e) Explanation and Assurances. Any written response by the Secretary under subsection (d) regarding a policy, question, or interpretation under part B shall include an explanation in the written response that–

---

[58] The Department of Education may not publish regulations that lessen the protections provided in the 1983 regulations, unless this reflects the clear and unequivocal intent of Congress.

(1) such response is provided as informal guidance and is not legally binding;

(2) when required, such response is issued in compliance with the requirements of section 553 of title 5, United States Code; and

(3) such response represents the interpretation by the Department of Education of the applicable statutory or regulatory requirements in the context of the specific facts presented.

(f) Correspondence From Department of Education Describing Interpretations of This Title.

(1) In General. The Secretary shall, on a quarterly basis, publish in the Federal Register, and widely disseminate to interested entities through various additional forms of communication, a list of correspondence from the Department of Education received by individuals during the previous quarter that describes the interpretations of the Department of Education of this title or the regulations implemented pursuant to this title.

(2) Additional Information. For each item of correspondence published in a list under paragraph (1), the Secretary shall—
   (A) identify the topic addressed by the correspondence and shall include such other summary information as the Secretary determines to be appropriate; and

   (B) ensure that all such correspondence is issued, where applicable, in compliance with the requirements of section 553 of title 5, United States Code.

20 U.S.C. § 1407 - State Administration.
➜ **OVERVIEW:** States must ensure that their rules, regulations, and policies conform to IDEA 2004.

 (a) Rulemaking. Each State that receives funds under this title **shall—**

(1) **ensure** that any State rules, regulations, and policies relating to this title **conform to the purposes of this title;**

(2) **identify in writing** to local educational agencies located in the State and the Secretary **any such rule, regulation, or policy as a State-imposed requirement that is not required by this title and Federal regulations;** and

(3) **minimize the number of rules, regulations, and policies** to which the local educational agencies and schools located in the State are subject under this title.

(b) Support and Facilitation. State rules, regulations, and policies under this title shall support and facilitate local educational agency and school-level system improvement designed to enable children with disabilities to meet the challenging State student academic achievement standards.

20 U.S.C. § 1408 - Paperwork Reduction.

➜ **OVERVIEW:** States may create pilot programs to reduce paperwork and other non-instructional burdens. The U. S. Department of Education may grants waivers to 15 States but may not waive procedural requirements under 20 U.S.C § 1415. Two years after IDEA is enacted, the Secretary must report to Congress on the effectiveness of these waivers.

(a) Pilot Program.

(1) Purpose. The purpose of this section is to provide an opportunity for States to identify ways to **reduce paperwork burdens** and other administrative duties that are directly associated with the requirements of this title, in order to increase the time and resources available for instruction and other activities aimed at improving educational and functional results for children with disabilities.
(2) Authorization.

(A) In General. In order to carry out the purpose of this section, the Secretary is **authorized to grant waivers of statutory requirements of, or regulatory requirements** relating to, part B for a period of time **not to exceed 4 years** with respect **to not more than 15 States** based on proposals submitted by States to reduce excessive paperwork and noninstructional time burdens that do not assist in improving educational and functional results for children with disabilities.

(B) Exception. The Secretary shall not waive under this section any statutory requirements of, or regulatory requirements relating to, applicable civil rights requirements.

(C) Rule of Construction. Nothing in this section shall be construed to--

(i) affect the right of a child with a disability to receive a **free appropriate public education** under part B; and
(ii) permit a State or local educational agency to **waive procedural safeguards under section 1415** of this title.

(3) Proposal.

(A) In General. A State desiring to participate in the program under this section shall submit a proposal to the Secretary at such time and in such manner as the Secretary may reasonably require.

(B) Content. The proposal shall include--

(i) a list of any statutory requirements of, or regulatory requirements relating to, part B that the State desires the Secretary to waive, in whole or in part; and
(ii) a list of any State requirements that the State proposes to waive or change, in whole or in part, to carry out a waiver granted to the State by the Secretary.

(4) Termination of Waiver. The Secretary shall terminate a State's waiver under this section if the Secretary determines that the State--

(A) needs assistance under section 1416(d)(2)(A)(ii) of this title and that the waiver has contributed to or caused such need for assistance;

(B) needs intervention under section 1416(d)(2)(A)(iii) of this title or needs substantial intervention under section 1416(d)(2)(A)(iv) of this title; or

(C) failed to appropriately implement its waiver.

(b) Report. Beginning 2 years after the date of enactment of the Individuals with Disabilities Education Improvement Act of 2004, the Secretary shall **include in the annual report to Congress** submitted pursuant to section 3486 of this title **information related to the effectiveness of waivers** granted under subsection (a), including any **specific recommendations for broader implementation of such waivers**, in--

(1) **reducing**--
  (A) the **paperwork burden** on teachers, principals, administrators, and related service providers; and

  (B) **noninstructional time** spent by teachers in complying with part B;

(2) **enhancing longer-term educational planning;**

(3) **improving positive outcomes** for children with disabilities;

(4) **promoting collaboration** between IEP Team members; and

(5) **ensuring satisfaction of family members.**

20 U.S.C. § 1409 - Freely Associated States.

➔ **OVERVIEW:** Grants are available to the "Freely Associated States."

The Republic of the Marshall Islands, the Federated States of Micronesia, and the Republic of Palau shall continue to be eligible for competitive grants administered by the Secretary under this title to the extent that such grants continue to be available to States and local educational agencies under this title.

END PART A

PART B- ASSISTANCE FOR EDUCATION OF ALL CHILDREN WITH DISABILITIES

➜ **OVERVIEW:** Part B, Assistance for Education of All Children with Disabilities, governs special education for children between the ages of 3 and 21 and includes Sections 1411 through Section 1419 of Title 20 of the United States Code (U.S.C.):

20 U.S.C. § 1411 - Authorization; allotment; use of funds; authorization of appropriations

20 U.S.C. § 1412 - State eligibility

20 U.S.C. § 1413 - Local educational agency eligibility

20 U.S.C. § 1414 - Evaluations, eligibility determinations, IEPs, and educational placements

20 U.S.C. § 1415 - Procedural safeguards

20 U.S.C. § 1416 - Monitoring, technical assistance, and enforcement

20 U.S.C. § 1417 - Administration

20 U.S.C. § 1418 - Program information

20 U.S.C. § 1419 - Preschool grants

For most readers, the most important sections are Section 1412, Section 1414, and Section 1415. Section 1412, State Eligibility, includes child find, least restrictive environment, unilateral placements, reimbursement, and state and district assessments. Section 1414 describes requirements for evaluations, reevaluations, eligibility, IEPs, and educational placements. Section 1415, Procedural Safeguards, describes the rules of procedure designed to protect the rights of children and their parents. These safeguards include the right to examine educational records and obtain an independent educational evaluation, and the legal requirements for prior written notice, procedural safeguard notice, due process complaint notice, due process hearings, resolution sessions, mediation, attorney's fees, and discipline.

20 U.S.C. § 1411. Authorization; Allotment; Use of Funds; Authorization of Appropriations.

➜ **OVERVIEW:** Section 1411 provides funding formulas, ratios, definitions, and requirements. New in IDEA 2004 is the optional Local Educational Agency (LEA) Risk Pool in Section 1411(e)(3) that allows states to reserve up to 10% of funds for "risk pools" to address the "high need children" with disabilities. Funds in the risk pool may not be used for litigation expenses.

(a) Grants to States.

(1) Purpose of Grants. The Secretary shall make grants to States, outlying areas, and freely associated States, and provide funds to the Secretary of the Interior, to assist them to provide special education and related services to children with disabilities in accordance with this part.

(2) Maximum amount. The **maximum amount of the grant** a State may receive under this section -

(A) for fiscal years 2005 and 2006 is -

(i) **the number of children with disabilities** in the State who are receiving special education and related services -

(I) aged 3 through 5 if the State is eligible for a grant under section 1419 of this title; and

(II) aged 6 through 21; **multiplied by**

(ii) **40 percent of the average per-pupil expenditure** in public elementary schools and secondary schools in the United States; and

(B) for fiscal year **2007** and subsequent fiscal years is -

(i) **the number of children with disabilities** in the 2004-2005 school year in the State who received special education and related services -

(I) aged 3 through 5 if the State is eligible for a grant under section 1419 of this title; and

(II) aged 6 through 21; **multiplied by**

(ii) **40 percent of the average per-pupil expenditure** in public elementary schools and secondary schools in the United States; **adjusted by**

(iii) **the rate of annual change** in the sum of -

(I) 85 percent of such State's population described in subsection (d)(3)(A)(i)(II); and

(II) 15 percent of such State's population described in subsection (d)(3)(A)(i)(III).

(b) Outlying Areas and Freely Associated States, Secretary of the Interior.

(1) Outlying Areas and Freely Associated States.

(A) Funds Reserved. From the amount appropriated for any fiscal year under subsection (i), the Secretary shall reserve not more than 1 percent, which shall be used -

(i) to provide assistance to the outlying areas in accordance with their respective populations of individuals aged 3 through 21; and

(ii) to provide each freely associated State a grant in the amount that such freely associated State received for fiscal year 2003 under this part, but only if the freely associated State meets the applicable requirements of this part, as well as the requirements of section 1411(b)(2)(C) of this title as such section was in effect on the day before the date of enactment of the Individuals with Disabilities Education Improvement Act of 2004.

(B) Special Rule. The provisions of Public Law 95-134, permitting the consolidation of grants by the outlying areas, shall not apply to funds provided to the outlying areas or the freely associated States under this section.

(C) Definition. In this paragraph, the term 'freely associated States' means the Republic of the Marshall Islands, the Federated States of Micronesia, and the Republic of Palau.

(2) Secretary of the Interior. From the amount appropriated for any fiscal year under subsection (i), the Secretary shall reserve 1.226 percent to provide assistance to the Secretary of the Interior in accordance with subsection (h).

(c) Technical Assistance.

(1) In General. The Secretary may reserve not more than 1/2 of 1 percent of the amounts appropriated under this part for each fiscal year to provide technical assistance activities authorized under section 1416(i) of this title.

(2) Maximum amount. The maximum amount the Secretary may reserve under paragraph (1) for any fiscal year is $25,000,000, cumulatively adjusted by the rate of inflation as measured by the percentage increase, if any, from the preceding fiscal year in the Consumer Price Index For All Urban Consumers, published by the Bureau of Labor Statistics of the Department of Labor.

(d) Allocations to States.

(1) In General. After reserving funds for technical assistance, and for payments to the outlying areas, the freely associated States, and the Secretary of the Interior under subsections (b) and (c) for a fiscal year, the Secretary shall allocate the remaining amount among the States in accordance with this subsection.

(2) Special Rule for use of Fiscal Year 1999 Amount. If a State received any funds under this section for fiscal year 1999 on the basis of children aged 3 through 5, but does not make a free appropriate public education available to all children with disabilities aged 3 through 5 in the State in any subsequent fiscal year, the Secretary shall compute the State's amount for fiscal year 1999, solely for the purpose of calculating the State's allocation in that subsequent year under paragraph (3) or (4), by subtracting the amount allocated to the State for fiscal year 1999 on the basis of those children.

(3) Increase in Funds. If the amount available for allocations to States under paragraph (1) for a fiscal year is equal to or greater than the amount allocated to the States under this paragraph for the preceding fiscal year, those allocations shall be calculated as follows:

> **(A) Allocation of Increase.**
> > **(i) In General.** Except as provided in subparagraph (B), the Secretary shall allocate for the fiscal year -
> > > (I) to each State the amount the State received under this section for fiscal year 1999;
> > > (II) 85 percent of any remaining funds to States on the basis of the States' relative populations of children aged 3 through 21 who are of the same age as children with disabilities for whom the State ensures the availability of a free appropriate public education under this part; and
> > > (III) 15 percent of those remaining funds to States on the basis of the States' relative populations of children described in subclause (II) who are living in poverty.
> > **(ii) Data.** For the purpose of making grants under this paragraph, the Secretary shall use the most recent population data, including data on children living in poverty, that are available and satisfactory to the Secretary.

> **(B) Limitations.** Notwithstanding subparagraph (A), allocations under this paragraph shall be subject to the following:
> > **(i) Preceding Year Allocation.** No State's allocation shall be less than its allocation under this section for the preceding fiscal year.
> > **(ii) Minimum.** No State's allocation shall be less than the greatest of -
> > > (I) the sum of -
> > > > (aa) the amount the State received under this section for fiscal year 1999; and
> > > > (bb) 1/3 of 1 percent of the amount by which the amount appropriated under subsection (i) for the fiscal year exceeds the amount appropriated for this section for fiscal year 1999;
> > > (II) the sum of—
> > > > (aa) the amount the State received under this section for the preceding fiscal year; and
> > > > (bb) that amount multiplied by the percentage by which the increase in the funds appropriated for this section from the preceding fiscal year exceeds 1.5 percent; or
> > > (III) the sum of—
> > > > (aa) the amount the State received under this section for the preceding fiscal year; and
> > > > (bb) that amount multiplied by 90 percent of the percentage increase in the amount appropriated for this section from the preceding fiscal year.
> > **(iii) Maximum.** Notwithstanding clause (ii), no State's allocation under this paragraph shall exceed the sum of -
> > > (I) the amount the State received under this section for the preceding fiscal year; and

(II) that amount multiplied by the sum of 1.5 percent and the percentage increase in the amount appropriated under this section from the preceding fiscal year.

(C) Ratable Reduction. If the amount available for allocations under this paragraph is insufficient to pay those allocations in full, those allocations shall be ratably reduced, subject to subparagraph (B)(i).

(4) Decrease in Funds. If the amount available for allocations to States under paragraph (1) for a fiscal year is less than the amount allocated to the States under this section for the preceding fiscal year, those allocations shall be calculated as follows:

(A) Amounts Greater than Fiscal Year 1999 Allocations. If the amount available for allocations is greater than the amount allocated to the States for fiscal year 1999, each State shall be allocated the sum of -
(i) the amount the State received under this section for fiscal year 1999; and
(ii) an amount that bears the same relation to any remaining funds as the increase the State received under this section for the preceding fiscal year over fiscal year 1999 bears to the total of all such increases for all States.

(B) Amounts Equal to or Less than Fiscal Year 1999 Allocations.
(i) In General. If the amount available for allocations under this paragraph is equal to or less than the amount allocated to the States for fiscal year 1999, each State shall be allocated the amount the State received for fiscal year 1999.
(ii) Ratable Reduction. If the amount available for allocations under this paragraph is insufficient to make the allocations described in clause (i), those allocations shall be ratably reduced.

(e) State Level Activities.

(1) State Administration.

(A) In General. For the purpose of administering this part, including paragraph (3), section 1419 of this title, and the coordination of activities under this part with, and providing technical assistance to, other programs that provide services to children with disabilities -
(i) each State may reserve for each fiscal year not more than the maximum amount the State was eligible to reserve for State administration under this section for fiscal year 2004 or $800,000 (adjusted in accordance with subparagraph (B)), whichever is greater; and
(ii) each outlying area may reserve for each fiscal year not more than 5 percent of the amount the outlying area receives under subsection (b)(1) for the fiscal year or $35,000, whichever is greater.

(B) Cumulative Annual Adjustments. For each fiscal year beginning with fiscal year 2005, the Secretary shall cumulatively adjust
(i) the maximum amount the State was eligible to reserve for State administration under this part for fiscal year 2004; and
(ii) $800,000, by the rate of inflation as measured by the percentage increase, if any, from the preceding fiscal year in the Consumer Price Index For All Urban Consumers, published by the Bureau of Labor Statistics of the Department of Labor.

(C) Certification. Prior to expenditure of funds under this paragraph, the State shall certify to the Secretary that the arrangements to establish responsibility for services pursuant to section 1412(a)(12)(A) of this title are current.

(D) Part C. Funds reserved under subparagraph (A) may be used for the administration of part C, if the State educational agency is the lead agency for the State under such part.

(2) Other State Level Activities.

(A) State Level Activities.
(i) In General. Except as provided in clause (iii), for the purpose of carrying out State-level activities, each State may reserve for each of the fiscal years 2005 and 2006 not more than 10 percent from the amount of the State's allocation under subsection (d) for each of the fiscal years 2005 and 2006, respectively. For fiscal year 2007 and each subsequent fiscal year, the State may reserve the maximum amount the State was eligible to reserve under the preceding sentence for fiscal year 2006 (cumulatively adjusted by the rate of inflation as measured by the percentage increase, if any, from the preceding fiscal year in the Consumer Price Index For All Urban Consumers, published by the Bureau of Labor Statistics of the Department of Labor).
(ii) Small State Adjustment. Notwithstanding clause (i) and except as provided in clause (iii), in the case of a State for which the maximum amount reserved for State administration is not greater than $850,000, the State may reserve for the purpose of carrying out State-level activities for each of the fiscal years 2005 and 2006, not more than 10.5 percent from the amount of the State's allocation under subsection (d) for each of the fiscal years 2005 and 2006, respectively. For fiscal year 2007 and each subsequent fiscal year, such State may reserve the maximum amount the State was eligible to reserve under the preceding sentence for fiscal year 2006 (cumulatively adjusted by the rate of inflation as measured by the percentage increase, if any, from the preceding fiscal year in the Consumer Price Index For All Urban Consumers, published by the Bureau of Labor Statistics of the Department of Labor).
(iii) Exception. If a State does not reserve funds under paragraph (3) for a fiscal year, then -
(I) in the case of a State that is not described in clause (ii), for fiscal year 2005 or 2006, clause (i) shall be applied by substituting 9.0 percent' for 10 percent'; and
(II) in the case of a State that is described in clause (ii), for fiscal year 2005 or 2006, clause (ii) shall be applied by substituting 9.5 percent' for 10.5 percent'.

(B) Required Activities. Funds reserved under subparagraph (A) shall be used to carry out the following activities:
(i) For monitoring, enforcement, and complaint investigation.
(ii) To establish and implement the mediation process required by section 1415(e) of this title, including providing for the cost of mediators and support personnel.

(C) Authorized Activities. Funds reserved under subparagraph (A) may be used to carry out the following activities:
(i) For support and direct services, including technical assistance, personnel preparation, and professional development and training.
(ii) To support paperwork reduction activities, including expanding the use of technology in the IEP process.
(iii) To assist local educational agencies in providing positive behavioral interventions and supports and appropriate mental health services for children with disabilities.
(iv) To improve the use of technology in the classroom by children with disabilities to enhance learning.
(v) To support the use of technology, including technology with universal design principles and assistive technology devices, to maximize accessibility to the general education curriculum for children with disabilities.
(vi) Development and implementation of transition programs, including coordination of services with agencies involved in supporting the transition of children with disabilities to postsecondary activities.

(vii) To assist local educational agencies in meeting personnel shortages.

(viii) To support capacity building activities and improve the delivery of services by local educational agencies to improve results for children with disabilities.

(ix) Alternative programming for children with disabilities who have been expelled from school, and services for children with disabilities in correctional facilities, children enrolled in State-operated or State-supported schools, and children with disabilities in charter schools.

(x) To support the development and provision of appropriate accommodations for children with disabilities, or the development and provision of alternate assessments that are valid and reliable for assessing the performance of children with disabilities, in accordance with sections 6311(b) and 7301 of this title.

(xi) To provide technical assistance to schools and local educational agencies, and direct services, including supplemental educational services as defined in 6316(e) of the this title to children with disabilities, in schools or local educational agencies identified for improvement under section 6316 of this title on the sole basis of the assessment results of the disaggregated subgroup of children with disabilities, including providing professional development to special and regular education teachers, who teach children with disabilities, based on scientifically based research to improve educational instruction, in order to improve academic achievement to meet or exceed the objectives established by the State under section 6311(b)(2)(G) of this title.

(3) Local Educational Agency Risk Pool.

(A) In General.

(i) Reservation of Funds. For the purpose of assisting local educational agencies (including a charter school that is a local educational agency or a consortium of local educational agencies) in addressing the needs of high need children with disabilities[59], each State shall have the option to reserve for each fiscal year 10 percent of the amount of funds the State reserves for State-level activities under paragraph (2)(A) -

(I) to establish and make disbursements from the high cost fund to local educational agencies in accordance with this paragraph during the first and succeeding fiscal years of the high cost fund; and

(II) to support innovative and effective ways of cost sharing by the State, by a local educational agency, or among a consortium of local educational agencies, as determined by the State in coordination with representatives from local educational agencies, subject to subparagraph (B)(ii).

(ii) Definition of Local Educational Agency. In this paragraph the term 'local educational agency' **includes a charter school** that is a local educational agency, or a consortium of local educational agencies.

(B) Limitation on Uses of Funds.

(i) Establishment of High Cost Fund. A State shall not use any of the funds the State reserves pursuant to subparagraph (A)(i), but may use the funds the State reserves under paragraph (1), to establish and support the high cost fund.

(ii) Innovative and Effective Cost Sharing. A State shall not use more than 5 percent of the funds the State reserves pursuant to subparagraph (A)(i) for each fiscal year to support innovative and effective ways of cost sharing among consortia of local educational agencies.

(C) State Plan for High Cost Fund.

---

[59] The provision for risk pools to address the needs of "high need children with disabilities" is new in IDEA 2004. Funds in the risk pool may be disbursed to school districts to support "innovative, effective ways of cost sharing" by districts and consortiums of districts. Funds in the risk pool may not be used to support litigation.

(i) Definition. The State educational agency **shall establish the State's definition of a high need child with a disability**, which definition shall be developed in consultation with local educational agencies.

(ii) State Plan. The State educational agency shall develop, not later than 90 days after the State reserves funds under this paragraph, annually review, and amend as necessary, a State plan for the high cost fund. Such State plan shall -

(i) establish, in coordination with representatives from local educational agencies, a definition of a high need child with a disability that, at a minimum—

(aa) addresses the financial impact a high need child with a disability has on the budget of the child's local educational agency; and

(bb) ensures that the cost of the high need child with a disability is greater than 3 times the average per pupil expenditure (as defined in section 7801 of the this title) in that State;

(II) establish eligibility criteria for the participation of a local educational agency that, at a minimum, takes into account the number and percentage of high need children with disabilities served by a local educational agency;

(III) develop a funding mechanism that provides distributions each fiscal year to local educational agencies that meet the criteria developed by the State under subclause (II); and

(IV) establish an annual schedule by which the State educational agency shall make its distributions from the high cost fund each fiscal year.

(iii) Public Availability. The State shall make its final **State plan publicly available** not less than 30 days before the beginning of the school year, including dissemination of such information on the State website.

(D) Disbursements from the High Cost Fund.

(i) In General. Each State educational agency shall make all annual disbursements from the high cost fund established under subparagraph (A)(i) in accordance with the State plan published pursuant to subparagraph (C).

(ii) Use of Disbursements. Each State educational agency shall make annual disbursements to eligible local educational agencies in accordance with its State plan under subparagraph (C)(ii).

(iii) Appropriate Costs. The costs associated with educating a high need child with a disability under subparagraph (C)(i) are only those costs associated with providing direct special education and related services to such child that are identified in such child's IEP.

(E) Legal Fees. The disbursements under subparagraph (D) **shall not support legal fees, court costs**, or other costs associated with a cause of action brought on behalf of a child with a disability to ensure a free appropriate public education for such child.

(F) Assurance of a Free Appropriate Public Education.- **Nothing** in this paragraph **shall be construed** -

(i) **to limit** or condition **the right** of a child with a disability who is assisted under this part **to receive a free appropriate public education** pursuant to section 1412(a)(1) of this title **in the least restrictive environment** pursuant to section 1412(a)(5) of this title; or

(ii) to authorize a State educational agency or local educational agency **to establish a limit on what may be spent** on the education of a child with a disability.

(G) Special Rule for Risk Pool and High Need Assistance Programs in Effect as of January 1, 2004. Notwithstanding the provisions of subparagraphs (A) through (F), a State may use funds reserved pursuant to this paragraph for implementing a placement neutral cost sharing and reimbursement program of high need, low incidence, catastrophic, or extraordinary aid to local educational agencies that provides services to high need students based on eligibility criteria for such programs that were created not later than January 1, 2004, and are currently in operation, if such program serves children that meet the requirement of the definition of a high need child with a disability as described in subparagraph (C)(ii)(I).

(H) Medicaid Services not Affected. Disbursements provided under this paragraph **shall not be used to pay costs** that otherwise would be reimbursed as medical assistance for a child with a disability under the State medicaid program under title XIX of the Social Security Act.

(I) Remaining Funds. Funds reserved under subparagraph (A) in any fiscal year but not expended in that fiscal year pursuant to subparagraph (D) shall be allocated to local educational agencies for the succeeding fiscal year in the same manner as funds are allocated to local educational agencies under subsection (f) for the succeeding fiscal year.

(4) Inapplicability of Certain Prohibitions. A State may use funds the State reserves under paragraphs (1) and (2) without regard to -

(A) the prohibition on commingling of funds in section 1412(a)(17)(B) of this title; and

(B) the prohibition on supplanting other funds in section 1412(a)(17)(C) of this title.

(5) Report on Use of Funds. As part of the information required to be submitted to the Secretary under section 1412 of this title, each State shall annually describe how amounts under this section -

(A) will be used to meet the requirements of this title; and

(B) will be allocated among the activities described in this section to meet State priorities based on input from local educational agencies.

(6) Special Rule for Increased Funds. A State may use funds the State reserves under paragraph (1)(A) as a result of inflationary increases under paragraph (1)(B) to carry out activities authorized under clause (i), (iii), (vii), or (viii) of paragraph (2)(C).

(7) Flexibility in Using Funds for Part C. Any State eligible to receive a grant under section 1419 of this title may use funds made available under paragraph (1)(A), subsection (f)(3), or section 1419(f)(5) of this title to develop and implement a State policy jointly with the lead agency under part C and the State educational agency to provide early intervention services (which shall include an educational component that promotes school readiness and incorporates preliteracy, language, and numeracy skills) in accordance with part C to children with disabilities who are eligible for services under section 1419 of this title and who previously received services under part C until such children enter, or are eligible under State law to enter, kindergarten, or elementary school as appropriate.

(f) Subgrants to Local Educational Agencies.

(1) Subgrants Required. Each State that receives a grant under this section for any fiscal year shall distribute any funds the State does not reserve under subsection (e) to local educational agencies (including public charter schools that operate as local educational agencies) in the State that have established their eligibility under section 1413 of this title for use in accordance with this part.

(2) Procedure for Allocations to Local Educational Agencies. For each fiscal year for which funds are allocated to States under subsection (d), each State shall allocate funds under paragraph (1) as follows:

(A) Base Payments. The State shall first award each local educational agency described in paragraph (1) the amount the local educational agency would have received under this section for fiscal year 1999, if the State had distributed 75 percent of its grant for that year under section 1411(d) of this title as section 1411(d) of this title was then in effect.

(B) Allocation of Remaining Funds. After making allocations under subparagraph (A), the State shall -
(i) allocate 85 percent of any remaining funds to those local educational agencies on the basis of the relative numbers of children enrolled in public and private elementary schools and secondary schools within the local educational agency's jurisdiction; and
(ii) allocate 15 percent of those remaining funds to those local educational agencies in accordance with their relative numbers of children living in poverty, as determined by the State educational agency.

(3) Reallocation of Funds. If a State educational agency determines that a local educational agency is adequately providing a free appropriate public education to all children with disabilities residing in the area served by that local educational agency with State and local funds, the State educational agency may reallocate any portion of the funds under this part that are not needed by that local educational agency to provide a free appropriate public education to other local educational agencies in the State that are not adequately providing special education and related services to all children with disabilities residing in the areas served by those other local educational agencies.

(g) Definitions. In this section:

(1) Average per Pupil Expenditure in Public Elementary Schools and Secondary Schools in the United States. The term 'average per-pupil expenditure in public elementary schools and secondary schools in the United States' means -

(A) without regard to the source of funds -
(i) the aggregate current expenditures, during the second fiscal year preceding the fiscal year for which the determination is made (or, if satisfactory data for that year are not available, during the most recent preceding fiscal year for which satisfactory data are available) of all local educational agencies in the 50 States and the District of Columbia; plus
(ii) any direct expenditures by the State for the operation of those agencies; divided by
(B) the aggregate number of children in average daily attendance to whom those agencies provided free public education during that preceding year.

(2) State. The term 'State' means each of the 50 States, the District of Columbia, and the Commonwealth of Puerto Rico.

(h) Use of Amounts by Secretary of the Interior.

(1) Provision of Amounts for Assistance.

(A) In General. The Secretary of Education shall provide amounts to the Secretary of the Interior to meet the need for assistance for the education of children with disabilities on reservations aged 5 to 21, inclusive, enrolled in elementary schools and secondary schools for Indian children operated or funded by the Secretary of the Interior. The amount of such payment for any fiscal year shall be equal to 80 percent of the amount allotted under subsection (b)(2) for that fiscal year. Of the amount described in the preceding sentence -
(i) 80 percent shall be allocated to such schools by July 1 of that fiscal year; and
(ii) 20 percent shall be allocated to such schools by September 30 of that fiscal year.

(B) Calculation of Number of Children. In the case of Indian students aged 3 to 5, inclusive, who are enrolled in programs affiliated with the Bureau of Indian Affairs (referred to in this subsection as the BIA') schools and that are required by the States in which such schools are located to attain or maintain State accreditation, and which schools have such accreditation prior to the date of enactment of the Individuals with Disabilities Education Act Amendments of 1991, the school shall be allowed to count those children for the purpose of distribution of the funds provided under this paragraph to the Secretary of the Interior. The Secretary of the Interior shall be responsible for meeting all of the requirements of this part for those children, in accordance with paragraph (2).

(C) Additional Requirement. With respect to all other children aged 3 to 21, inclusive, on reservations, the State educational agency shall be responsible for ensuring that all of the requirements of this part are implemented.

(2) Submission of Information. The Secretary of Education may provide the Secretary of the Interior amounts under paragraph (1) for a fiscal year only if the Secretary of the Interior submits to the Secretary of Education information that -

(A) demonstrates that the Department of the Interior meets the appropriate requirements, as determined by the Secretary of Education, of sections 1412 (including monitoring and evaluation activities) and 1413 of this title;

(B) includes a description of how the Secretary of the Interior will coordinate the provision of services under this part with local educational agencies, tribes and tribal organizations, and other private and Federal service providers;

(C) includes an assurance that there are public hearings, adequate notice of such hearings, and an opportunity for comment afforded to members of tribes, tribal governing bodies, and affected local school boards before the adoption of the policies, programs, and procedures related to the requirements described in subparagraph (A);

(D) includes an assurance that the Secretary of the Interior will provide such information as the Secretary of Education may require to comply with section 1418 of this title;

(E) includes an assurance that the Secretary of the Interior and the Secretary of Health and Human Services have entered into a memorandum of agreement, to be provided to the Secretary of Education, for the coordination of services, resources, and personnel between their respective Federal, State, and local offices and with State and local educational agencies and other entities to facilitate the provision of services to Indian children with disabilities residing on or near reservations (such agreement shall provide for the apportionment of responsibilities and costs, including child find, evaluation, diagnosis, remediation or therapeutic measures, and (where appropriate) equipment and medical or personal supplies as needed for a child to remain in school or a program); and

(F) includes an assurance that the Department of the Interior will cooperate with the Department of Education in its exercise of monitoring and oversight of this application, and any agreements entered into between the Secretary of the Interior and other entities under this part, and will fulfill its duties under this part.

(3) Applicability. The Secretary shall withhold payments under this subsection with respect to the information described in paragraph (2) in the same manner as the Secretary withholds payments under section 1416(e)(6) of this title.

(4) Payments for Education and Services for Indian Children with Disabilities Aged 3 Through 5.

(A) In General. With funds appropriated under subsection (i), the Secretary of Education shall make payments to the Secretary of the Interior to be distributed to tribes or tribal organizations (as defined under section 450b of title 25) or consortia of tribes or tribal organizations to provide for the coordination of assistance for special education and related services for children with disabilities aged 3 through 5 on reservations served by elementary schools and secondary schools for Indian children operated or funded by the Department of the Interior. The amount of such payments under subparagraph (B) for any fiscal year shall be equal to 20 percent of the amount allotted under subsection (b)(2).

(B) Distribution of Funds. The Secretary of the Interior shall distribute the total amount of the payment under subparagraph (A) by allocating to each tribe, tribal organization, or consortium an amount based on the number of children with disabilities aged 3 through 5 residing on reservations as reported annually, divided by the total of those children served by all tribes or tribal organizations.

(C) Submission of Information. To receive a payment under this paragraph, the tribe or tribal organization shall submit such figures to the Secretary of the Interior as required to determine the amounts to be allocated under subparagraph (B). This information shall be compiled and submitted to the Secretary of Education.

(D) Use of Funds. The funds received by a tribe or tribal organization shall be used to assist in child find, screening, and other procedures for the early identification of children aged 3 through 5, parent training, and the provision of direct services. These activities may be carried out directly or through contracts or cooperative agreements with the BIA, local educational agencies, and other public or private nonprofit organizations. The tribe or tribal organization is encouraged to involve Indian parents in the development and implementation of these activities. The tribe or tribal organization shall, as appropriate, make referrals to local, State, or Federal entities for the provision of services or further diagnosis.

(E) Biennial Report. To be eligible to receive a grant pursuant to subparagraph (A), the tribe or tribal organization shall provide to the Secretary of the Interior a biennial report of activities undertaken under this paragraph, including the number of contracts and cooperative agreements entered into, the number of children contacted and receiving services for each year, and the estimated number of children needing services during the 2 years following the year in which the report is made. The Secretary of the Interior shall include a summary of this information on a biennial basis in the report to the Secretary of Education required under this subsection. The Secretary of Education may require any additional information from the Secretary of the Interior.

(F) Prohibitions. None of the funds allocated under this paragraph **may be used** by the Secretary of the Interior **for administrative purposes,** including child count and the provision of technical assistance.

(5) Plan for Coordination of Services. The Secretary of the Interior shall develop and implement a plan for the coordination of services for all Indian children with disabilities residing on reservations covered under this title. Such plan shall provide for the coordination of services benefiting those children from whatever source, including tribes, the Indian Health Service, other BIA divisions, and other Federal agencies. In developing the plan, the Secretary of the Interior shall consult with all interested and involved parties. The plan shall be based on the needs of the children and the system best suited for meeting those needs, and may involve the establishment of cooperative agreements between the BIA, other Federal agencies, and other entities. The plan shall also be distributed upon request to States, State educational agencies and local educational agencies, and other agencies providing services to infants, toddlers, and children with disabilities, to tribes, and to other interested parties.

(6) Establishment of Advisory Board. To meet the requirements of section 1412(a)(21) of this title, the Secretary of the Interior shall establish, under the BIA, an advisory board composed of individuals involved in or concerned with the education and provision of services to Indian infants, toddlers, children, and youth with disabilities, including

Indians with disabilities, Indian parents or guardians of such children, teachers, service providers, State and local educational officials, representatives of tribes or tribal organizations, representatives from State Interagency Coordinating Councils under section 1441 of this title in States having reservations, and other members representing the various divisions and entities of the BIA. The chairperson shall be selected by the Secretary of the Interior. The advisory board shall -

(A) assist in the coordination of services within the BIA and with other local, State, and Federal agencies in the provision of education for infants, toddlers, and children with disabilities;

(B) advise and assist the Secretary of the Interior in the performance of the Secretary of the Interior's responsibilities described in this subsection;

(C) develop and recommend policies concerning effective inter - and intra-agency collaboration, including modifications to regulations, and the elimination of barriers to inter - and intra-agency programs and activities;

(D) provide assistance and disseminate information on best practices, effective program coordination strategies, and recommendations for improved early intervention services or educational programming for Indian infants, toddlers, and children with disabilities; and

(E) provide assistance in the preparation of information required under paragraph (2)(D).

(7) Annual Reports.

(A) In General. The advisory board established under paragraph (6) shall prepare and submit to the Secretary of the Interior and to Congress an annual report containing a description of the activities of the advisory board for the preceding year.

(B) Availability. The Secretary of the Interior shall make available to the Secretary of Education the report described in subparagraph (A).

(i) Authorizations of Appropriations. For the purpose of carrying out this part, other than section 1419 of this title, there are authorized to be appropriated -

(1) $12,358,376,571 for fiscal year 2005;
(2) $14,648,647,143 for fiscal year 2006;
(3) $16,938,917,714 for fiscal year 2007;
(4) $19,229,188,286 for fiscal year 2008;
(5) $21,519,458,857 for fiscal year 2009;
(6) $23,809,729,429 for fiscal year 2010;
(7) $26,100,000,000 for fiscal year 2011; and
(8) such sums as may be necessary for fiscal year 2012 and each succeeding fiscal year.

20 U.S.C. § 1412. State Eligibility. *Catch-All*

➡ **OVERVIEW:** Section 1412, State Eligibility, is often called the "**Catch-All**" statute because it includes diverse topics including child find, least restrictive environment, transition to preschool programs, equitable services for children in private schools, unilateral placements, tuition reimbursement, and assessments. Section 1412(a)(3) describes child find requirements. Section 1412(a)(5) describes requirements for educating children with disabilities in the least restrictive environment (LRE). Section 1412(a)(10) is about services to children who attend private schools and includes new requirements about consultation with private schools and equitable services for children who attend private schools. Section 1412(a)(11) clarifies that the State is ultimately responsible for ensuring that children with disabilities receive a free appropriate education. Section 1412(a)(14) about personnel qualifications describes new requirements for highly qualified special education teachers. Section 1412(a)(16) includes important new requirements about participation in assessments, accommodations guidelines, and alternate assessments. Section 1412(a)(23) includes requirements about access to instructional materials. Section 1412(a)(25) describes the new prohibition on mandatory medication.

(a) In General. A State is eligible for assistance under this part for a fiscal year **if the State submits a plan** that provides assurances to the Secretary **that the State has in effect policies and procedures** to ensure that the State meets each of the following conditions:

(1) Free Appropriate Public Education.

(A) In General. A free appropriate public education is available to all children with disabilities residing in the State between the ages of 3 and 21, inclusive, including children with disabilities **who have been suspended or expelled** from school.[60]

(B) Limitation. The obligation to make a free appropriate public education available to all children with disabilities does not apply with respect to children -
(i) aged 3 through 5 and 18 through 21 in a State to the extent that its application to those children would be inconsistent with State law or practice, or the order of any court, respecting the provision of public education to children in those age ranges; and
(ii) aged 18 through 21 to the extent that State law does not require that special education and related services under this part be provided to children with disabilities who, in the educational placement **prior to their incarceration** in an adult correctional facility -
(I) were **not actually identified** as being a child with a disability under section 1401 of this title; or
(II) did not have an individualized education program under this part.

(C) State Flexibility. A State that provides early intervention services in accordance with part C to a child who is eligible for services under section 1419 of this title, is not required to provide such child with a free appropriate public education.

(2) Full Educational Opportunity Goal. The State has established a goal of providing full educational opportunity to all children with disabilities and a detailed timetable for accomplishing that goal.

---

[60] All children who are eligible for special education services under IDEA are entitled to FAPE, including children who have been suspended or expelled from school. Before Congress enacted Public Law 94-142 in 1975, millions of children with disabilities were not allowed to attend public schools. (See Findings in Section 1400(c) and Discipline in Section 1415(k)).

✳ **(3) Child Find.**

(A) In General. All children with disabilities residing in the State, **including** children with disabilities who are **homeless children** or are **wards of the State** and children with disabilities **attending private schools,** regardless of the severity of their disabilities, and **who are in need of special education and related services, are identified, located, and evaluated** and a practical method is developed and implemented to determine which children with disabilities are currently receiving needed special education and related services.[61]

✳ **(B) Construction. Nothing in this title requires that children be classified by their disability** so long as each child who has a disability listed in section 1401 of this title and who, by reason of that disability, needs special education and related services is regarded as a child with a disability under this part.[62]

(4) Individualized Education Program. An individualized education program, or an individualized family service plan that meets the requirements of section 1436(d) of this title, is developed, reviewed, and revised for each child with a disability in accordance with section 1414(d) of this title.

(5) Least Restrictive Environment. *The law does not mandate inclusion - look at where the child learns*

(A) In General. To the maximum extent appropriate, children with disabilities, including children in public or private institutions or other care facilities, are educated with children who are not disabled, and special classes, separate schooling, or other removal of children with disabilities from the regular educational environment occurs only when the nature or severity of the disability of a child is such that education in regular classes with the use of supplementary aids and services cannot be achieved satisfactorily.[63]

(B) Additional Requirement.
(i) In General. A **State funding mechanism shall not result in placements that violate** the requirements of subparagraph (A), and a State shall not use a funding mechanism by which the State distributes funds on the basis of the type of setting in which a child is served that will result in the failure to provide a child with a disability a free appropriate public education according to the unique needs of the child as described in the child's IEP.
(ii) Assurance. If the State does not have policies and procedures to ensure compliance with clause (i), the State shall provide the Secretary an assurance that the State will revise the funding mechanism as soon as feasible to ensure that such mechanism does not result in such placements.

---

[61] Child find requires school districts to identify, locate, and evaluate all children with disabilities, including children who are home schooled, homeless, wards of the state, and children who attend private schools. See also Section 1412(a)(10) regarding the requirements that public schools consult with private school officials.

[62] If a child is eligible for special education services under Section 1401(3), the child does not have be labeled with a disability to receive special education services. The school does not have to determine the child's "label" before providing services. Schools often spend months evaluating a child before providing any special education services. During this time, the child falls further behind. See also Section 1414(a)(1)(C)(i)(I) about the new 60 calendar day timeline between parental consent and completion of the evaluation process.

[63] The definition of "least restrictive environment" did not change. Judicial decisions about "mainstreaming" and "least restrictive environment" (LRE) vary, even within the same state. Some school districts claim the law requires them to mainstream all children with disabilities, even children who need individualized instruction that cannot be delivered in general education classrooms. In other districts, parents must fight to have their disabled child "included" in general education classes. The law takes a commonsense approach to this issue: children with disabilities should be educated with children who are not disabled "to the maximum extent appropriate." However, children can receive one-to-one or small group instruction outside of regular classes if this is necessary for them to learn.

(6) Procedural Safeguards.

(A) In General. Children with disabilities and their parents are afforded the procedural safeguards required by section 1415 of this title.

(B) Additional Procedural Safeguards. Procedures to ensure that **testing and evaluation materials and procedures** utilized for the purposes of evaluation and placement of children with disabilities for services under this title will be selected and administered so as **not to be racially or culturally discriminatory.** Such materials or procedures shall be **provided and administered in the child's native language or mode of communication,** unless it clearly is not feasible to do so, and **no single procedure shall be the sole criterion** for determining an appropriate educational program for a child.[64]

(7) Evaluation. Children with disabilities are evaluated in accordance with subsections (a) through (c) of section 1414 of this title.

(8) Confidentiality. Agencies in the State comply with section 1417(c) of this title (relating to the confidentiality of records and information).

(9) Transition from Part C to Preschool Programs. Children participating in early intervention programs assisted under part C, and who will participate in preschool programs assisted under this part, **experience a smooth and effective transition to those preschool programs** in a manner consistent with section 1437(a)(9) of this title. By the third birthday of such a child, an individualized education program or, if consistent with sections 1414(d)(2)(B) and 1436(d) of this title, an individualized family service plan, has been developed and is being implemented for the child. The local educational agency will participate in transition planning conferences arranged by the designated lead agency under section 1435(a)(10) of this title.

(10) Children in Private Schools.

(A) Children Enrolled in Private Schools by Their Parents.
(i) In General. To the extent consistent with the number and location of **children with disabilities** in the State who are **enrolled by their parents in private elementary schools and secondary schools** in the school district served by a local educational agency, **provision is made for the participation of those children** in the program assisted or carried out under this part by providing for such children special education and related services in accordance with the following requirements, unless the Secretary has arranged for services to those children under subsection (f):[65]

---

[64] In "Findings" at Section 1400(c), Congress described the over-representation of minority children and limited English proficient children in special education. These children often do not perform as well on traditional measures of intelligence and educational achievement. The requirements that evaluations shall be administered in the child's native language or mode of communication and that "no single procedure shall be the sole criterion" for determining an appropriate educational program, attempt to remedy evaluations that have caused minority children to be over-represented in special education.

[65] School districts must keep and report data about the number of children who are evaluated, found eligible, and provided services. These requirements apply to all children who attend private schools in the district. Special education and related services may be provided on the premises of a private religious school.

(I) Amounts to be expended for the provision of those services (including **direct services to parentally placed private school children**) by the local educational agency shall be equal to a proportionate amount of Federal funds made available under this part.[66]

(II) In calculating the proportionate amount of Federal funds, the local educational agency, after **timely and meaningful consultation with representatives of private schools** as described in clause (iii), **shall conduct a thorough and complete child find process** to determine the number of parentally placed children with disabilities attending private schools located in the local educational agency.[67]

(III) Such **services to parentally placed private school children with disabilities may be provided to the children on the premises of private, including religious, schools,** to the extent consistent with law.

(IV) State and local funds may supplement and in no case shall supplant the proportionate amount of Federal funds required to be expended under this subparagraph.

(V) Each **local educational agency shall maintain in its records** and provide to the State educational agency **the number of children evaluated** under this subparagraph, the number of children determined to be **children with disabilities** under this paragraph, and the **number of children served** under this paragraph.

(ii) **Child Find Requirement.**

(I) **In General.** The **requirements of paragraph (3) (relating to child find) shall apply** with respect **to children with disabilities** in the State who are **enrolled in private, including religious, elementary schools and secondary schools.**

(II) **Equitable Participation.** The child find process shall be designed to ensure the **equitable participation of parentally placed private school children** with disabilities and an accurate count of such children.

(III) **Activities.** In carrying out this clause, the local educational agency, or where applicable, the State educational agency, shall undertake activities similar to those activities undertaken for the agency's public school children.

(IV) **Cost.** The **cost of carrying out this clause, including individual evaluations, may not be considered** in determining whether a local educational agency has met its obligations under clause (i).

(V) **Completion Period.** Such child find process shall be completed in a time period comparable to that for other students attending public schools in the local educational agency.

(iii) **Consultation.** To ensure timely and meaningful consultation, a local educational agency, or where appropriate, a State educational agency, **shall consult with private school representatives and representatives of parents of parentally placed private school children with disabilities during the design and development of special education and related services for the children,**[68] including regarding -

(I) the child find process and how parentally placed private school **children suspected of having a disability can participate equitably,** including how parents, teachers, and private school officials will be informed of the process;

---

[66] IDEA includes new requirements about consultation between public school and private school officials and equitable participation of children who attend private schools. The consultation process in Section 1412(a)(10)(A) includes written affirmation, compliance, complaints to the state by private schools, and the provision of equitable services to children who attend private schools. The language about consultation with private schools brings IDEA 2004 into conformity with No Child Left Behind. (20 U.S.C. § 6320)

[67] The consultation process includes written affirmation, compliance, complaints to the state by private schools. (Section 1412(a)(10)(A))

[68] The language about consultation with private schools brings IDEA 2004 into conformity with No Child Left Behind. (20 U.S.C. § 6320)

(II) the determination of the proportionate amount of Federal funds available to serve parentally placed private school children with disabilities under this subparagraph, including the determination of how the amount was calculated;

(III) the consultation process among the local educational agency, private school officials, and representatives of parents of parentally placed private school children with disabilities, including how such process will operate throughout the school year to ensure that parentally placed private school children with disabilities identified through the child find process can meaningfully participate in special education and related services;

(IV) how, where, and by whom special education and related services will be provided for parentally placed private school children with disabilities, including a discussion of types of services, including direct services and alternate service delivery mechanisms, how such services will be apportioned if funds are insufficient to serve all children, and how and when these decisions will be made; and

(V) how, **if the local educational agency disagrees with the views of the private school officials on the provision of services** or the types of services, **whether provided directly or through a contract**, the local educational agency **shall provide to the private school officials a written explanation** of the reasons why the local educational agency **chose not to provide services** directly or through a contract.

(iv) Written Affirmation. When timely and meaningful consultation as required by clause (iii) has occurred, **the local educational agency shall obtain a written affirmation signed by the representatives of participating private schools,** and if such representatives do not provide such affirmation within a reasonable period of time, the local educational agency shall forward the documentation of the consultation process to the State educational agency.

(v) Compliance.

(I) In General. A private school official shall have the **right to submit a complaint** to the State educational agency that the local educational agency did not engage in consultation that was meaningful and timely, or did not give due consideration to the views of the private school official.

(II) Procedure. If the private school official wishes to submit a complaint, the **official shall provide the basis of the noncompliance** with this subparagraph by the local educational agency to the State educational agency, and the local educational agency shall forward the appropriate documentation to the State educational agency. If the private school official is dissatisfied with the decision of the State educational agency, **such official may submit a complaint to the Secretary** by providing the basis of the noncompliance with this subparagraph by the local educational agency to the Secretary, and the State educational agency shall forward the appropriate documentation to the Secretary.

(vi) Provision of Equitable Services.

(I) Directly or Through Contracts. The provision of services pursuant to this subparagraph shall be provided

(aa) by employees of a public agency; or

(bb) through contract by the public agency with an individual, association, agency, organization, or other entity.

(II) Secular, Neutral, Nonideological. Special education and related services provided to parentally placed private school children with disabilities, including materials and equipment, shall be secular, neutral, and nonideological.[69]

(vii) Public Control of Funds. The control of funds used to provide special education and related services under this subparagraph, and title to materials, equipment, and property purchased with those

---

[69] Court decisions about whether school districts (LEAs) must provide special education and related services at a child's private school differ around the country. Many courts have held that the public school must make these services available, but that services do not have to be provided at the private school. IDEA 2004 may cause a shift in future legal rulings.

funds, shall be in a public agency for the uses and purposes provided in this title, and a public agency shall administer the funds and property.

(B) Children Placed in, or Referred to, Private Schools by Public Agencies.

(i) In General. Children with disabilities in private schools and facilities are provided special education and related services, in accordance with an individualized education program, at no cost to their parents, if such children are placed in, or referred to, such schools or facilities by the State or appropriate local educational agency as the means of carrying out the requirements of this part or any other applicable law requiring the provision of special education and related services to all children with disabilities within such State.

(ii) Standards. In all cases described in clause (i), the State educational agency shall determine whether such schools and facilities meet standards that apply to State educational agencies and local educational agencies and that **children so served have all the rights the children** would have if served by such agencies.[70]

(C) Payment for Education of Children Enrolled in Private Schools Without Consent of or Referral by the Public Agency.

(i) In General. Subject to subparagraph (A), this part does not require a local educational agency to pay for the cost of education, including special education and related services, of a child with a disability at a private school or facility if that agency made a free appropriate public education available to the child and the parents elected to place the child in such private school or facility.

(ii) Reimbursement for Private School Placement.[71] **If the parents** of a child with a disability, **who previously received special education and related services** under the authority of a public agency, **enroll the child in a private** elementary school or secondary **school without the consent** of or referral by the public agency, **a court or a hearing officer may require the agency to reimburse the parents** for the cost of that enrollment if the court or hearing officer finds that **the agency had not made a free appropriate public education available to the child in a timely manner prior to that enrollment.**[72]

(iii) Limitation on Reimbursement. The cost of **reimbursement** described in clause (ii) **may be reduced or denied** -

(I) **if** -

(aa) at the most recent IEP meeting that the parents attended prior to removal of the child from the public school, **the parents did not inform the IEP Team that they were rejecting the placement** proposed by the public agency to provide a free appropriate public education to their child, **including stating their concerns and their intent to enroll their child in a private school at public expense; or**

(bb) **10 business days** (including any holidays that occur on a business day) **prior to the removal** of the child from the public school, the parents **did not give written notice** to the public agency of the information described in item (aa);

(II) if, prior to the parents' removal of the child from the public school, the public agency informed the parents, through the notice requirements described in section 1415(b)(3) of this title, of its

---

[70] If a public school places a child in a private school, the child has the same rights under IDEA as if the child attended a public school.

[71] See **Appendix B – Tuition Reimbursement for Private Programs** in the back of this book.

[72] The law about reimbursement for parental placements in private schools is unchanged. If the parent removes the child from a public school program and places the child in a private program, the parent may be reimbursed for the costs of the private program if a hearing officer or court determines that the public school did not offer FAPE "in a timely manner." The language that reimbursement "shall not be reduced . . ." was modified in IDEA 2004 (IDEA 97 said "may not be reduced . . .") Changing the language to "shall not be reduced" eliminates the discretion of the hearing officer. Now hearing officers shall not reduce or deny reimbursement if the subsequent conditions are met.

intent to evaluate the child (including a statement of the purpose of the evaluation that was appropriate and reasonable), **but the parents did not make the child available for such evaluation**; or

(III) upon a **judicial finding of unreasonableness** with respect to actions taken by the parents.

(iv) Exception. Notwithstanding the notice requirement in clause (iii)(I), the cost of reimbursement

(I) **shall not be reduced or denied** for failure to provide such notice if -

(aa) the school prevented the parent from providing such notice;

(bb) the parents had not received notice, pursuant to section 1415 of this title, of the notice requirement in clause (iii)(I); or

(cc) compliance with clause (iii)(I) would likely result in physical harm to the child; and

(II) **may**, in the discretion of a court or a hearing officer, **not be reduced or denied** for failure to provide such notice if -

(aa) the parent is illiterate or cannot write in English; or

(bb) compliance with clause (iii)(I) would likely result in serious emotional harm to the child.

(11) State Educational Agency Responsible for General Supervision.

(A) In General. The State educational agency **is responsible for ensuring** that

(i) the requirements of this part are met;

(ii) all educational programs for children with disabilities in the State, including all such programs administered by any other State agency or local agency -

(I) are under the general supervision of individuals in the State who are responsible for educational programs for children with disabilities; and

(II) meet the educational standards of the State educational agency; and

(iii) in carrying out this part with respect to homeless children, the requirements of subtitle B of title VII of the McKinney-Vento Homeless Assistance Act (42 U.S.C. § 11431 *et. seq.*) are met.[73]

(B) Limitation. Subparagraph (A) shall not limit the responsibility of agencies in the State other than the State educational agency to provide, or pay for some or all of the costs of, a free appropriate public education for any child with a disability in the State.

(C) Exception. Notwithstanding subparagraphs (A) and (B), the Governor (or another individual pursuant to State law), consistent with State law, may assign to any public agency in the State the responsibility of ensuring that the requirements of this part are met with respect to children with disabilities who are convicted as adults under State law and incarcerated in adult prisons.

(12) Obligations Related to and Methods of Ensuring Services -

(A) Establishing Responsibility for Services. The Chief Executive Officer of a State or designee of the officer shall ensure that an interagency agreement or other mechanism for interagency coordination is in effect between each public agency described in subparagraph (B) and the State educational agency, in order to ensure that all services described in subparagraph (B)(i) that are needed **to** ensure a free appropriate public education are provided, including the provision of such services during the pendency of any dispute under clause (iii). Such agreement or mechanism shall include the following:

---

[73] State departments of education (SEAs) are responsible for supervising school districts (LEAs). Many state departments of education view their role as a source of funding, technical assistance and training, and not an enforcement agency. In lawsuits, States often argue that they have sovereign immunity despite the clear language in Section 1403, Abrogation of Sovereign Immunity.

(i) Agency Financial Responsibility. An identification of, or a method for defining, the financial responsibility of each agency for providing services described in subparagraph (B)(i) to ensure a free appropriate public education to children with disabilities, provided that the financial responsibility of each public agency described in subparagraph (B), including the State medicaid agency and other public insurers of children with disabilities, shall precede the financial responsibility of the local educational agency (or the State agency responsible for developing the child's IEP).

(ii) Conditions and Terms of Reimbursement. The conditions, terms, and procedures under which a local educational agency shall be reimbursed by other agencies.

(iii) Interagency Disputes. Procedures for resolving interagency disputes (including procedures under which local educational agencies may initiate proceedings) under the agreement or other mechanism to secure reimbursement from other agencies or otherwise implement the provisions of the agreement or mechanism.

(iv) Coordination of Services Procedures. Policies and procedures for agencies to determine and identify the interagency coordination responsibilities of each agency to promote the coordination and timely and appropriate delivery of services described in subparagraph (B)(i).

(B) Obligation of Public Agency.

(i) In General. If any public agency other than an educational agency is otherwise obligated under Federal or State law, or assigned responsibility under State policy pursuant to subparagraph (A), to provide or pay for any services that are also considered special education or related services (**such as, but not limited to**, services described in section 1401(1) of this title relating to assistive technology devices, 1401(2) of this title relating to assistive technology services, 1401(26) of this title relating to related services, 1401(33) of this title relating to supplementary aids and services, and 1401(34) of this title relating to transition services) that are necessary for ensuring a free appropriate public education to children with disabilities within the State, such public agency shall fulfill that obligation or responsibility, either directly or through contract or other arrangement pursuant to subparagraph (A) or an agreement pursuant to subparagraph (C).

(ii) Reimbursement for Services by Public Agency. If a public agency other than an educational agency fails to provide or pay for the special education and related services described in clause (i), the local educational agency (or State agency responsible for developing the child's IEP) shall provide or pay for such services to the child.[74] Such local educational agency or State agency is authorized to claim reimbursement for the services from the public agency that failed to provide or pay for such services and such public agency shall reimburse the local educational agency or State agency pursuant to the terms of the interagency agreement or other mechanism described in subparagraph (A)(i) according to the procedures established in such agreement pursuant to subparagraph (A)(ii).

(C) Special Rule. The requirements of subparagraph (A) may be met through -

(i) State statute or regulation;

(ii) signed agreements between respective agency officials that clearly identify the responsibilities of each agency relating to the provision of services; or

(iii) other appropriate written methods as determined by the Chief Executive Officer of the State or designee of the officer and approved by the Secretary.

---

[74] When other public agencies are responsible for providing services, they must comply with this section. Because IDEA focuses on the transition from school to work and further education, state Departments of Vocational Rehabilitation may be responsible for services.

(13) Procedural Requirements Relating to Local Educational Agency Eligibility. The State educational agency will not make a final determination that a local educational agency is not eligible for assistance under this part without first affording that agency reasonable notice and an opportunity for a hearing.

(14) Personnel Qualifications.[75]

(A) In General. The State educational agency has established and maintains qualifications to ensure that personnel necessary to carry out this part are appropriately and adequately prepared and trained, including that those personnel have the content knowledge and skills to serve children with disabilities.[76]

(B) Related Services Personnel and Paraprofessionals. The qualifications under subparagraph (A) include qualifications for related services personnel and paraprofessionals that
(i) are consistent with any State-approved or State-recognized **certification, licensing, registration, or other comparable requirements** that apply to the professional discipline in which those personnel are providing special education or related services;
(ii) ensure that **related services personnel** who deliver services in their discipline or profession meet the requirements of clause (i) and have **not had certification or licensure requirements waived** on an emergency, temporary, or provisional basis; and
(iii) allow paraprofessionals and assistants who are appropriately trained and supervised, in accordance with State law, regulation, or written policy, in meeting the requirements of this part to be used to assist in the provision of special education and related services under this part to children with disabilities.

(C) Qualifications for Special Education Teachers. The qualifications described in subparagraph (A) shall ensure that each person employed as a **special education teacher** in the State who teaches elementary school, middle school, or secondary school **is highly qualified** by the deadline established in section 6319(a)(2) of this title.[77]

(D) Policy. In implementing this section, a State shall adopt a policy that includes a requirement that local educational agencies in the State **take measurable steps to recruit, hire, train, and retain highly qualified personnel** to provide special education and related services under this part to children with disabilities.

(E) Rule of Construction. Notwithstanding any other individual right of action that a parent or student may maintain under this part, **nothing in this paragraph shall be construed to create a right of action on behalf of an individual student** for the failure of a particular State educational agency or local educational agency staff person to be highly qualified, or to prevent a parent from filing a complaint about staff qualifications with the State educational agency as provided for under this part.[78]

---

[75] The requirements about qualifications of special education teachers in Section 1412(a)(14) are new and track the highly qualified teacher requirements in No Child Left Behind. (20 U.S.C. § 6319) Teachers of core academic subjects must be highly qualified by the end of the 2005-2006 school year.(NCLB, Section 6319(a)(2)) The requirements for related services personnel and paraprofessionals did not change in IDEA 2004.

[76] IDEA 2004 requires states to take measurable steps "to recruit, hire, train, and retain highly qualified personnel to provide special education and related services." (Section 1412(a)(14)(D))

[77] For more information about requirements for teachers and paraprofessionals under No Child Left Behind, read Chapter 6, "NCLB for Teachers, Principals and Paraprofessionals" in *Wrightslaw: No Child Left Behind* and consult the Bibliography at the end of *Wrightslaw: IDEA 2004*.

[78] There is no right of action, i.e., right to sue a state or school district because a teacher is not highly qualified. Parents may file complaints about inadequately trained teachers with the State Department of Education.

⌐ **(15) Performance Goals and Indicators.** The State.

(A) has established goals for the performance of children with disabilities in the State that
(i) promote the purposes of this title, as stated in section 1400(d) of this title;
(ii) are the same as the State's definition of **adequate yearly progress**, including the State's objectives for progress by children with disabilities, under section 6311(b)(2)(C) of this title;
(iii) address **graduation rates and dropout rates**, as well as such other factors as the State may determine; and
(iv) are consistent, to the extent appropriate, with any other goals and standards for children established by the State;

(B) has established performance indicators the State will use to assess progress toward achieving the goals described in subparagraph (A), including **measurable annual objectives for progress** by children with disabilities under section 6311(b)(2)(C)(v)(II)(cc) of this title;

(C) will annually report to the Secretary and the public on the progress of the State, and of children with disabilities in the State, toward meeting the goals established under subparagraph (A), which may include elements of the reports required under section 6311(h) of this title.

⌐ **(16) Participation in Assessments.**[79]

(A) In General. All children with disabilities are included in all general State and districtwide assessment programs, including assessments described under section 6311 of this title, **with appropriate accommodations and alternate assessments** where necessary and as indicated **in their respective individualized education programs.**[80]

[handwritten: No Child Left Behind]

(B) Accommodation Guidelines. The State (or, in the case of a districtwide assessment, the local educational agency) has developed guidelines for the provision of appropriate accommodations.

(C) Alternate Assessments.[81]
(i) In General. The State (or, in the case of a districtwide assessment, the local educational agency) has developed and implemented guidelines for the participation of children with disabilities in alternate assessments for those children who cannot participate in regular assessments under subparagraph (A) with accommodations as indicated in their respective individualized education programs.
(ii) Requirements for Alternate Assessments. The guidelines under clause (i) shall provide for alternate assessments that
(I) are aligned with the State's challenging academic content standards and challenging student academic achievement standards; and
(II) if the State has adopted alternate academic achievement standards permitted under the regulations promulgated to carry out section 6311(b)(1) of this title, measure the achievement of children with disabilities against those standards.

---

[79] The language in Section 1414(a)(16) changed to: "**All** children with disabilities are included in **all** general State and districtwide assessment programs . . . **with appropriate accommodations** . . ." IDEA 2004 includes requirements for accommodations guidelines and alternate assessments.

[80] The requirement that schools include all children with disabilities in all State and district assessments may have a negative impact on schools that fail use research based methods to teach children with disabilities to read, write, and do arithmetic and who fail to assess these children's progress frequently.

[81] See *Alternate Assessments: Measuring What All Students Have Learned* by Sandra Thompson, Rachel Quenemoen and Martha L. Thurlow, National Center on Educational Outcomes. www.nasponline.org/futures/altassess.html

(iii) **Conduct of Alternate Assessments**. The State conducts the alternate assessments described in this subparagraph.

(D) **Reports**. The **State educational agency** (or, in the case of a districtwide assessment, the **local educational agency**) makes available to the public, and **reports to the public** with the same frequency and in the same detail as it reports on the assessment of nondisabled children, the following:

(i) The number of children with disabilities participating in regular assessments, and the number of those children who were provided accommodations in order to participate in those assessments.

(ii) The number of children with disabilities participating in alternate assessments described in subparagraph (C)(ii)(I).

(iii) The number of children with disabilities participating in alternate assessments described in subparagraph (C)(ii)(II).

(iv) **The performance of children with disabilities on regular assessments and on alternate assessments** (if the number of children with disabilities participating in those assessments is sufficient to yield statistically reliable information and reporting that information will not reveal personally identifiable information about an individual student), compared with the achievement of all children, including children with disabilities, on those assessments.

(E) **Universal Design**. The **State educational agency** (or, in the case of a districtwide assessment, the local educational agency) **shall,** to the extent feasible, **use universal design principles in** developing and administering any assessments under this paragraph.

(17) Supplementation of State, Local, and Other Federal Funds.

(A) **Expenditures**. Funds paid to a State under this part will be expended in accordance with all the provisions of this part.

(B) **Prohibition Against Commingling**. Funds paid to a State under this part will not be commingled with State funds.

(C) **Prohibition Against Supplantation and Conditions for Waiver by Secretary**. Except as provided in section 1413 of this title, funds paid to a State under this part will be used to supplement the level of Federal, State, and local funds (including funds that are not under the direct control of State or local educational agencies) expended for special education and related services provided to children with disabilities under this part and in no case to supplant such Federal, State, and local funds, except that, where the State provides clear and convincing evidence that all children with disabilities have available to them a free appropriate public education, the Secretary may waive, in whole or in part, the requirements of this subparagraph if the Secretary concurs with the evidence provided by the State.

(18) Maintenance of State Financial Support.

(A) **In General.** The State does not reduce the amount of State financial support for special education and related services for children with disabilities, or otherwise made available because of the excess costs of educating those children, below the amount of that support for the preceding fiscal year.

(B) **Reduction of Funds for Failure to Maintain Support.** The Secretary shall reduce the allocation of funds under section 1411 of this title for any fiscal year following the fiscal year in which the State fails to comply with the requirement of subparagraph (A) by the same amount by which the State fails to meet the requirement.

(C) Waivers for Exceptional or Uncontrollable Circumstances. The Secretary may waive the requirement of subparagraph (A) for a State, for 1 fiscal year at a time, if the Secretary determines that

(i) granting a waiver would be equitable due to exceptional or uncontrollable circumstances such as a natural disaster or a precipitous and unforeseen decline in the financial resources of the State; or

(ii) the State meets the standard in paragraph (17)(C) for a waiver of the requirement to supplement, and not to supplant, funds received under this part.

(D) Subsequent Years. If, for any year, a State fails to meet the requirement of subparagraph (A), including any year for which the State is granted a waiver under subparagraph (C), the financial support required of the State in future years under subparagraph (A) shall be the amount that would have been required in the absence of that failure and not the reduced level of the State's support.

✳ **(19) Public Participation.** Prior to the adoption of any policies and procedures needed to comply with this section (including any amendments to such policies and procedures), the State ensures that there are public hearings, adequate notice of the hearings, and an opportunity for comment available to the general public, including individuals with disabilities and parents of children with disabilities.

✳ **(20) Rule of Construction.** In complying with paragraphs (17) and (18), a State may not use funds paid to it under this part to satisfy State-law mandated funding obligations to local educational agencies, including funding based on student attendance or enrollment, or inflation.

✳ **(21) State Advisory Panel.**[82]

(A) In General. The State has established and maintains an advisory panel for the purpose of providing policy guidance with respect to special education and related services for children with disabilities in the State.

(B) Membership. Such advisory panel shall consist of members appointed by the Governor, or any other official authorized under State law to make such appointments, be representative of the State population, and be **composed of individuals involved in, or concerned with, the education of children with disabilities,** including -

(i) parents of children with disabilities (ages birth through 26);

(ii) individuals with disabilities;

(iii) teachers;

(iv) representatives of institutions of higher education that prepare special education and related services personnel;

(v) State and local education officials, including officials who carry out activities under subtitle B of title VII of the McKinney-Vento Homeless Assistance Act (42 U.S.C. 11431 et seq.);

(vi) administrators of programs for children with disabilities;

(vii) representatives of other State agencies involved in the financing or delivery of related services to children with disabilities;

(viii) representatives of private schools and public charter schools;

(ix) not less than 1 representative of a vocational, community, or business organization concerned with the provision of transition services to children with disabilities;

(x) a representative from the State child welfare agency responsible for foster care; and

(xi) representatives from the State juvenile and adult corrections agencies.

---

[82] Most members of state advisory panels shall be individuals with disabilities or parents of children with disabilities. Other members include representatives from private and charter schools, child welfare agencies, and corrections agencies.

(C) Special Rule. A majority of the members of the panel shall be individuals with disabilities or parents of children with disabilities (ages birth through 26).

(D) Duties. The advisory panel shall -
(i) advise the State educational agency of unmet needs within the State in the education of children with disabilities;
(ii) comment publicly on any rules or regulations proposed by the State regarding the education of children with disabilities;
(iii) advise the State educational agency in developing evaluations and reporting on data to the Secretary under section 1418 of this title;
(iv) advise the State educational agency in developing corrective action plans to address findings identified in Federal monitoring reports under this part; and
(v) advise the State educational agency in developing and implementing policies relating to the coordination of services for children with disabilities.

(22) Suspension and Expulsion Rates.

(A) In General. The State educational agency **examines data**, including data disaggregated by race and ethnicity, to determine if significant discrepancies are occurring in the **rate of long-term suspensions and expulsions** of children with disabilities -
(i) among local educational agencies in the State; or
(ii) compared to such rates for nondisabled children within such agencies.

(B) Review and Revision of Policies. If such discrepancies are occurring, the State educational agency reviews and, if appropriate, revises (or requires the affected State or local educational agency to revise) its **policies, procedures, and practices** relating to the **development and implementation of IEPs**, the use of **positive behavioral interventions and supports, and procedural safeguards,** to ensure that such policies, procedures, and practices comply with this title.

(23) Access to Instructional Materials.[83]

(A) In General. The State adopts the **National Instructional Materials Accessibility Standard** for the purposes of providing instructional materials to blind persons or other persons with print disabilities, **in a timely manner** after the publication of the National Instructional Materials Accessibility Standard in the Federal Register.

(B) Rights of State Educational Agency. Nothing in this paragraph shall be construed to require any State educational agency to coordinate with the National Instructional Materials Access Center. If a State educational agency chooses not to coordinate with the National Instructional Materials Access Center, such agency **shall provide an assurance** to the Secretary that the agency **will provide instructional materials to blind persons or other persons with print disabilities** in a timely manner.

(C) Preparation and Delivery of Files. If a State educational agency chooses to coordinate with the National Instructional Materials Access Center, not later than 2 years after the date of enactment of the Individuals with Disabilities Education Improvement Act of 2004, the agency, as part of any print instructional materials adoption process, procurement contract, or other practice or instrument used for

---

[83] The requirements about access to instructional materials and accessibility standards are new in IDEA 2004.

purchase of print instructional materials, shall enter into a written contract with the publisher of the print instructional materials to -

(i) require the publisher to prepare and, on or before delivery of the print instructional materials, provide to the National Instructional Materials Access Center electronic files containing the contents of the print instructional materials using the National Instructional Materials Accessibility Standard; or

(ii) purchase instructional materials from the publisher that are produced in, or may be rendered in, specialized formats.

(D) Assistive Technology. In carrying out this paragraph, the State educational agency, to the maximum extent possible, shall work collaboratively with the State agency responsible for assistive technology programs.

(E) Definitions. In this paragraph:

(i) National Instructional Materials Access Center. The term 'National Instructional Materials Access Center' means the center established pursuant to section 1474(e) of this title.

(ii) National Instructional Materials Accessibility Standard. The term 'National Instructional Materials Accessibility Standard' has the meaning given the term in section 1474(e)(3)(A) of this title.

(iii) Specialized Formats. The term 'specialized formats' has the meaning given the term in section 1474(e)(3)(D) of this title.

(24) Overidentification and Disproportionality.[84]

The State has in effect, consistent with the purposes of this title and with section 1418(d) of this title, **policies and procedures designed to prevent the inappropriate overidentification or disproportionate representation by race and ethnicity of children** as children with disabilities, including children with disabilities with a particular impairment described in section 1401 of this title.

(25) Prohibition on Mandatory Medication.[85]   *New in 2004*

(A) In General. The State educational agency **shall prohibit State and local educational agency personnel from requiring a child to obtain a prescription** for a substance covered by the Controlled Substances Act (21 U.S.C. 801 et seq.) **as a condition of attending school, receiving an evaluation** under subsection (a) or (c) of section 1414 of this title, or receiving services under this title.

(B) Rule of Construction. Nothing in subparagraph (A) **shall be construed to create a Federal prohibition against teachers** and other school personnel consulting or **sharing classroom-based observations with parents** or guardians regarding a student's academic and functional performance, or behavior in the classroom or school, or regarding the need for evaluation for special education or related services under paragraph (3).

---

[84] The section about Overidentification and Disproportionality is new. In Findings, Congress found that "African-American children are identified as having mental retardation and emotional disturbance at rates greater than their White counterparts. Schools with predominately white students and teachers have placed disproportionately high numbers of their minority students into special education." (Section 1400(c)(12)(C)) States must develop policies and procedures to correct these problems.

[85] The requirements that prohibit school personnel from requiring a child to obtain a prescription for a controlled substance (i.e., Ritalin, Adderal, etc.) in order to attend school, receive an evaluation, or receive special education services are new in IDEA 2004.

(b) State Educational Agency as Provider of Free Appropriate Public Education or Direct Services. If the State educational agency provides free appropriate public education to children with disabilities, or provides direct services to such children, such agency -

(1) shall comply with any additional requirements of section 1413(a) of this title, as if such agency were a local educational agency; and

(2) may use amounts that are otherwise available to such agency under this part to serve those children without regard to section 1413(a)(2)(A)(i) of this title (relating to excess costs).

(c) Exception for Prior State Plans.

(1) In General. If a State has on file with the Secretary policies and procedures that demonstrate that such State meets any requirement of subsection (a), including any policies and procedures filed under this part as in effect before the effective date of the Individuals with Disabilities Education Improvement Act of 2004, the Secretary shall consider such State to have met such requirement for purposes of receiving a grant under this part.

(2) Modifications Made by State. Subject to paragraph (3), an application submitted by a State in accordance with this section shall remain in effect until the State submits to the Secretary such modifications as the State determines necessary. This section shall apply to a modification to an application to the same extent and in the same manner as this section applies to the original plan.

(3) Modifications Required by the Secretary. If, after the effective date of the Individuals with Disabilities Education Improvement Act of 2004, the provisions of this title are amended (or the regulations developed to carry out this title are amended), there is a new interpretation of this title by a Federal court or a State's highest court, or there is an official finding of noncompliance with Federal law or regulations, then the Secretary may require a State to modify its application only to the extent necessary to ensure the State's compliance with this part.

(d) Approval by the Secretary.

(1) In General. If the Secretary determines that a State is eligible to receive a grant under this part, the Secretary shall notify the State of that determination.

(2) Notice and Hearing. The Secretary shall not make a final determination that a State is not eligible to receive a grant under this part until after providing the State -

(A) with reasonable notice; and

(B) with an opportunity for a hearing.

(e) Assistance Under Other Federal Programs. Nothing in this title permits a State to reduce medical and other assistance available, or to alter eligibility, under titles V and XIX of the Social Security Act with respect to the provision of a free appropriate public education for children with disabilities in the State.

(f) By-Pass for Children in Private Schools.

(1) In General. If, on the date of enactment of the Education of the Handicapped Act Amendments of 1983, a State educational agency was prohibited by law from providing for the **equitable participation** in special programs **of children with disabilities enrolled in private elementary schools and secondary schools** as required by subsection (a)(10)(A), or if the Secretary determines that a State educational agency, local educational agency, or other entity has substantially **failed or is unwilling to provide for such equitable participation**, then the Secretary shall, notwithstanding such provision of law, arrange for the provision of services to such children through arrangements that shall be subject to the requirements of such subsection.

(2) Payments.

(A) Determination of Amounts. If the Secretary arranges for services pursuant to this subsection, the Secretary, after consultation with the appropriate public and private school officials, shall pay to the provider of such services for a fiscal year an amount per child that does not exceed the amount determined by dividing -
(i) the total amount received by the State under this part for such fiscal year; by
(ii) the number of children with disabilities served in the prior year, as reported to the Secretary by the State under section 1418 of this title.

(B) Withholding of Certain Amounts. Pending final resolution of any investigation or complaint that may result in a determination under this subsection, the Secretary may withhold from the allocation of the affected State educational agency the amount the Secretary estimates will be necessary to pay the cost of services described in subparagraph (A).

(C) Period of Payments. The period under which payments are made under subparagraph (A) shall continue until the Secretary determines that there will no longer be any failure or inability on the part of the State educational agency to meet the requirements of subsection (a)(10)(A).

(3) Notice and Hearing.

(A) In General. The Secretary shall not take any final action under this subsection until the State educational agency affected by such action has had an opportunity, for not less than 45 days after receiving written notice thereof, to submit written objections and to appear before the Secretary or the Secretary's designee to show cause why such action should not be taken.

(B) Review of Action. If a State educational agency is dissatisfied with the Secretary's final action after a proceeding under subparagraph (A), such agency may, not later than 60 days after notice of such action, file with the United States court of appeals for the circuit in which such State is located a petition for review of that action. A copy of the petition shall be forthwith transmitted by the clerk of the court to the Secretary. The Secretary thereupon shall file in the court the record of the proceedings on which the Secretary based the Secretary's action, as provided in section 2112 of title 28, United States Code.

(C) Review of Findings of Fact. The findings of fact by the Secretary, if supported by substantial evidence, shall be conclusive, but the court, for good cause shown, may remand the case to the Secretary to take further evidence, and the Secretary may thereupon make new or modified findings of fact and may modify the Secretary's previous action, and shall file in the court the record of the further proceedings. Such new or modified findings of fact shall likewise be conclusive if supported by substantial evidence.

(D) Jurisdiction of Court of Appeals; Review by United States Supreme Court. Upon the filing of a petition under subparagraph (B), the United States court of appeals shall have jurisdiction to affirm the action of the Secretary or to set it aside, in whole or in part. The judgment of the court shall be subject to review by the Supreme Court of the United States upon certiorari or certification as provided in section 1254 of title 28, United States Code.

20 U.S.C. § 1413. Local Educational Agency Eligibility.

➡ **OVERVIEW:** Section 1413 includes requirements for school district (LEA) and charter school eligibility. IDEA 2004 includes new requirements about purchasing instructional materials, records of migratory children, and early intervening services. School districts must provide services to children with disabilities who attend charter schools in the same manner as children who attend other public schools and must provide supplementary services and related services on site at the charter school. Section 1413(a)(6) describes new requirements about access to instructional materials and the option of coordinating with the National Instructional Materials Access Center. Section 1413(f) describes new requirements for early intervening services in IDEA 2004. States can provide direct services if a district does not comply with the law.

(a) In General. A local educational agency is eligible for assistance under this part for a fiscal year if such agency submits a plan that provides assurances to the State educational agency that the local educational agency meets each of the following conditions:

(1) Consistency With State Policies. The local educational agency, in providing for the education of children with disabilities within its jurisdiction, has in effect policies, procedures, and programs that are consistent with the State policies and procedures established under section 1412 of this title.

(2) Use of Amounts.

(A) In General. Amounts provided to the local educational agency under this part shall be expended in accordance with the applicable provisions of this part and -
(i) shall be used only to pay the excess costs of providing special education and related services to children with disabilities;
(ii) shall be used to supplement State, local, and other Federal funds and not to supplant such funds; and
(iii) shall not be used, except as provided in subparagraphs (B) and (C), to reduce the level of expenditures for the education of children with disabilities made by the local educational agency from local funds below the level of those expenditures for the preceding fiscal year.

(B) Exception. Notwithstanding the restriction in subparagraph (A)(iii), a local educational agency may reduce the level of expenditures where such reduction is attributable to -
(i) the voluntary departure, by retirement or otherwise, or departure for just cause, of special education personnel;
(ii) a decrease in the enrollment of children with disabilities;
(iii) the termination of the obligation of the agency, consistent with this part, to provide a program of special education to a particular child with a disability that is an exceptionally costly program, as determined by the State educational agency, because the child -
(I) has left the jurisdiction of the agency;
(II) has reached the age at which the obligation of the agency to provide a free appropriate public education to the child has terminated; or
(III) no longer needs such program of special education; or
(iv) the termination of costly expenditures for long-term purchases, such as the acquisition of equipment or the construction of school facilities.

(C) Adjustment to Local Fiscal Effort in Certain Fiscal Years.
(i) Amounts in Excess. Notwithstanding clauses (ii) and (iii) of subparagraph (A), for any fiscal year for which the allocation received by a local educational agency under section 1411(f) of this title exceeds the amount the local educational agency received for the previous fiscal year, the local educational

agency may reduce the level of expenditures otherwise required by subparagraph (A)(iii) by not more than 50 percent of the amount of such excess.

(ii) Use of Amounts to Carry Out Activities Under ESEA. If a local educational agency exercises the authority under clause (i), the agency shall use an amount of local funds equal to the reduction in expenditures under clause (i) to carry out activities authorized under the Elementary and Secondary Education Act of 1965. [20 U.S.C. § 6301 et. seq.]

(iii) State Prohibition. Notwithstanding clause (i), if a State educational agency determines that a local educational agency is unable to establish and maintain programs of free appropriate public education that meet the requirements of subsection (a) or the State educational agency has taken action against the local educational agency under section 1416 of this title, the State educational agency shall prohibit the local educational agency from reducing the level of expenditures under clause (i) for that fiscal year.

(iv) Special Rule. The amount of funds expended by a local educational agency under subsection (f) shall count toward the maximum amount of expenditures such local educational agency may reduce under clause (i).

(D) Schoolwide Programs Under Title I of the ESEA. Notwithstanding subparagraph (A) or any other provision of this part, a local educational agency may use funds received under this part for any fiscal year to carry out a schoolwide program under section 6314 of this title, except that the amount so used in any such program shall not exceed -

(i) the number of children with disabilities participating in the schoolwide program; multiplied by

(ii)

(I) the amount received by the local educational agency under this part for that fiscal year; divided by

(II) the number of children with disabilities in the jurisdiction of that agency.

(3) Personnel Development. The local educational agency shall ensure that all personnel necessary to carry out this part are appropriately and adequately prepared, subject to the requirements of section 1412(a)(14) of this title and section 6622 of this title.

(4) Permissive Use of Funds.

(A) Uses Notwithstanding paragraph (2)(A) or section 1412(a)(17)(B) of this title (relating to commingled funds), funds provided to the local educational agency under this part may be used for the following activities:

(i) Services and Aids That Also Benefit Nondisabled Children. For the costs of special education and related services, and supplementary aids and services, provided in a regular class or other education-related setting to a child with a disability in accordance with the individualized education program of the child, even if 1 or more nondisabled children benefit from such services.

(ii) Early Intervening Services. To develop and implement coordinated, early intervening educational services in accordance with subsection (f).

(iii) High Cost Education and Related Services. To establish and implement cost or risk sharing funds, consortia, or cooperatives for the local educational agency itself, or for local educational agencies working in a consortium of which the local educational agency is a part, to pay for high cost special education and related services.

(B) Administrative Case Management. A local educational agency may use funds received under this part to purchase appropriate technology for recordkeeping, data collection, and related case management activities of teachers and related services personnel providing services described in the individualized education program of children with disabilities, that is needed for the implementation of such case management activities.

(5) Treatment of Charter Schools and Their Students. In carrying out this part with respect to charter schools that are public schools of the local educational agency, the local educational agency -

(A) **serves children with disabilities attending those charter schools in the same manner as** the local educational agency serves **children with disabilities in its other schools, including providing supplementary and related services on site** at the charter school to the same extent to which the local educational agency has a policy or practice of providing such services on the site to its other public schools; and

(B) provides funds under this part to those charter schools -
　(i) on the same basis as the local educational agency provides funds to the local educational agency's other public schools, including proportional distribution based on relative enrollment of children with disabilities; and
　(ii) at the same time as the agency distributes other Federal funds to the agency's other public schools, consistent with the State's charter school law.

(6) Purchase of Instructional Materials.

(A) In General. Not later than 2 years after the date of enactment of the Individuals with Disabilities Education Improvement Act of 2004, a local educational agency that chooses to **coordinate with the National Instructional Materials Access Center**, when purchasing print instructional materials, shall acquire the print instructional materials in the same manner and subject to the same conditions as a State educational agency acquires print instructional materials under section 1412(a)(23) of this title.

(B) Rights of Local Educational Agency. Nothing in this paragraph shall be construed to require a local educational agency to coordinate with the National Instructional Materials Access Center. If a local educational agency chooses not to coordinate with the National Instructional Materials Access Center, the local educational agency shall provide an assurance to the State educational agency that the local educational agency will provide instructional materials to blind persons or other persons with print disabilities in a timely manner.

(7) Information for State Educational Agency. The local educational agency **shall provide** the State educational agency with information necessary to enable the State educational agency to carry out its duties under this part, including, with respect to paragraphs (15) and (16) of section 1412(a) of this title, **information relating to the performance of children with disabilities** participating in programs carried out under this part.

(8) Public Information. The local educational agency **shall make available to parents of children with disabilities and to the general public** all documents relating to the eligibility of such agency under this part.

(9) Records Regarding Migratory Children with Disabilities. The local educational agency shall cooperate in the Secretary's efforts under section 6398 of this title to ensure the linkage of records pertaining to migratory children with a disability for the purpose of electronically exchanging, among the States, health and educational information regarding such children.

(b) Exception for Prior Local Plans.

(1) In General. If a local educational agency or State agency has on file with the State educational agency policies and procedures that demonstrate that such local educational agency, or such State agency, as the case may be, meets any requirement of subsection (a), including any policies and procedures filed under this part as in effect before the effective date of the Individuals with Disabilities Education Improvement Act of 2004, the State educational agency shall consider such local educational agency or State agency, as the case may be, to have met such requirement for purposes of receiving assistance under this part.

(2) Modification Made by Local Educational Agency. Subject to paragraph (3), an application submitted by a local educational agency in accordance with this section shall remain in effect until the local educational agency submits to the State educational agency such modifications as the local educational agency determines necessary.

(3) Modifications Required by State Educational Agency. If, after the effective date of the Individuals with Disabilities Education Improvement Act of 2004, the provisions of this title are amended (or the regulations developed to carry out this title are amended), there is a new interpretation of this title by Federal or State courts, or there is an official finding of noncompliance with Federal or State law or regulations, then the State educational agency may require a local educational agency to modify its application only to the extent necessary to ensure the local educational agency's compliance with this part or State law.

(c) Notification of Local Educational Agency or State Agency in Case of Ineligibility. If the State educational agency determines that a local educational agency or State agency is not eligible under this section, then the State educational agency shall notify the local educational agency or State agency, as the case may be, of that determination and shall provide such local educational agency or State agency with reasonable notice and an opportunity for a hearing.

(d) Local Educational Agency Compliance.[86]

(1) In General. If the State educational agency, after reasonable notice and an opportunity for a hearing, finds that a local educational agency or State agency that has been determined to be eligible under this section is failing to comply with any requirement described in subsection (a), the State educational agency **shall reduce or shall not provide any further payments** to the local educational agency or State agency until the State educational agency is satisfied that the local educational agency or State agency, as the case may be, is complying with that requirement.

(2) Additional Requirement. Any State agency or local educational agency in receipt of a notice described in paragraph (1) shall, by means of public notice, take such measures as may be necessary to bring the pendency of an action pursuant to this subsection to the attention of the public within the jurisdiction of such agency.

(3) Consideration. In carrying out its responsibilities under paragraph (1), the State educational agency shall **consider any decision made in a hearing** held under section 1415 of this title **that is adverse** to the local educational agency or State agency involved in that decision.

---

[86] If a school district fails to comply with the requirements described in Section 1413(a), the State must eliminate payments until the district is in compliance. This requirement is not discretionary.

(e) Joint Establishment of Eligibility.

(1) Joint Establishment.

(A) In General. A State educational agency may require a local educational agency to establish its eligibility jointly with another local educational agency if the State educational agency determines that the local educational agency will be ineligible under this section because the local educational agency will not be able to establish and maintain programs of sufficient size and scope to effectively meet the needs of children with disabilities.

(B) Charter School Exception. A State educational agency may not require a charter school that is a local educational agency to jointly establish its eligibility under subparagraph (A) unless the charter school is explicitly permitted to do so under the State's charter school law.

(2) Amount of Payments. If a State educational agency requires the joint establishment of eligibility under paragraph (1), the total amount of funds made available to the affected local educational agencies shall be equal to the sum of the payments that each such local educational agency would have received under section 1411(f) of this title if such agencies were eligible for such payments.

(3) Requirements. Local educational agencies that establish joint eligibility under this subsection shall -

(A) adopt policies and procedures that are consistent with the State's policies and procedures under section 1412(a) of this title; and

(B) be jointly responsible for implementing programs that receive assistance under this part.

(4) Requirements for Educational Service Agencies.

(A) In General. If an educational service agency is required by State law to carry out programs under this part, the joint responsibilities given to local educational agencies under this subsection shall -
(i) not apply to the administration and disbursement of any payments received by that educational service agency; and
(ii) be carried out only by that educational service agency.

(B) Additional Requirement. Notwithstanding any other provision of this subsection, an educational service agency shall provide for the education of children with disabilities in the least restrictive environment, as required by section 1412(a)(5) of this title.

(f) Early Intervening Services.[87]

(1) In General. A local educational agency **may not use more than 15 percent** of the amount such agency receives under this part for any fiscal year, less any amount reduced by the agency pursuant to subsection (a)(2)(C), if any, in combination with other amounts (which may include amounts other than education

---

[87] The new requirements for early intervening services reflect the requirement to use using "proven methods of teaching and learning" based on "replicable research." (See Findings, Section 1400(c)(4)) School districts may use up to 15 percent of their Part B funds to develop and implement early intervening services for students who need academic and behavioral assistance but have not been identified as needing special education services. Funds can be used for training so teachers have the knowledge and skills to deliver scientifically based academic instruction and literacy instruction. Funds can also be used to provide students with educational evaluations, services and supports, including scientifically based literacy instruction.

funds), **to develop and implement coordinated, early intervening services**, which may include interagency financing structures, for **students in kindergarten through grade 12** (with a particular **emphasis on students in kindergarten through grade 3**) who have **not been identified as needing special education** or related services **but who need additional academic and behavioral support** to succeed in a general education environment.

(2) Activities. In implementing coordinated, early intervening services under this subsection, a local educational agency may carry out activities that include -

(A) **professional development** (which may be provided by entities other than local educational agencies) for teachers and other school staff to enable such personnel to deliver **scientifically based academic instruction**[88] **and behavioral interventions, including scientifically based literacy instruction**[89], and, where appropriate, instruction on the use of adaptive and instructional software; and

(B) providing **educational and behavioral evaluations, services, and supports**, including **scientifically based literacy instruction**.

(3) Construction. Nothing in this subsection shall be construed to limit or create a right to a free appropriate public education under this part.

(4) Reporting. Each local educational agency that develops and maintains coordinated, early intervening services under this subsection shall annually report to the State educational agency on -

(A) the number of students served under this subsection; and

(B) the number of students served under this subsection who subsequently receive special education and related services under this title during the preceding 2-year period.

(5) Coordination with Elementary and Secondary Education Act of 1965. Funds made available to carry out this subsection may be used to carry out coordinated, early intervening services aligned with activities funded by, and carried out under, the Elementary and Secondary Education Act of 1965 if such funds are used to supplement, and not supplant, funds made available under the Elementary and Secondary Education Act of 1965 for the activities and services assisted under this subsection.

(g) Direct Services by the State Educational Agency.

(1) In General. A State educational agency **shall use the payments** that would otherwise have been available to a local educational agency or to a State agency **to provide special education and related services directly** to children with disabilities residing in the area served by that local educational agency, or for whom that State agency is responsible, if the State educational agency determines that the local educational agency or State agency, as the case may be -

(A) has not provided the information needed to establish the eligibility of such local educational agency or State agency under this section;

---

[88] See **Appendix F – Reading and Research Based Instruction**

[89] The definitions of reading, scientifically based reading research, the essential components of reading instruction, and screening, diagnostic, and classroom-based reading assessments are in No Child Left Behind at 20 U. S. C. Section 6368. (See *Wrightslaw: No Child Left Behind*)

(B) is unable to establish and maintain programs of free appropriate public education that meet the requirements of subsection (a);

(C) is unable or unwilling to be consolidated with 1 or more local educational agencies in order to establish and maintain such programs; or

(D) has 1 or more children with disabilities who can best be served by a regional or State program or service delivery system designed to meet the needs of such children.

(2) Manner and Location of Education and Services. The **State** educational agency **may provide special education and related services** under paragraph (1) **in such manner and at such locations** (including regional or State centers) **as the State** educational agency **considers appropriate.** Such education and services shall be provided in accordance with this part.

(h) State Agency Eligibility. Any State agency that desires to receive a subgrant for any fiscal year under section 1411(f) of this title shall demonstrate to the satisfaction of the State educational agency that –

(1) all children with disabilities who are participating in programs and projects funded under this part receive a free appropriate public education, and that those children and their parents are provided all the rights and procedural safeguards described in this part; and

(2) the agency meets such other conditions of this section as the Secretary determines to be appropriate.

(i) Disciplinary Information. The State **may** require that a local educational agency include in the records of a child with a disability a statement of any **current or previous disciplinary action** that has been taken against the child and transmit such statement to the same extent that such disciplinary information is included in, and transmitted with, the student records of nondisabled children. The statement may include a description of any behavior engaged in by the child that required disciplinary action, a description of the disciplinary action taken, and any other information that is relevant to the safety of the child and other individuals involved with the child. If the State adopts such a policy, and the child transfers from 1 school to another, the transmission of any of the child's records shall include both the child's current individualized education program and any such statement of current or previous disciplinary action that has been taken against the child.

(j) State Agency Flexibility.

(1) Adjustment to State Fiscal Effort in Certain Fiscal Years. For any fiscal year for which the allotment received by a State under section 1411 of this title exceeds the amount the State received for the previous fiscal year and if the State in school year 2003-2004 or any subsequent school year pays or reimburses all local educational agencies within the State from State revenue 100 percent of the non-Federal share of the costs of special education and related services, the State educational agency, notwithstanding paragraphs (17) and (18) of section 1412(a) of this title and section 1412(b) of this title, may reduce the level of expenditures from State sources for the education of children with disabilities by not more than 50 percent of the amount of such excess.

(2) Prohibition. Notwithstanding paragraph (1), if the Secretary determines that a State educational agency is unable to establish, maintain, or oversee programs of free appropriate public education that meet the requirements of this part, or that the State needs assistance, intervention, or substantial intervention under section 1416(d)(2)(A) of this title, the Secretary shall prohibit the State educational agency from exercising the authority in paragraph (1).

(3) Education Activities. If a State educational agency exercises the authority under paragraph (1), the agency shall use funds from State sources, in an amount equal to the amount of the reduction under paragraph (1), to support activities authorized under the Elementary and Secondary Education Act of 1965 or to support need based student or teacher higher education programs.

(4) Report. For each fiscal year for which a State educational agency exercises the authority under paragraph (1), the State educational agency shall report to the Secretary the amount of expenditures reduced pursuant to such paragraph and the activities that were funded pursuant to paragraph (3).

(5) Limitation. Notwithstanding paragraph (1), a State educational agency may not reduce the level of expenditures described in paragraph (1) if any local educational agency in the State would, as a result of such reduction, receive less than 100 percent of the amount necessary to ensure that all children with disabilities served by the local educational agency receive a free appropriate public education from the combination of Federal funds received under this title and State funds received from the State educational agency.

✳ ## 20 U.S.C. § 1414. Evaluations, Eligibility Determinations, Individualized Education Programs, and Educational Placements.

➡ **OVERVIEW:** Section 1414 includes requirements for evaluations, reevaluations, eligibility, Individualized Education Programs, and educational placements. Section 1414(a) describes new requirements for initial evaluations, parental consent, the new 60-day timeline to complete evaluations, and new limits on reevaluations. Section 1414(b) describes evaluation procedures, new requirements about determining educational needs, and the movement away from using discrepancy models to identify children with specific learning disabilities. Section 1414(c) clarifies that schools must review evaluations and information provided by parents and that schools must reevaluate before terminating eligibility, with two exceptions. IDEA 2004 made significant changes in Section 1414(d) about Individualized Education Programs (IEPs), IEP team members, meeting attendance, consolidated meetings, and reviewing and revising IEPs. Section 1414(e) clarifies that the parent is a member of any group that makes decisions about a child's educational placement. Section 1414(f) is new and describes alternate means of participating in meetings.

✳ **(a) Evaluations, Parental Consent, and Reevaluations.**

(1) Initial Evaluations.[90]

(A) In General. A State educational agency, other State agency, or local educational agency **shall** conduct a **full and individual initial evaluation** in accordance with this paragraph and subsection (b), **before the initial provision of special education** and related services to a child with a disability under this part.

(B) Request for Initial Evaluation. Consistent with subparagraph (D), either **a parent** of a child,[91] or a **State educational agency**, other **State agency, or local educational agency may initiate a request** for an initial evaluation to determine if the child is a child with a disability.

(C) Procedures.
(i) In General. Such initial evaluation shall consist of procedures -
(I) to determine whether a child is a child with a disability (as defined in section 1401 of this title) **within 60 days of receiving parental consent** for the evaluation,[92] or, if the State establishes a timeframe within which the evaluation must be conducted, within such timeframe; and
(II) to determine the educational needs of such child.
(ii) Exception. The relevant timeframe in clause (i)(I) **shall not apply** to a local educational agency if -
(I) a **child enrolls in a school** served by the local educational agency **after the relevant timeframe** in clause (i)(I) **has begun** and prior to a determination by the child's previous local educational agency as to whether the child is a child with a disability (as defined in section 1401 of this title), but only **if the subsequent local educational agency is making sufficient progress to ensure a prompt completion of the evaluation, and the parent and subsequent local educational agency agree to a specific time** when the evaluation will be completed; **or**
(II) the parent of a child **repeatedly fails or refuses to produce the child** for the evaluation.

Calendar

---

[90] Section 1414(a)(1)(B) is new and states that the parents, the state department of education, other state agencies, and the school district may request an initial evaluation.

[91] See **Wrightslaw: From Emotions to Advocacy** for sample letters, including a letter to request an evaluation for special education services.

[92] IDEA 2004 includes a new requirement that initial evaluations and eligibility be completed within **60 days** of receiving parental consent. When federal law and regulations create a timeline of "days," this means calendar days (not school days), unless the law or regulation specifies an alternative. Earlier reauthorizations of IDEA did not include a timeline, so some states adopted very long timelines, leading to delays that prevented children from receiving the services they needed. Some states are considering longer timelines.

(D) Parental Consent.[93]

(i) In General.

(I) Consent for Initial Evaluation. The agency proposing to conduct an initial evaluation to determine if the child qualifies as a child with a disability as defined in section 1401 of this title **shall obtain informed consent from the parent**[94] of such child **before conducting the evaluation.** Parental consent for evaluation **shall not be construed as consent for placement** for receipt of special education and related services.

(II) Consent for Services. An agency that is responsible for making a free appropriate public education available to a child with a disability under this part **shall seek to obtain informed consent from the parent of such child before providing special education** and related services to the child.

(ii) Absence of Consent.[95]

(I) For Initial Evaluation. If the **parent of such child does not provide consent for an initial evaluation** under clause (i)(I), or the parent fails to respond to a request to provide the consent, the local educational agency **may pursue the initial evaluation** of the child by utilizing the procedures described in section 1415 of this title, except to the extent inconsistent with State law relating to such parental consent.

(II) For Services. If the parent of such child **refuses to consent to services under** clause (i)(II), **the local educational agency shall not provide special education and related services to the child by utilizing the procedures described in section 1415 of this title.**

(III) Effect on Agency Obligations. If the parent of such child **refuses to consent to the receipt of special education** and related services, or the parent fails to respond to a request to provide such consent

(aa) the local educational agency **shall not** be considered to be in violation of the requirement to make available a free appropriate public education to the child for the failure to provide such child with the special education and related services for which the local educational agency requests such consent; and

(bb) the local educational agency **shall not** be required to convene an IEP meeting or develop an IEP under this section for the child for the special education and related services for which the local educational agency requests such consent.

(iii) Consent for Wards of the State.[96]

(I) In General. If the child is a ward of the State and is not residing with the child's parent, the agency shall make reasonable efforts to **obtain the informed consent from the parent** (as defined in section 1401 of this title) of the child for an initial evaluation to determine whether the child is a child with a disability.

---

[93] The school must obtain parental consent before conducting the initial evaluation. Parental consent for an evaluation is not consent for the child to receive special education services. The school must obtain **informed parental consent** before providing special education services.

[94] The definitions of "parent" and "foster parent" are at Section 1401(23). The definition of "ward of the state" is at Section 1401(36).

[95] "Absence of Consent" is new in IDEA 2004. If the parent does not consent to an evaluation, the district may request a due process hearing against the parent. However, if the parent does not consent to special education services, the district may **not** pursue a due process hearing against the parent. The "Effect on Agency Obligations" section is also new. If the parent refuses consent for services, the district has not violated the IDEA, and is not required to convene an IEP meeting or develop an IEP for the child.

[96] The consent requirements for children who are wards of the state are new. If the child is a ward of the state, the school must attempt to obtain parental consent for an initial evaluation. Exceptions to this requirement are listed in Section 1414(a)(1)(D)(ii)(II). If a judge terminates parental rights or takes educational decision-making rights from the parent, the judge may appoint another individual (i.e., probation officer, social worker) to make decisions for the child and who can give consent to an initial evaluation.

(II) Exception. The agency shall not be required to obtain informed consent from the parent of a child for an initial evaluation to determine whether the child is a child with a disability if -

(aa) despite reasonable efforts to do so, the agency cannot discover the whereabouts of the parent of the child;

(bb) the rights of the parents of the child have been terminated in accordance with State law; or

(cc) the rights of the parent to make educational decisions have been subrogated by a judge in accordance with State law and consent for an initial evaluation has been given by **an individual appointed by the judge to represent the child.**

(E) Rule of Construction. The **screening** of a student by a teacher or specialist to determine appropriate instructional strategies for curriculum implementation **shall not be considered to be an evaluation** for eligibility for special education and related services.[97]

(2) Reevaluations.[98]

(A) In General. A local educational agency **shall ensure that a reevaluation** of each child with a disability is conducted in accordance with subsections (b) and (c) -

(i) if the local educational agency determines that the **educational or related services needs**, including improved academic achievement and functional performance, of the child **warrant a reevaluation**; or

(ii) if the **child's parents or teacher requests a reevaluation.**

(B) Limitation. A reevaluation conducted under subparagraph (A) **shall occur -**

(i) **not more frequently than once a year, unless** the parent and the local educational agency agree otherwise; and

(ii) **at least once every 3 years**, unless the parent and the local educational agency agree that a reevaluation is unnecessary.[99]

(b) Evaluation Procedures.[100]

(1) Notice. The local educational agency shall provide notice to the parents of a child with a disability, in accordance with subsections (b)(3), (b)(4), and (c) of section 1415 of this title, that describes any evaluation procedures such agency proposes to conduct.

---

[97] A "screening" by a teacher or educational diagnostician to determine instructional strategies does not comply with the requirements for evaluations in Section 1414.

[98] The language about reevaluations changed in IDEA 2004. The school is not required to reevaluate a child more often than once a year, unless the parent and school agree otherwise. The school shall evaluate at least every three years, unless the parent and school agree that a reevaluation is unnecessary. The school must reevaluate if the child's educational needs change **or** if the child's parent or teacher request a reevaluation.

[99] These limits on the frequency of reevaluations are likely to cause difficulties in developing IEPs. The law requires that the IEP include "a statement of the child's **present levels** of academic achievement and functional performance" (Section 1414(d)(1)(A)(i)). If the child has not been evaluated for a year or more, the IEP team will not have valid information about the child's **present levels** of academic achievement and functional performance.

[100] The school "shall use a variety of assessment tools and strategies to gather relevant functional, developmental, and academic information" about the child. The school shall "not use any single measure or assessment as the sole criterion" for determining if a child is eligible. Information from the evaluation is to be used in determining the contents of the child's IEP, and how to help the child make progress in the general education curriculum.

(2) Conduct of Evaluation. In conducting the evaluation, the local educational agency **shall -**

(A) use a **variety of assessment tools and strategies to gather relevant functional, developmental, and academic information, including information provided by the parent,** that may assist in determining -
    (i) whether the **child is a child with a disability;** and
    (ii) the **content of the child's individualized education program,** including information related to enabling the child to be **involved in and progress in the general education curriculum,** or, for preschool children, to participate in appropriate activities;

(B) **not use any single measure or assessment as the sole criterion** for determining whether a child is a child with a disability or determining an appropriate educational program for the child; and

(C) use **technically sound instruments** that may assess the relative contribution of **cognitive and behavioral factors,** in addition to **physical or developmental factors.**

(3) Additional Requirements.[101] Each local educational agency **shall ensure that**

(A) **assessments and other evaluation materials** used to assess a child under this section -
    (i) are selected and administered so as **not to be discriminatory on a racial or cultural basis;**
    (ii) are provided and administered in the language and form most likely to yield **accurate information on what the child knows and can do academically, developmentally, and functionally,** unless it is not feasible to so provide or administer;
    (iii) are used for purposes for which the assessments or measures **are valid and reliable;**
    (iv) are administered by **trained and knowledgeable personnel;** and
    (v) are administered in accordance with any instructions provided by the producer of such assessments;

(B) the child is assessed in **all areas of suspected disability;**

(C) assessment tools and strategies that provide **relevant information** that directly assists persons in determining the **educational needs of the child** are provided; and

(D) assessments of children with disabilities who transfer from 1 school district to another school district in the same academic year are coordinated with such children's prior and subsequent schools, as necessary and as expeditiously as possible, to ensure prompt completion of full evaluations.

(4) Determination of Eligibility and Educational Need.[102] Upon completion of the administration of assessments and other evaluation measures -

---

[101] IDEA 2004 includes additional requirements about assessments. The school must ensure that assessments "are provided and administered in the language and form most likely to yield accurate information on what the child knows and can do academically, developmentally, and functionally . . ." When children transfer to new schools, the receiving school must complete assessments "as expeditiously as possible to ensure prompt completion of full evaluations." The language about assessing children "in all areas of suspected disability" and that assessments shall provide relevant information to determine the child's educational needs are unchanged.

[102] In IDEA 2004, "Determination of Eligibility" was changed to "Determination of Eligibility and **Educational Need**" (Section 1414(b)(4)) A team of qualified professionals and the parent determine "whether the child is a child with a disability . . . **and the educational needs of the child** . . ." The requirements about providing the parent with copies of the evaluation report and documentation of eligibility are unchanged.

(A) **the determination of whether the child is a child with a disability** as defined in section 1401(3) of this title **and the educational needs of the child shall** be made by a team of qualified professionals and the parent of the child in accordance with paragraph (5); and

(B) a copy of the evaluation report and the documentation of determination of eligibility **shall be given** to the parent.[103]

(5) Special Rule for Eligibility Determination. In making a determination of eligibility under paragraph (4)(A), a child shall not be determined to be a child with a disability if the determinant factor for such determination is -

(A) **lack of appropriate instruction in reading**, including in the **essential components of reading instruction** [104] (as defined in section 6368(3) of this title);[105]

(B) lack of instruction in math; or

(C) limited English proficiency.

(6) Specific Learning Disabilities.[106]

Severe discrepancy ✱

(A) **In General.** Notwithstanding section 1407(b) of this title, when determining whether a child has a specific learning disability as defined in section 1401 of this title, a local educational agency **shall not be required to take into consideration whether a child has a severe discrepancy between achievement and intellectual ability** in oral expression, listening comprehension, written expression, basic reading skill, reading comprehension, mathematical calculation, or mathematical reasoning.

(B) **Additional Authority.** In determining whether a child has a specific learning disability, a local educational agency may use a process that determines if the child responds to **scientific, research-based intervention**[107] as a part of the evaluation procedures described in paragraphs (2) and (3).

---

[103] If the school decides that a child with a disability is not eligible for special education services under IDEA, or if the parent disagrees with the school's classification of the child's disability, the parent must obtain a comprehensive psycho-educational evaluation from an expert in the private sector. For more on this topic, please read *Wrightslaw: From Emotions to Advocacy*

[104] For the essential components of reading instruction, see **Appendix F: Reading and Research Based Instruction.**

[105] The new language about "lack of appropriate instruction in reading, including the essential components of reading instruction" brings IDEA into conformity with NCLB. The essential components of reading instruction are defined as explicit and systematic instruction in - (A) phonemic awareness; (B) phonics; (C) vocabulary development; (D) reading fluency, including oral reading skills; and (E) reading comprehension strategies." (See 20 U.S.C. § 6368 in *Wrightslaw: No Child Left Behind*)

[106] Schools are not required to determine if a child has a severe discrepancy between achievement and intellectual ability to determine that a child has a specific learning disability and needs special education services, nor are schools prohibited from using a discrepancy model. Schools may use response to intervention (RTI) to determine if the child responds to scientific, research-based intervention as part of the evaluation process. See **Appendix C - Discrepancy Models, Response to Intervention and Specific Learning Disabilities.**

[107] The legal definition of "scientifically based reading research" is in No Child Left Behind, 20 U.S.C. § 6368(6). (See *Wrightslaw: No Child Left Behind*.) and **Appendix F** of *Wrightslaw: IDEA 2004.*

✄ **(c) Additional Requirements for Evaluation and Reevaluations.**

(1) Review of Existing Evaluation Data. As part of an **initial evaluation** (if appropriate) and as part of **any reevaluation** under this section, the IEP Team and other qualified professionals, as appropriate, **shall -**
   (A) review existing evaluation data on the child, including -
      (i) **evaluations and information provided by the parents** of the child;
      (ii) current classroom-based, **local, or State assessments**, and classroom-based observations; and
      (iii) observations by teachers and related services providers; and

   (B) on the basis of that review, and input from the child's parents, **identify what additional data**, if any, **are needed** to determine -
      (i) whether the child is a child with a disability as defined in section 1401(3) of this title, and **the educational needs of the child**[108], or, in case of a reevaluation of a child, whether the child continues to have such a disability and such educational needs;
      (ii) the **present levels of academic achievement and related developmental needs** of the child;
      (iii) whether the child needs special education and related services, or in the case of a reevaluation of a child, whether the child continues to need special education and related services; and
      (iv) **whether any additions or modifications** to the special education and related services **are needed** to enable the child to **meet the measurable annual goals set out** in the individualized education program of the child and to participate, as appropriate, in the general education curriculum.

(2) Source of Data. The local educational agency shall administer such assessments and other evaluation measures as may be needed to produce the data identified by the IEP Team under paragraph (1)(B).

(3) Parental Consent. Each local educational agency **shall obtain informed parental consent**, in accordance with subsection (a)(1)(D), **prior to conducting any reevaluation of a child with a disability**, except that such informed parental consent need not be obtained if the local educational agency can demonstrate that it had taken reasonable measures to obtain such consent and the child's parent has failed to respond.

(4) Requirements If Additional Data Are Not Needed.[109] If the IEP Team and other qualified professionals, as appropriate, determine that **no additional data are needed** to determine whether the child continues to be a child with a disability and to **determine the child's educational needs,**[110] the local educational agency -

   (A) **shall** notify the child's parents of -
      (i) that **determination** and the **reasons for the determination**; and
      (ii) the **right** of such parents **to request an assessment** to determine whether the child continues to be a child with a disability and **to determine the child's educational needs**; and
   (B) shall not be required to conduct such an assessment **unless requested to by the child's parents.**[111]

---

[108] The language about using evaluations and reevaluations to determine the "educational needs of the child" and "present levels of academic achievement and related developmental needs of the child" are new. (Section 1414(c)(1))

[109] The law includes new language that allows school personnel to decide that "no additional data are needed" in determining educational needs or eligibility. (Section 1414(c)(4)) This language is at odds with the requirement that the school reevaluate "at least once every 3 years." (Section 1414 (a)(2)(B)(ii))

[110] IEP teams must determine the child's "educational needs" and "present levels of academic achievement and related developmental needs." If a child is not evaluated at frequent intervals, information about the child's educational needs, "present levels of academic achievement" and "related developmental needs" will not be available. (Section 1414(d)(1)(A)(i)(I))

(5) Evaluations Before Change in Eligibility.

(A) In General. Except as provided in subparagraph (B), a local educational agency **shall evaluate** a child with a disability in accordance with this section **before determining that the child is no longer a child with a disability.**

(B) Exception.
(i) In General. The evaluation described in subparagraph (A) **shall not be required** before the termination of a child's eligibility under this part **due to graduation from secondary school with a regular diploma, or due to exceeding the age eligibility** for a free appropriate public education under State law.
(ii) Summary of Performance. For a child whose eligibility under this part terminates under circumstances described in clause (i), a local educational agency **shall provide** the child with a summary of the child's **academic achievement and functional performance**, which shall include **recommendations on how to assist the child in meeting the child's postsecondary goals.**

✗ (d) Individualized Education Programs.

(1) Definitions. In this title:

(A) Individualized Education Program.[112]
(i) In General. The term 'individualized education program' or IEP' means a **written statement** for each child with a disability that is developed, reviewed, and revised in accordance with this section and **that includes -**
(I) a statement of the child's **present levels of academic achievement and functional performance,**[113] including[114] -
(aa) how the child's disability affects the **child's involvement and progress in the general education curriculum;**
(bb) for preschool children, as appropriate, how the disability affects the child's participation in appropriate activities; and
(cc) for children with disabilities **who take alternate assessments** aligned to alternate achievement standards, a **description of benchmarks or short-term objectives;**
(II) a **statement of measurable annual goals, including academic and functional goals,**[115] designed to -

---

[111] Parents have a right to request an assessment to determine their child's educational needs. (Section 1414(a)(4)(ii)). To ensure that your request is honored, make your request for an assessment of your child's educational needs in writing.

[112] To learn how the IEP law is organized and how the legal requirements for IEPs changed, read **Appendix D: Roadmap to the IEP.**

[113] To learn what the scores in your child's evaluations mean (i.e., standard scores, percentile ranks, age and grade equivalent scores), read Chapters 10 and 11 about "Tests and Measurements" in *Wrightslaw: From Emotions to Advocacy.*

[114] The IEP must include "a statement of the child's present levels of academic achievement and functional performance . . ." For children who take alternate assessments, the IEP must include "a description of benchmarks or short-term objectives."

[115] To learn how to write IEPs that are Specific, Measurable, use Action words, are Realistic and Time specific, read Chapter 11, SMART IEPs, in *Wrightslaw: From Emotions to Advocacy.*

(aa) meet the child's needs that result from the child's disability to enable the child to be involved in and make progress in the general education curriculum; and

(bb) meet each of the child's other educational needs that result from the child's disability;

(III) a **description of how the child's progress** toward meeting the annual goals described in subclause (II) **will be measured**[116] and **when periodic reports on the progress** the child is making toward meeting the annual goals (such as through the use of quarterly or other periodic reports, concurrent with the issuance of report cards) **will be provided**;

(IV) a **statement of the special education and related services and supplementary aids and services, based on peer-reviewed research**[117] to the extent practicable, to be provided to the child, or on behalf of the child, **and** a statement of the **program modifications or supports for school personnel** that will be provided for the child -

(aa) to advance appropriately toward attaining the annual goals;

(bb) to be involved in and make progress in the general education curriculum in accordance with subclause (I) and to participate in extracurricular and other nonacademic activities; and

(cc) to be educated and participate with other children with disabilities and nondisabled children in the activities described in this subparagraph;

(V) an **explanation** of the extent, if any, to which the **child will not participate with nondisabled children in the regular class** and in the activities described in subclause (IV)(cc);

(VI)

(aa) a statement of **any individual appropriate accommodations** that are necessary **to measure the academic achievement and functional performance** of the child[118] on State and districtwide assessments consistent with section 1412(a)(16)(A) of this title; and

(bb) **if** the IEP Team determines that **the child shall take an alternate assessment**[119] on a particular State or districtwide assessment of student achievement, **a statement of why** -

(AA) the child cannot participate in the regular assessment; and

(BB) the particular alternate assessment selected is appropriate for the child;

(VII) **the projected date for the beginning of the services** and modifications described in subclause (IV), and the anticipated **frequency, location, and duration of those services** and modifications; and

(VIII) beginning not later than the first IEP to be in effect **when the child is 16**, and updated annually thereafter -

(aa) appropriate **measurable postsecondary goals based upon age appropriate transition assessments**[120] related to training, education, employment, and, where appropriate, independent living skills;

---

[116] The IEP must include measurable annual goals that address the child's "present levels of academic achievement and functional performance."

[117] Congress added new language about research based instruction to IDEA 2004. The child's IEP must include "a statement of the special education and related services and supplementary aids and services, **based on peer-reviewed research to the extent practicable,** to be provided to the child . . . and a statement of the program modifications or supports for school personnel that will be provided…"

[118] IDEA contains new language about "individual appropriate accommodations" on state and district testing and new requirements for alternate assessments. The child's IEP must include: "a statement of any individual appropriate accommodations that are necessary to measure the academic achievement and functional performance of the child on State and districtwide assessments…"

[119] If the IEP Team determines that the child shall take an alternate assessment on a State or district assessment, the team must include a statement about "why the child cannot participate in the regular assessment" and [why] "the particular alternate assessment selected is appropriate for the child…"

(bb) the **transition services (including courses of study)** needed to assist the child in reaching (aa) appropriate **measurable postsecondary goals based upon age appropriate transition assessments** related to training, education, employment, and, where appropriate, independent living skills;

(bb) the **transition services (including courses of study)** needed to assist the child in reaching; *and these goals*

(cc) beginning not later than 1 year before the child reaches the age of majority under State law, a statement that the child has been informed of the child's rights under this title, if any, that will transfer to the child on reaching the **age of majority** under section 1415(m) of this title.

(ii) **Rule of Construction.** Nothing in this section shall be construed to require -

(I) that additional information be included in a child's IEP beyond what is explicitly required in this section; and

(II) the IEP Team to include information under 1 component of a child's IEP that is already contained under another component of such IEP.

(B) Individualized Education Program Team. The term 'individualized education program team' or IEP Team' means a group of individuals composed of -

(i) the **parents** of a child with a disability;

(ii) **not less than 1 regular education teacher of such child** (if the child is, or may be, participating in the regular education environment);

(iii) **not less than 1 special education teacher**, or where appropriate, not less than 1 special education **provider** of such child;

(iv) a **representative of the local educational agency who** -

(I) is qualified to provide, or supervise the provision of, specially designed instruction to meet the unique needs of children with disabilities;

(II) is knowledgeable about the general education curriculum; and

(III) is knowledgeable about the availability of resources of the local educational agency;

(v) an **individual who can interpret the instructional implications of evaluation results**, who may be a member of the team described in clauses (ii) through (vi);

(vi) at the discretion of the parent or the agency, **other individuals who have knowledge or special expertise regarding the child**, including related services personnel as appropriate; and

(vii) whenever appropriate, **the child** with a disability.

(C) IEP Team Attendance.[121]

(i) **Attendance Not Necessary.** A member of the IEP Team shall not be required to attend an IEP meeting, in whole or in part, if the parent of a child with a disability and the local educational agency agree that the attendance of such member is not necessary because the member's area of the curriculum or related services is not being modified or discussed in the meeting.

(ii) **Excusal.** A member of the IEP Team may be excused from attending an IEP meeting, in whole or in part, when the meeting involves a modification to or discussion of the member's area of the curriculum or related services, if -

---

[120] The requirements for transition in IEPs changed. The first IEP after the child is 16 (and updated annually) must include "appropriate measurable postsecondary goals based upon age appropriate transition assessments related to training, education, employment, and, where appropriate, independent living skills…and the transition services (including courses of study) needed to assist the child in reaching these goals."

[121] A member of the IEP team may be excused from attending an IEP meeting if their area of curriculum or service will not be discussed or modified during the meeting. An IEP team member may also be excused from an IEP meeting that involves their area of curriculum or service if they submit input in writing and if the parent and schools consent. The parent's consent must be in writing.

(I) the parent and the local educational agency consent to the excusal; and
(II) the member submits, in writing to the parent and the IEP Team, input into the development of the IEP prior to the meeting. *written agreement*
(iii) **Written Agreement and Consent Required**. A parent's agreement under clause (i) and consent under clause (ii) shall be in writing.

(D) IEP Team Transition. In the case of a child who was previously served under part C, an invitation to the initial IEP meeting shall, at the request of the parent, be sent to the part C service coordinator or other representatives of the part C system to assist with the smooth transition of services.

(2) Requirement That Program Be in Effect.

(A) In General. At the beginning of each school year, each local educational agency, State educational agency, or other State agency, as the case may be, **shall have in effect, for each child with a disability in the agency's jurisdiction, an individualized education program,**[122] as defined in paragraph (1)(A).

(B) Program for Child Aged 3 Through 5. In the case of a child with a disability aged 3 through 5 (or, at the discretion of the State educational agency, a 2-year-old child with a disability who will turn age 3 during the school year), the IEP Team **shall consider** the individualized family service plan that contains the material described in section 1436 of this title, and that is developed in accordance with this section, and the individualized family service plan may serve as the IEP of the child if using that plan as the IEP is -
(i) consistent with State policy; and
(ii) agreed to by the agency and the child's parents.

(C) Program for Children Who Transfer School Districts.[123]
    (i) In General.
        (I) Transfer within the Same State. In the case of a child with a disability who **transfers school districts within the same academic year,** who enrolls in a new school, and **who had an IEP** that was in effect in the same State, the local educational agency shall provide such child with a free appropriate public education, **including services comparable to those described in the previously held IEP**, in consultation with the parents **until such time** as the local educational agency adopts the previously held IEP or develops, adopts, and implements a new IEP that is consistent with Federal and State law.
        (II) Transfer Outside State. In the case of a child with a disability who transfers school districts within the same academic year, who enrolls in a new school, and who had an IEP that was in effect in another State, the local educational agency shall provide such child with a free appropriate public education, including services comparable to those described in the previously held IEP, in consultation with the parents until such time as the local educational agency conducts an evaluation pursuant to subsection (a)(1), if determined to be necessary by such agency, and develops a new IEP, if appropriate, that is consistent with Federal and State law.

---

[122] IEPs must be in effect at the beginning of the school year for all children with disabilities, including children who attend private programs. Under IDEA 2004, public schools may be responsible for offering IEPs to students who attend private schools. See Sections 1412(a)(3)+(10) about child find and private schools. However, if the parent refuses to consent to an evaluation or to special education services, the school is not required to develop an IEP. (Section 1414(a)(1)(D)(ii)) If the parent refuses to permit the school to evaluate the child, any entitlement to reimbursement for a private school program may be reduced or barred. (Section 1412(a)(10))

[123] The subsection about programs for children who transfer is new. If the child transfers to a district in the same state or another state, the receiving school must provide comparable services to those in the sending district's IEP until they develop and implement a new IEP.

(ii) **Transmittal of Records.** To facilitate the transition for a child described in clause (i) -

(I) the new school in which the child enrolls shall take reasonable steps to promptly obtain the child's records, including the IEP and supporting documents and any other records relating to the provision of special education or related services to the child, from the previous school in which the child was enrolled, pursuant to section 99.31(a)(2) of title 34, Code of Federal Regulations; and

(II) the previous school in which the child was enrolled shall take reasonable steps to promptly respond to such request from the new school.

(3) Development of IEP.

(A) In General. In developing each child's IEP, the IEP Team, subject to subparagraph (C), **shall consider**[124]
(i) the **strengths of the child**;
(ii) the **concerns of the parents** for enhancing the education of their child;
(iii) the results of the initial evaluation or **most recent evaluation** of the child; and
(iv) the **academic, developmental, and functional needs** of the child.[125]

(B) Consideration of Special Factors. The IEP Team **shall -**
(i) in the case of a **child whose behavior impedes the child's learning or that of others**, consider the use of positive behavioral interventions and supports, and other strategies, to address that behavior;
(ii) in the case of a **child with limited English proficiency**, consider the language needs of the child as such needs relate to the child's IEP;
(iii) in the case of a **child who is blind or visually impaired**, provide for instruction in Braille and the use of Braille unless the IEP Team determines, after an evaluation of the child's reading and writing skills, needs, and appropriate reading and writing media (including an evaluation of the child's future needs for instruction in Braille or the use of Braille), that instruction in Braille or the use of Braille is not appropriate for the child;
(iv) consider the **communication needs of the child**, and in the case of a **child who is deaf or hard of hearing**, consider the child's language and communication needs, opportunities for direct communications with peers and professional personnel in the child's language and communication mode, academic level, and full range of needs, including opportunities for direct instruction in the child's language and communication mode; and
(v) consider whether the child needs **assistive technology devices** and services.

(C) Requirement with Respect to Regular Education Teacher.[126] A regular education teacher **of the child**, as a member of the IEP Team, **shall**, to the extent appropriate, participate in the development of the IEP of the child, including the determination of appropriate positive behavioral interventions and supports, and other strategies, and the determination of supplementary aids and services, program modifications, and support for school personnel consistent with paragraph (1)(A)(i)(IV).

(D) Agreement. In making changes to a child's IEP **after the annual IEP meeting for a school year**, the parent of a child with a disability and the local educational agency **may agree not to convene** an IEP

---

[124] In developing the IEP, the IEP team must consider the parents' concerns about the child's education, including concerns about inadequate progress. Some IEP teams refuse to accept or use information from private sector evaluations on the child. Schools **shall consider** the most recent evaluation on the child.

[125] The Department of Education will publish model Individualized Education Program (IEP) and Individualized Family Service Plan (IFSP) forms when the final regulations are published.

[126] The IEP Team shall include "not less than one regular education teacher" of the child who will participate in developing the IEP.

meeting for the purposes of making such changes, and instead **may develop a written document to amend or modify the child's current IEP.**

(E) Consolidation of IEP Team Meetings. To the extent possible, the local educational agency **shall encourage the consolidation of reevaluation** meetings for the child **and other IEP Team meetings** for the child.

(F) Amendments. Changes to the IEP may be made either by the entire IEP Team or, as provided in subparagraph (D), by amending the IEP rather than by redrafting the entire IEP. Upon request, a parent shall be provided with a revised copy of the IEP with the amendments incorporated.

(4) Review and Revision of IEP.[127]

(A) In General. The local educational agency shall ensure that, subject to subparagraph (B), the IEP Team -
(i) reviews the child's IEP periodically, **but not less frequently than annually,** to determine whether the annual goals for the child are being achieved; and
(ii) revises the IEP as appropriate to address -
(I) any **lack of expected progress** toward the annual goals and in the general education curriculum, where appropriate;
(II) the **results of any reevaluation** conducted under this section;
(III) **information** about the child **provided to, or by, the parents**, as described in subsection (c)(1)(B);
(IV) the child's **anticipated needs**; or
(V) other matters.

(B) Requirement with Respect to Regular Education Teacher. A regular education teacher of the child, as a member of the IEP Team, shall, consistent with paragraph (1)(C), participate in the review and revision of the IEP of the child.

(5) Multi-Year IEP Demonstration.[128]

(A) Pilot Program.
(i) Purpose. The purpose of this paragraph is to provide an opportunity for States to allow parents and local educational agencies the opportunity for long-term planning by offering the option of developing a **comprehensive multi-year IEP, not to exceed 3 years**, that is designed to coincide with the natural transition points for the child.
(ii) Authorization. In order to carry out the purpose of this paragraph, the Secretary is authorized to **approve not more than 15 proposals** from States to carry out the activity described in clause (i).
(iii) Proposal.

---

[127] IDEA 2004 made significant changes to the section about reviewing and revising IEPs. If the parent and school decide to amend or modify the IEP developed at the annual IEP meeting, and do not want to convene another IEP meeting, they may revise the IEP by agreement. The IEP team must create a written document to amend or modify the IEP. This document should describe the changes or modifications in the IEP and note that, by agreement of the parties, an IEP meeting was not convened. The parent should be provided with a copy of the revised IEP.

[128] IDEA 2004 added a multi-year IEP pilot project. Fifteen states may apply for approval to use three-year IEPs. IEP review dates must be based on "natural transition points." The parent has a right to "opt-out" of this program. The parent of a child served under a multi-year IEP can have a review of the IEP without waiting for the date of the "natural transition point."

(I) In General. A State desiring to participate in the program under this paragraph shall submit a proposal to the Secretary at such time and in such manner as the Secretary may reasonably require.

(II) Content. The proposal shall include -

(aa) **assurances that the development of a multi-year IEP under this paragraph is optional for parents;**

(bb) assurances that the parent is required to provide informed consent before a comprehensive multi-year IEP is developed;

(cc) a list of required elements for each multi-year IEP, including -

(AA) measurable goals pursuant to paragraph (1)(A)(i)(II), coinciding with natural transition points for the child, that will enable the child to be involved in and make progress in the general education curriculum and that will meet the child's other needs that result from the child's disability; and

(BB) measurable annual goals for determining progress toward meeting the goals described in subitem (AA); and

(dd) **a description of** the process for the review and revision of each multi-year IEP, including -

(AA) a review by the IEP Team of the child's multi-year IEP at each of the child's natural transition points;

(BB) in years other than a child's natural transition points, **an annual review of the child's IEP** to determine the child's current levels of progress and whether the annual goals for the child are being achieved, and a requirement to amend the IEP, as appropriate, to enable the child to continue to meet the measurable goals set out in the IEP;

(CC) if the IEP Team determines on the basis of a review that the child is not making sufficient progress toward the goals described in the multi-year IEP, a requirement that the local educational agency shall ensure that the IEP Team carries out a more thorough review of the IEP in accordance with paragraph (4) within 30 calendar days; and

(DD) **at the request of the parent,** a requirement that the IEP Team shall conduct **a review of the child's multi-year IEP** rather than or subsequent to an annual review.

(B) Report. Beginning 2 years after the date of enactment of the Individuals with Disabilities Education Improvement Act of 2004, the Secretary shall submit an annual report to the Committee on Education and the Workforce of the House of Representatives and the Committee on Health, Education, Labor, and Pensions of the Senate regarding the effectiveness of the program under this paragraph and any specific recommendations for broader implementation of such program, including

(i) reducing -

(I) the paperwork burden on teachers, principals, administrators, and related service providers; and

(II) noninstructional time spent by teachers in complying with this part;

(ii) enhancing longer-term educational planning;

(iii) improving positive outcomes for children with disabilities;

(iv) promoting collaboration between IEP Team members; and

(v) ensuring satisfaction of family members.

(C) Definition. In this paragraph, the term **'natural transition points'** means those periods that are close in time to the transition of a child with a disability from preschool to elementary grades, from elementary grades to middle or junior high school grades, from middle or junior high school grades to secondary school grades, and from secondary school grades to post-secondary activities, but in no case a period longer than 3 years.

(6) Failure to Meet Transition Objectives. If a participating agency, other than the local educational agency, fails to provide the transition services described in the IEP in accordance with paragraph (1)(A)(i)(VIII), the local educational agency shall reconvene the IEP Team to identify alternative strategies to meet the transition objectives for the child set out in the IEP.

—— **(7) Children with Disabilities in Adult Prisons.**[129]

(A) In General. The following requirements **shall not apply to children with disabilities who are convicted as adults** under State law **and incarcerated in adult prisons:**

(i) The requirements contained in section 1412(a)(16) of this title and paragraph (1)(A)(i)(VI) (relating to participation of children with disabilities in general assessments).

(ii) The requirements of items (aa) and (bb) of paragraph (1)(A)(i)(VIII) (relating to transition planning and transition services), do not apply with respect to such children whose eligibility under this part will end, because of such children's age, before such children will be released from prison.

(B) Additional Requirement. If a child with a disability is convicted as an adult under State law and incarcerated in an adult prison, the child's IEP Team may modify the child's IEP or placement notwithstanding the requirements of sections 1412(a)(5)(A) of this title and paragraph (1)(A) if the State has demonstrated a bona fide security or compelling penological interest that cannot otherwise be accommodated.

✕ **(e) Educational Placements.** Each local educational agency or State educational agency shall ensure that **the parents** of each child with a disability **are members of any group** that makes **decisions on the educational placement** of their child.[130]

✳ **(f) Alternative Means of Meeting Participation.**[131] When conducting IEP team meetings and placement meetings pursuant to this section, section 1415(e) of this title, and section 1415(f)(1)(B) of this title, and carrying out administrative matters under section 1415 of this title (such as scheduling, exchange of witness lists, and status conferences), the parent of a child with a disability and a local educational agency may agree to use alternative means of meeting participation, such as video conferences and conference calls.

---

[129] A school district is not required to offer an IEP in the least restrictive environment to a child who has been convicted as an adult and who is incarcerated in an adult prison. A child with a disability who was convicted as an adult and is in prison (not jail) shall not be tested on the statewide assessments. The "appropriate measurable postsecondary goals" "transition services" and "courses of study" are not required. Sentences of less than one year are usually served in jails. Longer sentences are usually served in prisons. In general, individuals who are convicted of misdemeanors serve sentences in jails while individuals convicted of felonies usually serve their sentences in prisons.

[130] Decisions about the child's placement cannot be made until after the IEP team, including the child's parent(s), meets and reaches consensus about the IEP goals. Although the law is clear on this issue, school personnel often decide on the child's placement before the IEP meeting. These unilateral actions prevent parents from "meaningful participation" in the educational decision-making process. When Congress added this provision to the statute in 1997, they sent a message that unilateral educational placement decisions by school officials are illegal.

[131] School meetings do not have to be face-to-face. IEP and placement meetings (Sections 1414(d)+(e)), mediation meetings (Section 1415(e)) and due process (IEP) resolution sessions (Section 1415(f)(1)(B)) may be convened by conference calls or video conferences.

✈ 20 U.S.C. § 1415. Procedural Safeguards.

➡ **OVERVIEW:** Section 1415 describes the safeguards designed to protect the rights of children with disabilities and their parents, including the right to participate in all meetings, to examine all educational records, and to obtain an independent educational evaluation (IEE) of the child. Parents have the right to written notice when the school proposes to change or refuses to change the identification, evaluation or placement of the child as well as the right to participate in mediation, present a complaint, and request a due process hearing.

Section 1415(c) describes requirements for the Prior Written Notice and the new Due Process Complaint Notice. Section 1415(d) describes the Procedural Safeguards Notice that schools must provide to parents and what this notice must include. Section 1415(e) describes requirements about using mediation to resolve disputes, legally binding written mediation agreements, and confidentiality. Section 1415(f) describes the legal requirements for due process hearings and the Resolution Session that may allow the parties to resolve disputes before a due process hearing. Section 1415(f) includes new requirements for hearing officers and timelines, including the new two-year statute of limitations. Section 1415(i) describes the appeals process and the new 90 day deadline on appeals. Section 1415(j) is the "stay put" statute that allows the child to remain in the "current educational placement" during litigation.

Section 1415(k) is the discipline statute. This statute includes authority for school personnel to place children in interim alternative educational settings and new requirements for children who violate a "code of student conduct." The statute includes manifestation determinations, placement as determined by the IEP team, appeals, authority of the hearing officer, and transfer of rights at the age of majority.

— **(a) Establishment of Procedures.** Any State educational agency, State agency, or local educational agency that receives assistance under this part **shall establish and maintain procedures** in accordance with this section to ensure that **children with disabilities and their parents are guaranteed procedural safeguards** with respect to the provision of a free appropriate public education by such agencies.

— **(b) Types of Procedures.**[132] The procedures required by this section shall include the following:

(1) An opportunity for the parents of a child with a disability to **examine all records** relating to such child and **to participate in meetings** with respect to the identification, evaluation, and educational placement of the child, and the provision of a free appropriate public education to such child, and **to obtain an independent educational evaluation**[133] of the child.

(2)

(A) Procedures to **protect the rights of the child whenever the parents of the child are not known**, the agency cannot, after reasonable efforts, locate the parents, or the child is a ward of the State, including the assignment of an individual to act as a surrogate for the parents, which surrogate shall not be an employee of the State educational agency, the local educational agency, or any other agency that is involved in the education or care of the child. In the case of -

(i) a **child who is a ward of the State**, such surrogate may alternatively be appointed by the judge overseeing the child's care provided that the surrogate meets the requirements of this paragraph; and

(ii) an **unaccompanied homeless youth** as defined in section 11434a(6) of title 42, the local educational agency shall appoint a surrogate in accordance with this paragraph.

---

[132] Parents have the right to examine all educational records, including test data. The right to examine records may include personal notes, if the notes have been shared with other staff. Parents should request test data (i.e., standard scores, percentile ranks, age equivalent scores, and grade equivalent scores) in writing.

[133] Parents have the right to obtain an Independent Educational Evaluation of their child. Many school districts attempt to restrict the parent's choice of evaluators to a list of approved evaluators selected by the school. The Office of Special Education Programs issued a policy letter clarifying that parents have the right to choose their own independent evaluator. (OSEP, Letter to Parker, 2004 located on the Wrightslaw website.)

(B) The State shall make reasonable efforts to ensure the assignment of a surrogate not more than **30 days** after there is a determination by the agency that the child needs a surrogate.

(3) **Written prior notice**[134] to the parents of the child, in accordance with subsection (c)(1), **whenever** the local educational agency -

(A) **proposes to initiate or change**; or

(B) **refuses to initiate or change, the identification, evaluation, or educational placement of the child,** or the provision of a free appropriate public education to the child.

(4) Procedures designed to ensure that the notice required by paragraph (3) is in the **native language of the parents**, unless it clearly is not feasible to do so.

(5) An opportunity for **mediation**, in accordance with subsection (e).

(6) An **opportunity** for any party **to present a complaint**

(A) with respect to **any matter relating to the identification, evaluation, or educational placement of the child,** or the provision of a free appropriate public education to such child; and

(B) which sets forth an alleged violation that occurred **not more than 2 years before the date**[135] the parent or public agency knew or should have known about the alleged action that forms the basis of the complaint, or, if the State has an explicit time limitation for presenting such a complaint under this part, in such time as the State law allows, except that the exceptions to the timeline described in subsection (f)(3)(D) shall apply to the timeline described in this subparagraph.

(7)
(A) Procedures that **require either party**, or the attorney representing a party, to **provide due process complaint notice**[136] in accordance with subsection (c)(2) (which shall remain confidential) -
(i) **to the other party**, in the complaint filed under paragraph (6), and **forward a copy** of such notice **to the State educational agency**; and
(ii) that **shall include** -
(I) the name of the child, the address of the residence of the child (or available contact information in the case of a homeless child), and the name of the school the child is attending;
(II) in the case of a homeless child or youth (within the meaning of section 11434a(2) of title 42), available contact information for the child and the name of the school the child is attending;
(III) a **description of the nature of the problem** of the child relating to such proposed initiation or change, including facts relating to such problem; and
(IV) a **proposed resolution of the problem** to the extent known and available to the party at the time.[137]

---

[134] The school district is to provide the parent, in writing, with the reason for refusing to evaluate a child or change the educational program.

[135] The two-year statute of limitations to present a complaint is new in IDEA 2004.

[136] The party who requests a due process hearing must provide a detailed notice to the other party that includes identifying information about the child, the nature of the problem, facts, and proposed resolution. The party that requests the due process hearing may not have the hearing until they provide this notice. See **Appendix E: Due Process Procedures and Timelines**.

(B) A requirement that a party **may not have** a due process hearing until the party, or the attorney representing the party, files a notice that meets the requirements of subparagraph (A)(ii).

(8) Procedures that **require** the State educational agency to develop **a model form to assist parents** in filing a complaint and due process complaint notice in accordance with paragraphs (6) and (7), respectively.

— **(c) Notification Requirements.**

(1) **Content of Prior Written Notice.**[138] The **notice** required by subsection (b)(3) **shall** include -

(A) a **description of the action proposed or refused** by the agency;

refusal — (B) an **explanation of why** the agency **proposes or refuses** to take the action and a **description of each evaluation procedure, assessment, record, or report the agency used** as a basis for the proposed or refused action;

(C) a statement that the parents of a child with a disability have protection under the procedural safeguards of this part and, if this notice is not an initial referral for evaluation, the means by which a copy of a description of the procedural safeguards can be obtained;

(D) **sources for parents** to contact **to obtain assistance** in understanding the provisions of this part;

(E) a **description of other options considered** by the IEP Team and the **reason why those options were rejected**; and

(F) a **description of the factors that are relevant** to the agency's proposal or refusal.

---

[137] A Due Process Complaint Notice can be a letter requesting a due process hearing that includes the required components. To learn how to write persuasive letters that make the reader want to help, read Chapter 24, "Letter to the Stranger," in *Wrightslaw: From Emotions to Advocacy*.

[138] Prior Written Notice (PWN) is easier to understand if you eliminate the word "prior" from your analysis. Assume a parent requests that the school increase the child's speech language therapy from three 15-minute sessions per week (45 minutes per week) to three 30-minute sessions per week (90 minutes per week). If the school refuses, they must provide "written notice" about their refusal. This written notice must describe what they refused to do and their alternate proposal, if any. The notice must explain their rationale and must describe each evaluation procedure, assessment, record, or report used as the basis of their refusal. The notice must also provide a description of all other options the IEP team considered and the reasons why the team rejected these options. Finally, the notice must describe any other factors that are relevant to their proposal or refusal. Schools often fail to provide Prior Written Notice when parents request more services or different services. IDEA 2004 strengthened the prior written notice requirements and requires schools to provide this notice in the event of a due process hearing. See Section 1415(2)(B)(i)(I) below.

(2) Due Process Complaint Notice.[139]

(A) Complaint. The **due process complaint notice** required under subsection (b)(7)(A) shall be deemed to be sufficient **unless** the party receiving the notice notifies the hearing officer and the other party in writing that the receiving party believes the notice has not met the requirements of subsection (b)(7)(A).

(B) Response to Complaint.
    (i) Local Educational Agency Response.
        (I) In General. If the local educational agency **has not sent a prior written notice** to the parent regarding the subject matter contained in the **parent's due process complaint notice**, such local educational agency **shall, within 10 days** of receiving the complaint, send to the parent a response that shall include -
            (aa) an explanation of why the agency proposed or refused to take the action raised in the complaint;
            (bb) a description of other options that the IEP Team considered and the reasons why those options were rejected;
            (cc) a description of each evaluation procedure, assessment, record, or report the agency used as the basis for the proposed or refused action; and
            (dd) a description of the factors that are relevant to the agency's proposal or refusal.
        (II) Sufficiency. A response filed by a local educational agency pursuant to subclause (I) shall not be construed to preclude such local educational agency from asserting that the parent's due process complaint notice was insufficient where appropriate.
    (ii) Other Party Response. Except as provided in clause (i), the **non-complaining party shall, within 10 days** of receiving the complaint, send to the complainant a response that specifically addresses the issues raised in the complaint.

(C) Timing. The party providing a hearing officer notification under subparagraph (A) shall provide the notification **within 15 days** of receiving the complaint.

(D) Determination. Within 5 days of receipt of the notification provided under subparagraph (C), the hearing officer **shall make a determination** on the face of the notice of whether the notification meets the requirements of subsection (b)(7)(A), and shall immediately notify the parties in writing of such determination.

(E) Amended Complaint Notice.
    (i) In General. A party **may amend its due process complaint notice only if** -
        (I) the other party **consents in writing** to such amendment **and** is **given the opportunity to resolve** the complaint through a meeting held pursuant to subsection (f)(1)(B); **or**
        (II) the **hearing officer grants permission**, except that the hearing officer may only grant such permission at any time not later than 5 days before a due process hearing occurs.
    (ii) Applicable Timeline. The applicable **timeline for a due process hearing under this part shall recommence at the time the party files an amended notice**, including the timeline under subsection (f)(1)(B).

---

[139] Section 1415(c)(2) includes requirements and timelines for the Due Process Complaint Notice and the Amended Complaint Notice. If the school did not provide Prior Written Notice to the parent, the school must send the notice within 10 days. The non-complaining party must respond to the complaint within 10 days. If the notice is insufficient, the receiving party must complain to the Hearing Officer within 15 days. (See Section 1415(c)(2)(C)) The Hearing Officer has 5 days to determine whether the complaint is sufficient. If it is not sufficient, an amended complaint may be filed. See **Appendix E: Due Process Procedure and Timelines**.

— **(d) Procedural Safeguards Notice.**[140]   *1 time a year*

(1) In General.

(A) Copy to Parents. A copy of the procedural safeguards available to the parents of a child with a disability shall be given to the parents **only 1 time a year, except** that a copy also shall be given to the parents -
   (i) upon **initial referral** or **parental request for evaluation;**
   (ii) upon the first occurrence of the **filing of a complaint** under subsection (b)(6); and
   (iii) upon **request by a parent.**

(B) Internet Websites. A local educational agency may place a current copy of the procedural safeguards notice on its Internet website if such website exists.

(2) Contents. The **procedural safeguards notice**[141] **shall include** a full explanation of the procedural safeguards, written in the **native language of the parents** (unless it clearly is not feasible to do so) and written **in an easily understandable manner**, available under this section and under regulations promulgated by the Secretary relating to -

(A) independent educational evaluation;

(B) prior written notice;

(C) parental consent;

(D) access to educational records;

(E) the opportunity to present and resolve complaints, including -
   (i) the **time period in which to make a complaint;**
   (ii) the opportunity for the agency to resolve the complaint; and
   (iii) the availability of mediation;

(F) the child's placement during pendency of due process proceedings;

(G) procedures for students who are subject to placement in an interim alternative educational setting;

(H) requirements for unilateral placement by parents of children in private schools at public expense;

(I) due process hearings, including requirements for disclosure of evaluation results and recommendations;

(J) State-level appeals (if applicable in that State);

(K) civil actions, including the time period in which to file such actions; and

(L) attorneys' fees.

---

[140] The purpose of the Procedural Safeguards Notice is to provide parents with information about their rights and protections under the law. Parents must be provided with notice of the time period (**statute of limitations**) within which "**to make a complaint.**" The Procedural Safeguards Notice also includes rights about mediation, "stay put," discipline, reimbursement for private placements, and attorneys' fees.

[141] The Department of Education will publish a model procedural safeguards notice form at the time the final special education regulations are published. (Section 1417(c))

(e) Mediation.[142]

(1) **In General.** Any State educational agency or local educational agency that receives assistance under this part shall ensure that procedures are established and implemented to allow **parties to disputes** involving any matter, including matters arising **prior to the filing of a complaint** pursuant to subsection (b)(6), to **resolve such disputes through a mediation process.**

(2) **Requirements.** Such procedures **shall** meet the following requirements:

(A) The procedures shall ensure that the mediation process -
  (i) is **voluntary** on the part of the parties;
  (ii) **is not used to deny or delay a parent's right to a due process hearing** under subsection (f), or to deny any other rights afforded under this part; and
  (iii) is conducted by a **qualified and impartial mediator** who is trained in effective mediation techniques.[143]

(B) **Opportunity to Meet with a Disinterested Party.** A local educational agency or a State agency may establish procedures to offer to parents and schools **that choose not to use the mediation process**, an opportunity to meet, at a time and location convenient to the parents, with a **disinterested party** who is under contract with -
  (i) a **parent training and information center or community parent resource center** in the State established under section 1471 of this title or 1472 of this title; **or**
  (ii) an appropriate **alternative dispute resolution entity**, to encourage the use, and explain the benefits, of the mediation process to the parents.

(C) **List of Qualified Mediators.**[144] The State **shall maintain a list of individuals who are qualified mediators** and knowledgeable in laws and regulations relating to the provision of special education and related services.

(D) **Costs.** The State shall bear the cost of the mediation process, including the costs of meetings described in subparagraph (B).

(E) **Scheduling and Location.** Each session in the mediation process shall be scheduled in a **timely manner** and shall be held in a **location that is convenient to the parties** to the dispute.[145]

---

[142] Mediation is a confidential process that allows parties to resolve disputes without litigation. The mediator helps the parties express their views and positions and understand the other's views and positions. A successful mediation requires both parties to discuss their views and differences frankly, without the presence of lawyers. Before entering into mediation, both parties should understand their rights and the law. A due process hearing does not have to be pending to request mediation.

[143] When you mediate or negotiate, your goals are to resolve the problems an protect the parent-school relationship. The Bibliography includes recommended books that will help you learn to negotiate effectively.

[144] The mediator's role is to facilitate the communication process. Mediators should not take positions or take sides. Good mediators do not have to be knowledgeable about special education law and practice but must know how to facilitate communication between parties. If mediators are not well trained in the process of mediation, their personal and professional biases and opinions will adversely affect the mediation process. Mediators are not arbitrators. Arbitrators issue rulings in favor of one party or the other.

[145] Mediation sessions and Resolution Sessions do not have to be face-to-face and may be may be convened by conference calls or video conferences. (Section 1414(f))

(F) Written Agreement.[146] In the case that a **resolution is reached** to resolve the complaint through the mediation process, the parties shall execute **a legally binding agreement** that sets forth such resolution and that -

(i) states that all **discussions that occurred during the mediation process shall be confidential and may not be used as evidence** in any subsequent due process hearing or civil proceeding;

(ii) is signed by both the parent and a representative of the agency who has the authority to bind such agency; and

(iii) is **enforceable in** any State court of competent jurisdiction or **in a district court of the United States.**

(G) Mediation Discussions. Discussions that occur during the mediation process **shall be confidential and may not be used as evidence** in any subsequent due process hearing or civil proceeding.[147]

— **(f) Impartial Due Process Hearing.**[148]

(1) In General.

(A) Hearing. Whenever a complaint has been received under subsection (b)(6) or (k), the parents or the local educational agency involved in such complaint shall have an opportunity for an impartial due process hearing, which shall be conducted by the **State educational agency or by the local educational agency**, as determined by State law or by the State educational agency.[149]

(B) Resolution Session.[150]

(i) **Preliminary Meeting.** Prior to the opportunity for an impartial due process hearing under subparagraph (A), the local educational agency **shall convene a meeting with the parents and the relevant member or members of the IEP Team** who have specific knowledge of the facts identified in the complaint

(I) **within 15 days** of receiving notice of the parents' complaint;

---

[146] Legally binding written settlement agreements are new in IDEA 2004. Previously, when a party breached a mediation agreement, the other party had to enforce the agreement by filing suit under a breach of contract theory, usually in state court. Now a party can use the power of federal courts to ensure that settlement agreements are honored.

[147] In mediation, discussions and admissions by the parties are confidential. If the case is not settled, information from settlement discussions may not be used or disclosed in a subsequent trial. An attempt to use confidential disclosures from mediation or settlement discussions in court could cause the case to be dismissed or the judge to issue an adverse ruling.

[148] Many pre-trial procedures and timelines for due process hearings are new in IDEA 2004. See **Appendix E: Due Process, Procedures, Timelines** for specific information.

[149] States have "one-tier" or "two-tier" systems for due process hearings. In one-tier systems, the state department of education conducts the due process hearing and the losing party can appeal to state or federal court. In two-tier systems, the due process hearing is conducted by the school district. The losing party must appeal to the state department of education which appoints a review officer or review panel. After the review officer or panel issues a decision, the losing party can appeal to state for federal court.

[150] The Resolution Session provides the parties with an opportunity to resolve their complaint before the due process hearing. The school district is required to convene the Resolution Session within 15 days of receiving the parent's Due Process Complaint Notice. The school district must send "the relevant member or members of the IEP team" who have knowledge about the facts in the parent's complaint and a school district representative who has decision-making authority (settlement authority). The school board attorney may not attend the Resolution Session unless the parent is accompanied by an attorney. The parents and district may agree to waive the Resolution Session or use the mediation process.

(II) which **shall include a representative of the agency who has decisionmaking authority** on behalf of such agency;

(III) which **may not include an attorney** of the local educational agency unless the parent is accompanied by an attorney; **and**

(IV) **where the parents of the child discuss their complaint,** and the facts that form the basis of the complaint, **and the local educational agency is provided the opportunity to resolve the complaint,** unless the parents and the local educational agency **agree in writing to waive such meeting,** or agree to use the mediation process described in subsection (e).

(ii) **Hearing.** If the local educational agency has not resolved the complaint to the satisfaction of the parents **within 30 days** of the receipt of the complaint, the due process hearing may occur, and **all of the applicable timelines for a due process hearing under this part shall commence.**

(iii) **Written Settlement Agreement.**[151] In the case that a resolution is reached to resolve the complaint at a meeting described in clause (i), the parties **shall execute a legally binding agreement** that is -

(I) signed by both the parent and a representative of the agency who has the authority to bind such agency; and

(II) **enforceable** in any State court of competent jurisdiction or in a **district court of the United States.**

(iv) **Review Period.** If the parties execute an agreement pursuant to clause (iii), a party may **void such agreement within 3 business days** of the agreement's execution.

(2) Disclosure of Evaluations and Recommendations.[152]

(A) In General. Not less than **5 business days** prior to a hearing conducted pursuant to paragraph (1), each party shall disclose to all other parties **all evaluations completed by that date, and recommendations** based on the offering party's evaluations, **that the party intends to use** at the hearing.

(B) Failure to Disclose. A hearing officer **may bar** any party that fails to comply with subparagraph (A) from introducing the relevant evaluation or recommendation at the hearing without the consent of the other party.

(3) Limitations on Hearing.

(A) Person Conducting Hearing.[153] A hearing officer conducting a hearing pursuant to paragraph (1)(A) **shall, at a minimum -**

---

[151] The requirements for legally binding written Settlement Agreements are new. Previously, when a party breached a settlement agreement, the other party had to enforce the agreement by filing suit under a breach of contract theory. Now the power of the federal courts may be used to ensure that settlement agreements are honored. Either party **may void a settlement agreement within 3 business days.** Note: The three-day rule does not apply to settlement agreements created in mediation.

[152] IDEA requires that evaluations and recommendations be disclosed no later than 5 business days before a due process hearing. Most state statutes and regulations, and the standard of practice, requires that all exhibits (including evaluations and recommendations), exhibit lists, and witness lists, be disclosed at least 5 days prior to a hearing. Failure to comply with requirements about disclosure often causes hearing officers to dismiss or postpone cases. For a sample document list that can be used as an exhibit list, see "The File: Do It Right," Chapter 9, *Wrightslaw: From Emotions to Advocacy.*

[153] The law includes new standards for hearing officers. Hearing officers must be knowledgeable about the law, federal and state regulations, and caselaw. Hearing officers must also have the knowledge and ability to "conduct hearings and write decisions in accordance with appropriate standard legal practice." Hearing Officers may not be employees of the state department of education or the school district that is involved in the child's education, nor may they have a "personal or professional conflict of interest" that may affect their ability to be objective.

(i) **not be** -
(I) an employee of the State educational agency or the local educational agency involved in the education or care of the child; or
(II) a person **having a personal or professional interest that conflicts** with the person's objectivity in the hearing;
(ii) **possess knowledge of, and the ability to understand**, the provisions of this title, Federal and State regulations pertaining to this title, and **legal interpretations** of this title by Federal and State courts;
(iii) possess the knowledge and ability to conduct hearings in accordance with appropriate, **standard legal practice**; and
(iv) possess the knowledge and ability to render and write decisions in accordance with appropriate, **standard legal practice.**

(B) Subject Matter of Hearing. The party requesting the due process hearing **shall not be allowed to raise issues** at the due process hearing **that were not raised in the notice** filed under subsection (b)(7), unless the other party agrees otherwise.

(C) Timeline for Requesting Hearing.[154] A parent or agency shall request an impartial due process hearing **within 2 years** of the date the parent or agency knew or should have known about the alleged action that forms the basis of the complaint, **or,** if the State has an explicit time limitation for requesting such a hearing under this part, in such time as the State law allows.

(D) Exceptions to the Timeline. The timeline described in subparagraph (C) **shall not apply to a parent if** the parent was prevented from requesting the hearing due to -
(i) **specific misrepresentations by the local educational agency that it had resolved** the problem forming the basis of the complaint; or
(ii) the local educational agency's **withholding of information from the parent** that was required under this part to be provided to the parent.

(E) Decision of Hearing Officer.[155]
(i) In General. Subject to clause (ii), **a decision** made by a hearing officer **shall be made on substantive grounds** based on a determination of whether the child received a free appropriate public education.[156]
(ii) Procedural Issues.[157] In matters alleging a **procedural violation**, a hearing officer may find that a child did not receive a free appropriate public education **only if the procedural inadequacies** -
(I) impeded the **child's right** to a free appropriate public education;
(II) significantly **impeded the parents' opportunity to participate** in the decisionmaking process regarding the provision of a free appropriate public education to the parents' child; **or**
(III) caused **a deprivation of educational benefits.**

---

[154] The two-year statute of limitations to present a complaint is new. If your state does not have a statute of limitations, you must request a due process hearing within two years. (Section 1415(b)(6)(B)) The two-year statute of limitations may not apply if the parent was prevented from requesting a hearing because of misrepresentations by the school district or because the district withheld information it was required to provide.

[155] Rulings by hearing officers should be based substantive issues, not procedural issues, unless the procedural violation impeded the child's right to a free appropriate public education, significantly impeded the parents' opportunity to participate in decision-making, or deprived the child of educational benefit. This language in the statute is new and incorporates existing caselaw about procedural and substantive issues.

[156] Issues of substance include determining whether a child has a disability that adversely affects educational performance (eligibility), whether a child has received FAPE (a free appropriate public education), or whether a child needs extended school year (ESY) services.

[157] Procedural issues include delays in scheduling evaluations, delays in determining eligibility, delays in convening IEP meetings, and failure to include the appropriate personnel in IEP meetings. The facts of a case will determine whether the procedural breach rises to the level identified in Section 1400(f)(3)(E)(ii).

(iii) Rule of Construction. Nothing in this subparagraph shall be construed to preclude a hearing officer from ordering a local educational agency to comply with procedural requirements under this section.

(F) Rule of Construction. Nothing in this paragraph shall be construed to affect the right of a parent to file a complaint with the State educational agency.

(g) Appeal.

(1) In General. If the hearing required by subsection (f) is conducted by a local educational agency, any party aggrieved by the findings and decision rendered in such a hearing may appeal such findings and decision to the State educational agency.

(2) Impartial Review and Independent Decision. The State educational agency shall conduct an impartial review of the findings and decision appealed under paragraph (1). The officer conducting such review shall make an independent decision upon completion of such review.

(h) Safeguards.[158] Any party to a hearing conducted pursuant to subsection (f) or (k), or an appeal conducted pursuant to subsection (g), shall be accorded -

(1) the **right to be accompanied and advised by counsel and by individuals with special knowledge or training** with respect to the problems of children with disabilities;

(2) the **right to present evidence and confront, cross-examine, and compel the attendance of witnesses;**

(3) the **right to a written, or**, at the option of the parents, **electronic verbatim record** of such hearing; and

(4) the **right to written, or**, at the option of the parents, **electronic findings of fact and decisions**, which findings and decisions -

(A) shall be **made available to the public** consistent with the requirements of section 1417(b) of this title (relating to the confidentiality of data, information, and records); and

(B) shall be **transmitted to the advisory panel** established pursuant to section 1412(a)(21) of this title.

(i) Administrative Procedures.

(1) In General.

(A) **Decision Made in Hearing** - A decision made in a hearing conducted pursuant to subsection (f) or (k) shall be final, except that any party involved in such hearing may appeal such decision under the provisions of subsection (g) and paragraph (2).[159]

---

[158] In a due process hearing, parents, or their attorney, have the right to present evidence and cross-examine witnesses, and to issue subpoenas for witnesses. Parents have a right to a written verbatim record (transcript) of the hearing and to written findings of fact and decisions. In some states you can be represented by a lay advocate. See **Appendix E: Due Process Procedures and Timelines.**

(B) Decision Made at Appeal. A decision made under subsection (g) shall be final, except that any party may bring an action under paragraph (2).[160]

(2) Right to Bring Civil Action.

(A) In General. Any party **aggrieved by the findings and decision** made under subsection (f) or (k) who does not have the right to an appeal under subsection (g), and any party aggrieved by the findings and decision made under this subsection, **shall have the right to bring a civil action** with respect to the complaint presented pursuant to this section, which action may be brought **in any State court** of competent jurisdiction **or in a district court of the United States**, without regard to the amount in controversy.[161]

(B) Limitation. The party bringing the action **shall have 90 days from the date of the decision of the hearing officer** to bring such an action, **or**, if the State has an explicit time limitation for bringing such action under this part, in such time as the State law allows.[162]

(C) Additional Requirements. In any action brought under this paragraph, the court
(i) shall receive the records of the administrative proceedings;
(ii) shall hear additional evidence at the request of a party;[163] and
(iii) basing its decision on the **preponderance of the evidence**, shall grant such relief as the court determines is appropriate.

(3) Jurisdiction of District Courts; Attorneys' Fees.

(A) In General. The district courts of the United States shall have jurisdiction of actions brought under this section without regard to the amount in controversy.

(B) Award of Attorneys' Fees.
(i) **In General.** In any action or proceeding brought under this section, the court, in its discretion, may award reasonable attorneys' fees as part of the costs -
(I) **to a prevailing party who is the parent of a child with a disability;**
(II) to a prevailing party who is a State educational agency or local educational agency **against the attorney of a parent** who files a complaint or subsequent cause of action that is **frivolous,**

---

[159] A case is pending before the U. S. Supreme Court about whether parents or school districts have the burden of proof in a due process hearing. A decision in *Schaffer v. Weast* is expected in late 2005 or early 2006. For updates on the case, go to www.wrightslaw.com/news/05/schaffer.weast.htm. The outcome of this case will have a significant impact on special education litigation. The decision in *Schaffer v. Weast* will be published in *Wrightslaw: Special Education Law, 2nd Edition* which is scheduled for publication in the winter of 2006.

[160] In two-tier states (discussed in Section 1415(f)(1)(A)), the losing party must first appeal to the state department of education (SEA). If the party does not appeal, the due process decision is the final decision.

[161] In two-tier states, the losing party does not have a right to appeal to state or federal court until after a decision is rendered by the SEA. After an adverse decision from the state, the losing party has a right to appeal to state or federal court.

[162] The losing party has 90 days to appeal to state or federal court. **This 90-day timeline is new.** States may provide different or **shorter timelines.** You need to know your state's statute of limitations for filing appeals in Court. If it is longer than 90 days, assume that the longer timeline does not apply because IDEA requires an appeal within 90 days.

[163] Despite language in IDEA that the Court "shall hear additional evidence at the request of a party," many Courts will not hear evidence that could have been offered at the due process hearing. Parties should put all their evidence into the record during the due process hearing.

unreasonable, or without foundation, or **against the attorney** of a parent **who continued to litigate** after the litigation clearly **became frivolous, unreasonable, or without foundation;**[164] **or**

(III) to a prevailing State educational agency or local educational agency **against the attorney of a parent, or against the parent**, if the parent's complaint or subsequent cause of action was presented for any **improper purpose, such as to harass, to cause unnecessary delay, or to needlessly increase the cost of litigation.**[165]

(ii) **Rule of Construction.** Nothing in this subparagraph shall be construed to affect section 327 of the District of Columbia Appropriations Act, 2005.

(C) Determination of Amount of Attorneys' Fees. Fees awarded under this paragraph shall be based on **rates prevailing in the community** in which the action or proceeding arose for the kind and quality of services furnished. **No bonus or multiplier may be used** in calculating the fees awarded under this subsection.

(D) Prohibition of Attorneys' Fees and Related Costs for Certain Services.
(i) **In General.** Attorneys' fees may not be awarded and related costs may **not be reimbursed** in any action or proceeding under this section for services performed subsequent to the time of a written offer of settlement to a parent if -
(I) the offer is made within the time prescribed by **Rule 68 of the Federal Rules of Civil Procedure** or, in the case of an administrative proceeding, at any time **more than 10 days before the proceeding begins;**
(II) the offer is not accepted within 10 days; and
(III) the court or administrative hearing officer finds that **the relief finally obtained by the parents is not more favorable to the parents** than the offer of settlement.[166]

(ii) **IEP Team Meetings. Attorneys' fees may not be awarded relating to any meeting of the IEP Team** unless such meeting is convened as a result of an administrative proceeding or judicial action, or, at the discretion of the State, for a mediation described in subsection (e).

(iii) **Opportunity to Resolve Complaints.** A meeting conducted pursuant to subsection (f)(1)(B)(i) shall not be considered -
(I) a meeting convened as a result of an administrative hearing or judicial action; or
(II) an administrative hearing or judicial action for purposes of this paragraph.

(E) Exception to Prohibition on Attorneys' Fees and Related Costs. Notwithstanding subparagraph (D), an award of attorneys' fees and related costs **may be made to a parent who is the prevailing party and who was substantially justified in rejecting the settlement offer.**

---

[164] Parents who prevail can recover attorneys fees from school districts. Now, school districts may recover attorneys' fees from the parent's attorney under specific, limited circumstances. If the parent or parent's attorney files a complaint that is frivolous, unreasonable, or for an improper purpose (i.e., to harass, cause unnecessary delay, or needlessly increase the cost of litigation), the Court may award attorneys' fees to the school district.

[165] Some parents, driven by anger and frustration, request due process hearings when they have not prepared a case. They may be focused on perceived wrongs by the school, not on a program that will meet their child's needs. Unfortunately, many hearing officers and judges view parents of children with disabilities as "loose cannons." These parents not only lose their cases, but they create ill will for other parents who use the due process procedure to resolve disputes.

[166] If the school district makes a written settlement offer 10 days before the due process hearing and the terms of the offer are the same or similar to the relief obtained through litigation, the parents may not be entitled to attorneys' fees. Attorneys' fees will not be awarded for IEP meetings. Some courts have held that only federal courts can award attorney's fees. Other courts have held that a state court or federal court can award attorneys' fees.

(F) Reduction in Amount of Attorneys' Fees. Except as provided in subparagraph (G), whenever the court finds that

(i) the parent, or the parent's attorney, during the course of the action or proceeding, **unreasonably protracted** the final resolution of the controversy;

(ii) the amount of the attorneys' fees otherwise authorized to be awarded unreasonably exceeds the hourly rate prevailing in the community for similar services by attorneys of reasonably comparable skill, reputation, and experience;

(iii) the **time spent** and legal services furnished **were excessive** considering the nature of the action or proceeding; or

(iv) the attorney representing the parent did not provide to the local educational agency the appropriate information in the notice of the complaint described in subsection (b)(7)(A), the court shall reduce, accordingly, the amount of the attorneys' fees awarded under this section.

(G) Exception to Reduction in Amount of Attorneys' Fees. The provisions of subparagraph (F) shall not apply in any action or proceeding if the court finds that the State or local educational agency unreasonably protracted the final resolution of the action or proceeding or there was a violation of this section.

Stay Put — **(j) Maintenance of Current Educational Placement.**[167] Except as provided in subsection (k)(4), **during the pendency of any proceedings** conducted pursuant to this section, unless the State or local educational agency and the parents otherwise agree, the child shall remain in the then-current educational placement of the child, or, if applying for initial admission to a public school, shall, with the consent of the parents, be placed in the public school program until all such proceedings have been completed.[168]

discipline — **(k) Placement in Alternative Educational Setting.**[169]

(1) Authority of School Personnel.

(A) Case-by-Case Determination. School personnel **may** consider any unique circumstances on a **case-by-case basis**[170] when determining **whether to order a change in placement** for a child with a disability who **violates a code of student conduct.**

---

[167] The "Stay Put" statute holds that during the due process hearing and appeals, the child will remain (stay put) in the current educational placement. Many courts have held that the "current educational placement" is not the physical location of services, but the nature of the educational program.

[168] Pursuant to the U. S. Supreme Court decisions in *Burlington* and *Carter*, parents may remove their child from an inappropriate placement, place their child into a private placement, and request reimbursement for the private placement, subject to the restrictions in Section 1412(a)(10). The First Circuit (in *Burlington*), Ninth Circuit (in *Clovis),* and the Third Circuit (in *Raelee S.*) held that when a State Review Officer awards reimbursement for a private placement, the private placement is the "current educational placement." If the school district appeals this decision, they must pay for the child's private placement while the case is being appealed. The 1997 IDEA regulations made this provision mandatory and the same language is included in the proposed regulations for IDEA 2004 at 34 C.F.R. § 300.518(c).

[169] "A free appropriate public education is available to **all children with disabilities** residing in the State between the ages of 3 and 21, inclusive, including children with disabilities who have been suspended or expelled from school." (Section 1412(a)(1)(A))

[170] Many administrators and school boards refuse to exercise discretion in disciplinary matters. They claim "the law" does not allow them to analyze the unique circumstances of a particular child's case. Congress added the language that school personnel "consider any unique circumstances on a case-by-case basis" in determining whether to order a change of placement in IDEA 2004. This clarifies that school officials may use discretion and consider each situation individually and rebuts the arguments of administrators who refuse to exercise discretion.

(B) Authority. School personnel under this subsection **may remove a child with a disability who violates a code of student conduct**[171] from their current placement to an appropriate interim alternative educational setting, another setting, or **suspension, for not more than 10 school days** (to the extent such alternatives are applied to children without disabilities).

(C) Additional Authority. If school personnel seek to order a change in placement that would **exceed 10 school days** and the behavior that gave rise to the violation of the school code is determined **not to be a manifestation** of the child's disability pursuant to subparagraph (E), the relevant disciplinary procedures applicable to **children without disabilities may be applied**[172] to the child in the same manner and for the same duration in which the procedures would be applied to children without disabilities, except as provided in section 1412(a)(1) of this title although it may be provided in an interim alternative educational setting.

(D) Services. A child with a disability who is **removed from the child's current placement** under subparagraph (G) (**irrespective** of whether the behavior is determined to be a manifestation of the child's disability) or subparagraph (C) **shall** –

    (i) continue to receive **educational services**, as provided in section 1412(a)(1) of this title, so as to enable the child to continue to participate **in the general education curriculum**, although in another setting, and to progress toward meeting the goals set out in the child's IEP; and

    (ii) receive, as appropriate, a **functional behavioral assessment, behavioral intervention services** and modifications, that are designed to address the behavior violation **so that it does not recur.**[173]

(E) Manifestation Determination.[174] [175]

    (i) **In General.** Except as provided in subparagraph (B), **within 10 school days of any decision to change the placement** of a child with a disability because of **a violation of a code of student conduct,**

---

[171] If a child with a disability violates a code of student conduct, school officials may suspend the child for **up to 10 days.** Codes of Conduct are usually written policies adopted by the School Board.

[172] If the school suspends the child with a disability for **more than 10 days** and determines that the child's behavior was not a manifestation of the disability, they may use the same procedures as with non-disabled children, but they must continue to provide the child with a free appropriate public education (FAPE) (Section 1412(a)(1)(A)) If the child has a **Section 504 plan,** and the behavior was not a manifestation of the disability, the school may suspend or expel the child. The child is not entitled to receive a free appropriate public education. See **Appendix A: Section 504 and IDEA.**

[173] If the school district suspends a child with a disability for **more than 10 days,** regardless of severity of the child's misconduct (i.e. violation of a code of conduct v. possession of a weapon), the child must continue to receive FAPE (see Section 1412(a)(1)(A)), so the child can participate in the general education curriculum, make progress on the IEP goals, and receive a functional behavioral assessment, behavioral intervention services and modifications to prevent the behavior from reoccurring.

[174] The IEP team must review all information about the child and determine if the negative behavior was caused by the child's disability, had a direct and substantial relationship to the disability, or was the result of the school's failure to implement the IEP. The IEP team must answer several questions. Is the child's IEP appropriate? Is the child's placement appropriate? Did the school provide appropriate behavior intervention strategies? Did the child's disability impair the child's ability to understand the impact and consequences of the behavior?

[175] If you are dealing with a discipline issue, you need to obtain a comprehensive psycho-educational evaluation of the child by an evaluator in the private sector who has expertise in the disability (i.e., autism, attention deficit, bipolar disorder, Asperger's Syndrome, auditory processing deficits). The evaluator must analyze the relationship between the child's disability and behavior. If there is a causal relationship, the evaluator should write a detailed report that describes the child's disability, the basis for determining that the behavior was a manifestation of the disability, and recommendations for an appropriate program. If you are dealing with a manifestation review, ask the evaluator to attend the hearing to explain the findings and make recommendations about alternative plans. Your goal is to develop a win-win solution to the problem.

the local educational agency, the **parent**, and relevant **members of the IEP Team** (as determined by the parent and the local educational agency) **shall review all relevant information** in the student's file, **including the child's IEP**, any teacher observations, and **any relevant information provided by the parents** to determine -

(I) if the conduct in question was **caused by, or had a direct and substantial relationship** to, the child's disability; or

(II) if the conduct in question was **the direct result of the local educational agency's failure to implement the IEP.**

(ii) Manifestation. If the local educational agency, the parent, and relevant members of the IEP Team determine that either subclause (I) or (II) of clause (i) is applicable for the child, the conduct shall be determined to be a manifestation of the child's disability.

(F) Determination That Behavior Was a Manifestation. If the local educational agency, the parent, and relevant members of the IEP Team make the determination that the conduct **was a manifestation of the child's disability, the IEP Team shall -**

(i) **conduct a functional behavioral assessment, and implement a behavioral intervention plan**[176] for such child, provided that the local educational agency had not conducted such assessment prior to such determination before the behavior that resulted in a change in placement described in subparagraph (C) or (G);

(ii) in the situation where a behavioral intervention plan has been developed, **review the behavioral intervention plan** if the child already has such a behavioral intervention plan, and **modify it**, as necessary, **to address the behavior;** and

(iii) except as provided in subparagraph (G), return the child to the placement from which the child was removed, unless the parent and the local educational agency agree to a change of placement as part of the modification of the behavioral intervention plan.

(G) Special Circumstances. School personnel may remove a student to an interim alternative educational setting for **not more than 45 school days without regard to whether the behavior is determined to be a manifestation** of the child's disability, in cases where a child -

(i) carries or possesses a **weapon**[177] to or at school, on school premises, or to or at a school function under the jurisdiction of a State or local educational agency;

(ii) knowingly **possesses or uses illegal drugs,** or sells or solicits the sale of a controlled substance[178], while **at school**, on school premises, or at a school function under the jurisdiction of a State or local educational agency; or

(iii) has inflicted **serious bodily injury** upon another person while at school, on school premises, or at a school function under the jurisdiction of a State or local educational agency.[179] [180]

---

[176] If the child's behavior was a manifestation of the disability, the IEP Team shall conduct a Functional Behavioral Assessment (assuming one has not been completed previously) and implement a Behavioral intervention plan (BIP). If a Behavior Intervention Plan was developed previously, it should be modified to address behavior as necessary. If the child's behavior did not involve weapons, drugs, or seriously bodily injury (see Section 1415(k)(1)(G)), the child should return to the prior placement.

[177] Section 1415(k)(7)(C) clarifies that the term "weapon" means a "dangerous weapon" capable of causing death or serious bodily injury.

[178] If the child is prescribed a controlled substance by a doctor, and the child has possession of the medication at school, this is not illegal possession or illegal use. The school may not expel or suspend the child for possessing prescribed medication. If the child attempts to sell or solicit the sale of the controlled substance, this "special circumstance" warrants a suspension for 45 school days and possible criminal prosecution.

[179] See Section 1415(k)(7) for the statutory differences between "controlled drugs" (Schedule I - V) and "illegal drugs," and definitions of "weapon" and "serious bodily injury."

(H) Notification. Not later than the date on which the decision to take disciplinary action is made, the local educational agency **shall** notify the parents of that decision, **and of all procedural safeguards accorded under this section.**

(2) Determination of Setting. The interim **alternative educational setting** in subparagraphs (C) and (G) of paragraph (1) **shall be determined by the IEP Team.**[181]

(3) Appeal.

(A) In General. The parent of a child with a disability who disagrees with any decision regarding **placement,** or the **manifestation determination** under this subsection, **or a local educational agency** that believes that maintaining the current placement of the child is **substantially likely to result in injury** to the child or to others, **may** request a hearing.[182]

(B) Authority of Hearing Officer.[183]
    (i) In General. A hearing officer **shall hear**, and make a determination regarding, **an appeal** requested under subparagraph (A).
    (ii) Change of Placement Order. In making the determination under clause (i), **the hearing officer may order a change in placement** of a child with a disability. In such situations, the hearing officer may
    (I) **return a child** with a disability to the placement from which the child was removed; or
        (II) **order a change in placement** of a child with a disability to an appropriate interim alternative educational setting for **not more than 45 school days if** the hearing officer determines that maintaining the current placement of such child is **substantially likely to result in injury to the child or to others.**

(4) Placement During Appeals. When an appeal under paragraph (3) has been requested by either the parent or the local educational agency -

(A) the child **shall remain in the interim alternative educational setting** pending the decision of the hearing officer **or** until the expiration of the time period provided for in paragraph (1)(C), whichever occurs first, unless the parent and the State or local educational agency agree otherwise; and

---

[180] If the child's behavior involves a dangerous weapon, illegal drugs, or serious bodily injury, the child may be suspended for 45 school days even if the behavior was a manifestation of the disability. The child is still entitled to FAPE pursuant to Section 1412(a)(1)(A) and Section 1415(k)(1)(D).

[181] The decision to place a child into an interim alternative educational setting shall be made by the IEP Team, not by an administrator or school board member. This is mandatory. The educational setting is an interim placement, not a permanent placement. Remember: parents are full members of the IEP team.

[182] The parent can request a hearing to appeal the manifestation determination or the decision to place the child in an interim alternative educational setting. The school can request a hearing to maintain the current educational placement if they think changing the placement is "substantially likely to result in injury." (See Section 1415(j) regarding "stay-put.") Appeal of a manifestation determination may be futile in a case that involves a dangerous weapon, illegal drugs, or serious bodily injury. The school can suspend a student for 45 school days for these behaviors even if the behavior was a manifestation of the child's disability.

[183] A hearing officer has the authority to return the child to the original placement. If the hearing officer concludes that the child is likely to injure himself or others, the hearing officer may order the child to be placed in an interim alternative educational setting for not more than 45 school days.

(B) the State or local educational agency shall arrange for an **expedited hearing**, which **shall occur within 20 school days** of the date the hearing is requested and shall result in a determination within 10 school days after the hearing.[184]

(5) Protections for Children Not Yet Eligible for Special Education and Related Services.

(A) In General. A child who has **not been determined to be eligible** for special education and related services under this part and who has engaged in behavior that violates a code of student conduct, **may assert any of the protections provided for in this part if the local educational agency had knowledge** (as determined in accordance with this paragraph) that the child was a child with a disability **before the behavior** that precipitated the disciplinary action occurred.

(B) Basis of Knowledge. A local educational agency **shall be deemed to have knowledge**[185] that a child is a child with a disability if, before the behavior that precipitated the disciplinary action occurred -
   (i) **the parent of the child has expressed concern in writing** to supervisory or administrative personnel of the appropriate educational agency, or a teacher of the child, **that the child is in need of special education** and related services;
   (ii) the parent of the child has **requested an evaluation** of the child pursuant to section 1414(a)(1)(B) of this title; **or**
   (iii) the **teacher of the child, or other personnel** of the local educational agency, has expressed **specific concerns about a pattern of behavior** demonstrated by the child, directly to the director of special education of such agency or to other supervisory personnel of the agency.[186]

(C) Exception. A local educational agency shall not be deemed to have knowledge that the child is a child with a disability if the parent of the child has not allowed an evaluation of the child pursuant to section 1414 of this title or has refused services under this part or the child has been evaluated and it was determined that the child was not a child with a disability under this part.

(D) Conditions that Apply if No Basis of Knowledge.
   (i) In General. If a local educational agency **does not** have knowledge that a child is a child with a disability (in accordance with subparagraph (B) or (C)) **prior** to taking disciplinary measures against the child, the child may be subjected to disciplinary measures applied to children without disabilities who engaged in comparable behaviors consistent with clause (ii).
   (ii) Limitations. If a **request is made for an evaluation** of a child during the time period in which the child is subjected to disciplinary measures under this subsection, the **evaluation shall be conducted in an expedited manner.** If the child is determined to be a child with a disability, taking into consideration information from the evaluation conducted by the agency and information provided by the parents, the

---

[184] Expedited hearings must be held within 20 school days and a decision rendered within 10 school days. While the decision is pending, the child shall remain in the alternative setting, unless the time limit for this placement expired.

[185] If the school knew, or should have known, that the child is a child with a disability and entitled to an IEP, then the child is protected under IDEA. The factors affecting "knowledge" are listed above. If the parent refused to permit an evaluation or special education services, the child loses the protections of this subsection.

[186] If you are concerned that your child may have a disability, you must put your concerns in writing. You should document important conversations, meetings, and telephone calls with notes or letters that describe what happened, what you were told, and your concerns. To do less is unwise. Courts have little sympathy for individuals who know or should know they have rights, fail to safeguard their rights, then complain that their rights were violated. Courts believe that the party who complains that their rights were violated must prove that they took reasonable steps to protect themselves, yet their rights were still violated.

agency **shall provide special education and related services**[187] in accordance with this part, except that, **pending the results** of the evaluation, the **child shall remain in the educational placement determined by school authorities.**

(6) Referral to and Action by Law Enforcement and Judicial Authorities.[188]

(A) Rule of Construction. Nothing in this part shall be construed to **prohibit** an agency from reporting a crime committed by a child with a disability to appropriate authorities or to prevent State law enforcement and judicial authorities from exercising their responsibilities with regard to the application of Federal and State law to crimes committed by a child with a disability.

(B) Transmittal of Records. An agency reporting a crime committed by a child with a disability shall ensure that copies of the special education and disciplinary records of the child are transmitted for consideration by the appropriate authorities to whom the agency reports the crime.

(7) Definitions. In this subsection:

(A) Controlled Substance. The term 'controlled substance' means a drug or other substance identified under schedule I, II, III, IV, or V in section 812(c) of title 21, United States Code.

(B) Illegal Drug. The term 'illegal drug' means a **controlled substance** but does not include a controlled substance that is **legally possessed** or used under the supervision of a licensed health-care professional or that is legally possessed[189] or used under any other authority under that Act or under any other provision of Federal law.

(C) Weapon. The term 'weapon'[190] has the meaning given the term **'dangerous weapon'** under section 930(g)(2) of title 18, United States Code.

(D) Serious Bodily Injury. The term 'serious bodily injury'[191] has the meaning given the term **'serious bodily injury'** under paragraph (3) of subsection (h) of section 1365 of title 18, United States Code.

---

[187] If the school did not have knowledge that the child had a disability and was entitled to an IEP, the child may be treated like a non-disabled child. If an evaluation is requested, it shall be expedited. Once it is determined that the child is eligible for special education and is entitled to an IEP, the child will receive all rights and protections under IDEA, including the detailed procedures provided in Section 1415(k).

[188] The school is not prohibited or required to report crimes committed by children with disabilities. Discretion and common sense should prevail. The practice of reporting behavior caused by emotional disturbances as "crimes" puts law enforcement personnel into positions for which they have not been trained. Treating emotionally distraught or emotionally disturbed children as criminals may inflict permanent emotional damage on vulnerable children.

[189] Many schools suspend and expel students who bring over-the-counter medications (i. e., aspirin, ibuprofen, Tums) to school, claiming that these medications are "drugs." This subsection clarifies that over-the-counter medications are not illegal drugs nor controlled substances. A child with a disability who receives services under IDEA is protected from these abuses of power by school officials. A child who has a Section 504 Plan does not have these protections.

[190] The term 'dangerous weapon' means a weapon, device, instrument, material, or substance, animate or inanimate, that is used for, or is readily capable of, **causing death or serious bodily injury,** except that such term does not include a pocket knife with a blade of less than 2 1/2 inches in length." 18 U.S.C. § 930(g)(2)

[191] The term 'serious bodily injury' means bodily injury which involves - (A) **a substantial risk of death;** (B) extreme physical pain; (C) protracted and obvious **disfigurement;** or (D) protracted loss or impairment of the function of a bodily member, organ, or mental faculty . . ." 18 U.S.C. § 1365(h)(3)

—— **(l) Rule of Construction.** Nothing in this title shall be construed to restrict or limit the rights, procedures, and remedies available under the Constitution, the Americans with Disabilities Act of 1990, [42 U.S.C. § 12101] title V of the Rehabilitation Act of 1973, [29 U.S.C. § 790] or other Federal laws protecting the rights of children with disabilities, except that before the filing of a civil action under such laws seeking relief that is also available under this part, the procedures under subsections (f) and (g) **shall be exhausted** to the same extent as would be required had the action been brought under this part.[192]

—— **(m) Transfer of Parental Rights at Age of Majority.**[193]

(1) In General. A State that receives amounts from a grant under this part may provide that, when a child with a disability **reaches the age of majority** under State law (except for a child with a disability who has been determined to be incompetent under State law) -

(A) the agency **shall provide** any **notice** required by this section **to both the individual and the parents**;

(B) all other rights accorded to parents under this part transfer to the child;

(C) the agency shall notify the individual and the parents of the transfer of rights; and

(D) all rights accorded to parents under this part transfer to children who are incarcerated in an adult or juvenile Federal, State, or local correctional institution.

(2) Special Rule.[194] If, under State law, a child with a disability who has reached the age of majority under State law, who has not been determined to be incompetent, but who is determined **not to have the ability to provide informed consent** with respect to the educational program of the child, the State **shall** establish procedures for appointing the parent of the child, or if the parent is not available, another appropriate individual, to represent the educational interests of the child throughout the period of eligibility of the child under this part.

---

[192] If a parent or child with a disability has a case against a school district or school employee for reasons, facts, and events that are not related to IDEA, they may file suit under that legal theory, but must usually initiate their case through a due process hearing. This often occurs when a lawsuit for dollar damages under Section 504 of the Rehabilitation Act is initiated. According to Section 1415(I): "before the filing of a civil action . . . the (due process) procedures under subsections (f) and (g) shall be exhausted . . ." This is called the "exhaustion of administrative remedies requirement." The case law in this area continues to evolve.

[193] The school district must provide notice to the parent and child that the parents' rights will transfer to child when the child reaches the "age of majority," which is usually age eighteen. States must establish procedures so parents can continue to represent the educational interests of their children.

[194] If possible, have your child write a statement that says, "I [child's name], pursuant to 20 U. S. C. Section 1415(m) and [your state's special education regulation section], hereby appoint my parent, [your name], to represent my educational interests." If the child is able, have this statement written out longhand, signed and dated. Use the above statute and your state's special education regulation language verbatim. Do not add or subtract from it, or rephrase it.

(n) Electronic Mail. A parent of a child with a disability may elect to receive notices required under this section by an electronic mail (e-mail) communication, if the agency makes such option available.[195]

(o) Separate Complaint. Nothing in this section shall be construed to preclude a parent from filing a separate due process complaint on an issue separate from a due process complaint already filed.[196]

20 U.S.C. § 1416. Monitoring, Technical Assistance, and Enforcement.

➡ **OVERVIEW:** Section 1416 is the enforcement statute. Although the U.S. Department of Education is responsible for enforcing IDEA, this provision has carried little weight over the past 30 years. In "Back to School on Civil Rights," the National Council on Disability found that no state was in compliance with the law and that the Department of Education did not require states to enforce the law. Instead, the law was enforced by parents who requested due process hearings. The National Council on Disability recommended that enforcement be vested with the U. S. Department of Justice. Congress has the power to amend the statute and provide the Department of Justice with this power but has not done so.

After passing the No Child Left Behind Act in 2001, Congress focused on special education outcomes in IDEA 2004. The law includes new language about Focused Monitoring. Previously, enforcement focused on procedural compliance, with little attention on whether children with disabilities were learning to read, write, spell, do arithmetic or were being prepared for employment and independent living.

Section 1416 includes stronger language about accountability. If the Department of Education determines that a state department of education (SEA) "needs assistance" for two consecutive years, the Department shall take corrective action that may include labeling the state as a "high risk grantee" and imposing special conditions. If the state continues in the "needs assistance" category for three consecutive years, the Department of Education may recover funds paid, withhold further funds, and refer the matter to the Department of Justice.

(a) Federal and State Monitoring.

(1) In General. The Secretary shall -

(A) monitor implementation of this part through -
(i) oversight of the exercise of general supervision by the States, as required in section 1412(a)(11) of this title; and
(ii) the State performance plans, described in subsection (b);

(B) enforce this part in accordance with subsection (e); and

(C) require States to -
(i) monitor implementation of this part by local educational agencies; and
(ii) enforce this part in accordance with paragraph (3) and subsection (e).

---

[195] At the parent's option, the school district can send notices by e-mail. Given the prevalence of email problems, including the automatic deletion or rejection of suspected spam, this option is not recommended as the primary means of providing or receiving notice. You may want receive notice by email as a supplement to the usual notification procedures.

[196] If a due process hearing is pending on one issue, and a new issue or issues arise, the parent may file a separate due process complaint notice. In the alternative, if the hearing officer and both sides agree, and the hearing has not yet been held, it may be possible to file an Amended Complaint as described in Section 1415(c)(2)(E).

(2) **Focused Monitoring.**[197] The **primary focus of Federal and State monitoring activities** described in paragraph (1) **shall** be on -

(A) **improving educational results and functional outcomes** for all children with disabilities; and

(B) ensuring that States **meet the program requirements** under this part, with a particular emphasis on those requirements that are most closely related to **improving educational results** for children with disabilities.

(3) **Monitoring Priorities.** The Secretary shall monitor the States, and shall require each State to monitor the local educational agencies located in the State (except the State exercise of general supervisory responsibility), using **quantifiable indicators** in each of the following priority areas, and using such qualitative indicators as are needed to adequately measure performance in the following priority areas:

(A) Provision of a free appropriate public education in the least restrictive environment.

(B) State exercise of general supervisory authority, including child find, effective monitoring, the use of resolution sessions, mediation, voluntary binding arbitration, and a system of transition services as defined in sections 1401(34) and 1437(a)(9) of this title.

(C) Disproportionate representation of racial and ethnic groups in special education and related services, to the extent the representation is the result of inappropriate identification.

(4) **Permissive Areas of Review.** The Secretary shall consider other relevant information and data, including data provided by States under section 1418 of this title.

(b) State Performance Plans.

(1) **Plan.**

(A) **In General.** Not later than **1 year after the date of enactment of the Individuals with Disabilities Education Improvement Act of 2004,** each State **shall have in place a performance** plan that evaluates that State's efforts to implement the requirements and purposes of this part and describes how the State will improve such implementation.

(B) **Submission for Approval.** Each State shall submit the State's performance plan to the Secretary for approval in accordance with the approval process described in subsection (c).

(C) **Review.** Each State shall review its State performance plan at least once every 6 years and submit any amendments to the Secretary.

---

[197] Monitoring will focus on **educational results and functional outcomes.** This is similar to No Child Left Behind and a refreshing change from procedural compliance issues. When the special education law was passed in 1975 (Public Law 94-142), many children with disabilities were denied services without due process of law. The law focused on protecting the rights of children and their parents (Section 1400(d)(1)(B)) and providing remedies for violations. (Section 1415) Educational outcomes took a back seat to procedural compliance.

Before the law was reauthorized in 1997, the word "measurable" (or a variation of that word) was rarely used to describe outcomes, goals, or objectives. When the law was reauthorized in 1997, the word "measurable" (or a variation of that word) appeared in the statute 16 times. In IDEA 2004, the word "measurable" is used 30 times. This measurable change in the frequency of the word "measure" may bode well for the future.

(2) Targets.

(A) In General. As a part of the State performance plan described under paragraph (1), each State shall establish **measurable** and rigorous targets for the indicators established under the priority areas described in subsection (a)(3).

(B) Data Collection.
(i) In General. Each State shall collect valid and reliable information as needed to report annually to the Secretary on the priority areas described in subsection (a)(3).
(ii) Rule of Construction. Nothing in this title shall be construed to authorize the development of a nationwide database of personally identifiable information on individuals involved in studies or other collections of data under this part.

(C) Public Reporting and Privacy.
(i) In General. The State shall use the targets established in the plan and priority areas described in subsection (a)(3) to analyze the performance of each local educational agency in the State in implementing this part.
(ii) Report.
(I) Public Report. The State shall report annually to the public on the performance of each local educational agency located in the State on the targets in the State's performance plan. The State shall make the State's performance plan available through public means, including by posting on the website of the State educational agency, distribution to the media, and distribution through public agencies.
(II) State Performance Report. The State shall report annually to the Secretary on the performance of the State under the State's performance plan.
(iii) Privacy. The State shall not report to the public or the Secretary any information on performance that would result in the disclosure of personally identifiable information about individual children or where the available data is insufficient to yield statistically reliable information.

(c) Approval Process.

(1) Deemed Approval. The Secretary shall review (including the specific provisions described in subsection (b)) each performance plan submitted by a State pursuant to subsection (b)(1)(B) and the plan shall be deemed to be approved by the Secretary unless the Secretary makes a written determination, prior to the expiration of the 120-day period beginning on the date on which the Secretary received the plan, that the plan does not meet the requirements of this section, including the specific provisions described in subsection (b).

(2) Disapproval. The Secretary shall not finally disapprove a performance plan, except after giving the State notice and an opportunity for a hearing.

(3) Notification. If the Secretary finds that the plan does not meet the requirements, in whole or in part, of this section, the Secretary shall -

(A) give the State notice and an opportunity for a hearing; and

(B) notify the State of the finding, and in such notification shall -
(i) cite the specific provisions in the plan that do not meet the requirements; and

(ii) request additional information, only as to the provisions not meeting the requirements, needed for the plan to meet the requirements of this section.

(4) Response. If the State responds to the Secretary's notification described in paragraph (3)(B) during the 30-day period beginning on the date on which the State received the notification, and resubmits the plan with the requested information described in paragraph (3)(B)(ii), the Secretary shall approve or disapprove such plan prior to the later of -

(A) the expiration of the 30-day period beginning on the date on which the plan is resubmitted; or

(B) the expiration of the 120-day period described in paragraph (1).

(5) Failure to Respond. If the State does not respond to the Secretary's notification described in paragraph (3)(B) during the 30-day period beginning on the date on which the State received the notification, such plan shall be deemed to be disapproved.

(d) Secretary's Review and Determination.

(1) Review. The Secretary shall annually review the State performance report submitted pursuant to subsection (b)(2)(C)(ii)(II) in accordance with this section.

(2) Determination.
(A) In General. Based on the information provided by the State in the State performance report, information obtained through monitoring visits, and any other public information made available, the Secretary shall determine if the State -
(i) meets the requirements and purposes of this part;
(ii) needs assistance in implementing the requirements of this part;
(iii) needs intervention in implementing the requirements of this part; or
(iv) needs substantial intervention in implementing the requirements of this part.

(B) Notice and Opportunity for a Hearing. For determinations made under clause (iii) or (iv) of subparagraph (A), the Secretary shall provide reasonable notice and an opportunity for a hearing on such determination.

(e) Enforcement.

(1) Needs Assistance. If the Secretary determines, **for 2 consecutive years,** that a State needs assistance under subsection (d)(2)(A)(ii) in implementing the requirements of this part, the Secretary **shall** take 1 or more of the following actions:

(A) Advise the State of available sources of technical assistance that may help the State address the areas in which the State needs assistance, which may include assistance from the Office of Special Education Programs, other offices of the Department of Education, other Federal agencies, technical assistance providers approved by the Secretary, and other federally funded nonprofit agencies, and require the State to work with appropriate entities. Such technical assistance may include -
(i) the provision of advice by experts to address the areas in which the State needs assistance, including explicit plans for addressing the area for concern within a specified period of time;
(ii) assistance in identifying and implementing professional development, instructional strategies, **and methods of instruction that are based on scientifically based research;**

(iii) designating and using distinguished superintendents, principals, special education administrators, special education teachers, and other teachers to provide advice, technical assistance, and support; and

(iv) devising additional approaches to providing technical assistance, such as collaborating with institutions of higher education, educational service agencies, national centers of technical assistance supported under part D, and private providers of scientifically based technical assistance.

(B) Direct the use of State-level funds under section 1411(e) of this title on the area or areas in which the State needs assistance.

(C) Identify the State as a **high-risk grantee and impose special conditions** on the State's grant under this part.

(2) Needs Intervention. If the Secretary determines, for **3 or more consecutive years**, that a State needs intervention under subsection (d)(2)(A)(iii) in implementing the requirements of this part, the following shall apply:

(A) The Secretary may take any of the actions described in paragraph (1).

(B) The Secretary shall take 1 or more of the following actions:

(i) Require the State to **prepare a corrective action plan or improvement plan** if the Secretary determines that the State should be able to correct the problem within 1 year.

(ii) Require the State to **enter into a compliance agreement** under section 1234f of this title, if the Secretary has reason to believe that the State **cannot correct the problem within 1 year**.

(iii) **For each year** of the determination, **withhold not less than 20 percent and not more than 50 percent of the State's funds** under section 1411(e) of this title, until the Secretary determines the State has sufficiently addressed the areas in which the State needs intervention.

(iv) Seek to **recover funds** under section 1234a this title.

(v) **Withhold, in whole or in part, any further payments** to the State under this part pursuant to paragraph (5).

(vi) **Refer the matter for appropriate enforcement action, which may include referral to the Department of Justice.**

(3) Needs Substantial Intervention. Notwithstanding paragraph (1) or (2), at any time that the Secretary determines that a State needs substantial intervention in implementing the requirements of this part or that there is a substantial failure to comply with any condition of a State educational agency's or local educational agency's eligibility under this part, the Secretary shall take 1 or more of the following actions:

(A) Recover funds under section 1234a of this title.

(B) Withhold, in whole or in part, any further payments to the State under this part.
(C) Refer the case to the Office of the Inspector General at the Department of Education.

(D) Refer the matter for appropriate enforcement action, which may include referral to the Department of Justice.

(4) Opportunity for Hearing.

(A) Withholding Funds. Prior to withholding any funds under this section, the Secretary shall provide reasonable notice and an opportunity for a hearing to the State educational agency involved.

(B) Suspension. Pending the outcome of any hearing to withhold payments under subsection (b), the Secretary may suspend payments to a recipient, suspend the authority of the recipient to obligate funds under this part, or both, after such recipient has been given reasonable notice and an opportunity to show cause why future payments or authority to obligate funds under this part should not be suspended.

(5) Report to Congress. The Secretary shall report to the Committee on Education and the Workforce of the House of Representatives and the Committee on Health, Education, Labor, and Pensions of the Senate within 30 days of taking enforcement action pursuant to paragraph (1), (2), or (3), on the specific action taken and the reasons why enforcement action was taken.

(6) Nature of Withholding.

(A) Limitation. If the Secretary withholds further payments pursuant to paragraph (2) or (3), the Secretary may determine -
(i) that such withholding will be limited to programs or projects, or portions of programs or projects, that affected the Secretary's determination under subsection (d)(2); or
(ii) that the State educational agency shall not make further payments under this part to specified State agencies or local educational agencies that caused or were involved in the Secretary's determination under subsection (d)(2).

(B) Withholding Until Rectified. Until the Secretary is satisfied that the condition that caused the initial withholding has been substantially rectified -
(i) payments to the State under this part shall be withheld in whole or in part; and
(ii) payments by the State educational agency under this part shall be limited to State agencies and local educational agencies whose actions did not cause or were not involved in the Secretary's determination under subsection (d)(2), as the case may be.

(7) Public Attention. Any State that has received notice under subsection (d)(2) shall, by means of a public notice, take such measures as may be necessary to bring the pendency of an action pursuant to this subsection to the attention of the public within the State.

(8) Judicial Review.

(A) In General. If any State is dissatisfied with the Secretary's action with respect to the eligibility of the State under section 1412 of this title, such State may, not later than 60 days after notice of such action, file with the United States court of appeals for the circuit in which such State is located a petition for review of that action. A copy of the petition shall be transmitted by the clerk of the court to the Secretary. The Secretary thereupon shall file in the court the record of the proceedings upon which the Secretary's action was based, as provided in section 2112 of title 28, United States Code.

(B) Jurisdiction; Review by United States Supreme Court. Upon the filing of such petition, the court shall have jurisdiction to affirm the action of the Secretary or to set it aside, in whole or in part. The judgment of the court shall be subject to review by the Supreme Court of the United States upon certiorari or certification as provided in section 1254 of title 28, United States Code.

(C) Standard of Review. The findings of fact by the Secretary, if supported by substantial evidence, shall be conclusive, but the court, for good cause shown, may remand the case to the Secretary to take further evidence, and the Secretary may thereupon make new or modified findings of fact and may modify the

Secretary's previous action, and shall file in the court the record of the further proceedings. Such new or modified findings of fact shall be conclusive if supported by substantial evidence.

(f) State Enforcement. If a State educational agency determines that a local educational agency is not meeting the requirements of this part, including the targets in the State's performance plan, the State educational agency shall prohibit the local educational agency from reducing the local educational agency's maintenance of effort under section 1413(a)(2)(C) of this title for any fiscal year.

(g) Rule of Construction. Nothing in this section shall be construed to restrict the Secretary from utilizing any authority under the General Education Provisions Act to monitor and enforce the requirements of this title.

(h) Divided State Agency Responsibility. For purposes of this section, where responsibility for ensuring that the requirements of this part are met with respect to children with disabilities who are convicted as adults under State law and incarcerated in adult prisons is assigned to a public agency other than the State educational agency pursuant to section 1412(a)(11)(C) of this title, the Secretary, in instances where the Secretary finds that the failure to comply substantially with the provisions of this part are related to a failure by the public agency, shall take appropriate corrective action to ensure compliance with this part, except that

(1) any reduction or withholding of payments to the State shall be proportionate to the total funds allotted under section 1411 of this title to the State as the number of eligible children with disabilities in adult prisons under the supervision of the other public agency is proportionate to the number of eligible individuals with disabilities in the State under the supervision of the State educational agency; and

(2) any withholding of funds under paragraph (1) shall be limited to the specific agency responsible for the failure to comply with this part.

(i) Data Capacity and Technical Assistance Review. The Secretary shall -

(1) review the data collection and analysis capacity of States to ensure that data and information determined necessary for implementation of this section is collected, analyzed, and accurately reported to the Secretary; and

(2) provide technical assistance (from funds reserved under section 1411(c) of this title), where needed, to improve the capacity of States to meet the data collection requirements.

20 U.S.C. § 1417. Administration.

➡ **OVERVIEW:** Section 1417 describes requirements for administering the law. The Department of Education may not mandate, direct, or control specific instructional content, curriculum or programs of instruction. When the special education regulations are published, the Department of Education is required to publish a model Individualized Education Program (IEP) form, an Individualized Family Service Plan (IFSP) form, procedural safeguards notice form, and prior written notice form.

(a) Responsibilities of Secretary. The Secretary shall -

(1) cooperate with, and (directly or by grant or contract) furnish technical assistance necessary to, a State in matters relating to -

(A) the education of children with disabilities; and

(B) carrying out this part; and

(2) provide short-term training programs and institutes.

(b) Prohibition Against Federal Mandates, Direction, or Control. Nothing in this title shall be construed to authorize an officer or employee of **the Federal Government to mandate, direct, or control** a State, local educational agency, or school's **specific instructional content**, academic achievement standards and assessments, **curriculum, or program of instruction.**

(c) Confidentiality. The Secretary shall take appropriate action, in accordance with section 1232g of this title, to ensure the protection of the confidentiality of any personally identifiable data, information, and records collected or maintained by the Secretary and by State educational agencies and local educational agencies pursuant to this part.

(d) Personnel. The Secretary is authorized to hire qualified personnel necessary to carry out the Secretary's duties under subsection (a), under section 1418 of this title, and under subpart 4 of part D, without regard to the provisions of title 5, United States Code, relating to appointments in the competitive service and without regard to chapter 51 and subchapter III of chapter 53 of such title relating to classification and general schedule pay rates, except that no more than 20 such personnel shall be employed at any time.

(e) Model Forms. Not later than the date that the Secretary publishes final regulations under this title, to implement amendments made by the Individuals with Disabilities Education Improvement Act of 2004, **the Secretary shall publish and disseminate widely** to States, local educational agencies, and parent and community training and information centers -

(1) **a model IEP form;**

(2) **a model individualized family service plan (IFSP) form;**

(3) **a model form of the notice of procedural safeguards** described in section 1415(d) of this title; and

(4) **a model form of the prior written notice** described in subsections (b)(3) and (c)(1) of section 1415 of this title that is consistent with the requirements of this part and is sufficient to meet such requirements.

20 U.S.C. § 1418. Program Information.

➡️ **OVERVIEW:** IDEA 2004 requires States to provide detailed reports about the number and percentage of children with disabilities by race, ethnicity, English proficiency, gender, and disability category, in specific categories, including children removed from school. The state must report Information about litigation and due process.

To address the issues of over-identification of minority children and the disproportionate number of minority children in special education, the Department of Education requires states to review and revise policies, procedures, and practices, and school districts to publicly report on their revised policies, procedures and practices. School districts are to provide early intervening services to groups of children who are over-identified.

(a) In General. Each State that receives assistance under this part, and the Secretary of the Interior, shall provide data each year to the Secretary of Education and the public on the following:

(1)

(A) The **number and percentage of children** with disabilities, by race, ethnicity, limited English proficiency status, gender, and disability category, who are **in each of the following separate categories**:

(i) Receiving a free appropriate public education.

(ii) Participating in regular education.

(iii) In separate classes, separate schools or facilities, or public or private residential facilities.

(iv) For each year of age from age 14 through 21, **stopped receiving special education** and related services because of program completion (including graduation with a regular secondary school diploma), or other reasons, **and the reasons why those children stopped receiving special education** and related services.

(v)

(I) Removed to an **interim alternative educational setting** under section 1415(k)(1) of this title.

(II) The **acts** or items **precipitating those removals**.

(III) The number of children with disabilities who are subject to **long-term suspensions or expulsions**.

(B) The number and percentage of children with disabilities, by race, gender, and ethnicity, who are **receiving early intervention services**.

(C) The number and percentage of children with disabilities, by race, gender, and ethnicity, who, from birth through age 2, **stopped receiving early intervention services** because of program completion or for other reasons.

(D) The **incidence and duration of disciplinary actions** by race, ethnicity, limited English proficiency status, gender, and disability category, of children with disabilities, **including suspensions of 1 day or more**.

(E) The number and percentage of children with disabilities who are **removed to alternative educational settings or expelled** as compared to children without disabilities who are removed to alternative educational settings or expelled.

(F) The **number of due process complaints** filed under section 1415 of this title and the **number of hearings conducted**.

(G) The number of **hearings requested** under section 1415(k) of this title and the number of **changes in placements ordered as a result of those hearings**.

(H) The number of **mediations held** and the **number of settlement agreements reached** through such mediations.

(2) The number and percentage of infants and toddlers, by race, and ethnicity, who are **at risk of having substantial developmental delays** (as defined in section 1432 of this title), and who are receiving early intervention services under part C.

(3) Any other information that may be required by the Secretary.

(b) Data Reporting.

(1) **Protection of Identifiable Data.** The data described in subsection (a) shall be publicly reported by each State in a manner that does not result in the disclosure of data identifiable to individual children.

(2) **Sampling.** The Secretary may permit States and the Secretary of the Interior to obtain the data described in subsection (a) through sampling.

(c) Technical Assistance. The Secretary may provide technical assistance to States to ensure compliance with the data collection and reporting requirements under this title.

(d) Disproportionality.[198]

(1) **In General.** Each State that receives assistance under this part, and the Secretary of the Interior, shall provide for the collection and examination of data to determine if significant disproportionality based on race and ethnicity is occurring in the State and the local educational agencies of the State with respect to -

(A) the identification of children as children with disabilities, including the identification of children as children with disabilities in accordance with a particular impairment described in section 1401(3) of this title;
(B) the placement in particular educational settings of such children; and
(C) the incidence, duration, and type of disciplinary actions, including suspensions and expulsions.

(2) **Review and Revision of Policies, Practices, and Procedures.** In the case of a **determination of significant disproportionality** with respect to the **identification** of children as children with disabilities, or the **placement** in particular educational settings of such children, in accordance with paragraph (1), the State or the Secretary of the Interior, as the case may be, **shall -**

(A) provide for the review and, if appropriate, **revision of the policies**, procedures, and practices used in such identification or placement to ensure that such policies, procedures, and practices comply with the requirements of this title;

(B) require any local educational agency identified under paragraph (1) to reserve the maximum amount of funds under section 1413(f) of this title to provide comprehensive coordinated early intervening services to serve children in the local educational agency, particularly children in those groups that were significantly overidentified under paragraph (1); and

(C) require the local educational agency to **publicly report on the revision of policies, practices, and procedures** described under subparagraph (A).

---

[198] See Section 1412(a)(24) about policies and practices regarding the over-identification or disproportionate representation by race and ethnicity.

20 U.S.C. § 1419. Preschool Grants.

➜ **OVERVIEW:** This section provides requirements for preschool grants.

(a) In General. The Secretary **shall** provide grants under this section to assist States to provide special education and related services, in accordance with this part

(1) to children with disabilities **aged 3 through 5, inclusive; and**

(2) at the State's discretion, to **2-year-old children** with disabilities who will turn 3 during the school year.

(b) Eligibility. A State shall be **eligible for a grant** under this section if such State -

(1) is eligible under section 1412 of this title to receive a grant under this part; and

(2) makes a **free appropriate public education available to all children with disabilities, aged 3 through 5,** residing in the State.

(c) Allocations to States.

(1) In General. The Secretary shall allocate the amount made available to carry out this section for a fiscal year among the States in accordance with paragraph (2) or (3), as the case may be.

(2) Increase in Funds. If the amount available for allocations to States under paragraph (1) for a fiscal year is equal to or greater than the amount allocated to the States under this section for the preceding fiscal year, those allocations shall be calculated as follows:

> **(A) Allocation.**
> **(i) In General.** Except as provided in subparagraph (B), the Secretary shall -
> (I) allocate to each State the amount the State received under this section for fiscal year 1997;
> (II) allocate 85 percent of any remaining funds to States on the basis of the States' relative populations of children aged 3 through 5; and
> (III) allocate 15 percent of those remaining funds to States on the basis of the States' relative populations of all children aged 3 through 5 who are living in poverty.
> **(ii) Data.** For the purpose of making grants under this paragraph, the Secretary shall use the most recent population data, including data on children living in poverty, that are available and satisfactory to the Secretary.

> **(B) Limitations.** Notwithstanding subparagraph (A), allocations under this paragraph shall be subject to the following:
> **(i) Preceding Years.** No State's allocation shall be less than its allocation under this section for the preceding fiscal year.
> **(ii) Minimum.** No State's allocation shall be less than the greatest of -
> (I) the sum of -
> (aa) the amount the State received under this section for fiscal year 1997; and
> (bb) 1/3 of 1 percent of the amount by which the amount appropriated under subsection (j) for the fiscal year exceeds the amount appropriated for this section for fiscal year 1997;
> (II) the sum of -
> (aa) the amount the State received under this section for the preceding fiscal year; and

(bb) that amount multiplied by the percentage by which the increase in the funds appropriated under this section from the preceding fiscal year exceeds 1.5 percent; or

(III) the sum of -

(aa) the amount the State received under this section for the preceding fiscal year; and

(bb) that amount multiplied by 90 percent of the percentage increase in the amount appropriated under this section from the preceding fiscal year.

(iii) Maximum. Notwithstanding clause (ii), no State's allocation under this paragraph shall exceed the sum of

(I) the amount the State received under this section for the preceding fiscal year; and

(II) that amount multiplied by the sum of 1.5 percent and the percentage increase in the amount appropriated under this section from the preceding fiscal year.

(C) Ratable Reductions. If the amount available for allocations under this paragraph is insufficient to pay those allocations in full, those allocations shall be ratably reduced, subject to subparagraph (B)(i).

(3) Decrease in Funds. If the amount available for allocations to States under paragraph (1) for a fiscal year is less than the amount allocated to the States under this section for the preceding fiscal year, those allocations shall be calculated as follows:

(A) Allocations. If the amount available for allocations is greater than the amount allocated to the States for fiscal year 1997, each State shall be allocated the sum of -

(i) the amount the State received under this section for fiscal year 1997; and

(ii) an amount that bears the same relation to any remaining funds as the increase the State received under this section for the preceding fiscal year over fiscal year 1997 bears to the total of all such increases for all States.

(B) Ratable Reductions. If the amount available for allocations is equal to or less than the amount allocated to the States for fiscal year 1997, each State shall be allocated the amount the State received for fiscal year 1997, ratably reduced, if necessary.

(d) Reservation for State Activities.

(1) In General. Each State may reserve not more than the amount described in paragraph (2) for administration and other State-level activities in accordance with subsections (e) and (f).

(2) Amount Described. For each fiscal year, the Secretary shall determine and report to the State educational agency an amount that is 25 percent of the amount the State received under this section for fiscal year 1997, cumulatively adjusted by the Secretary for each succeeding fiscal year by the lesser of -

(A) the percentage increase, if any, from the preceding fiscal year in the State's allocation under this section; or

(B) the percentage increase, if any, from the preceding fiscal year in the Consumer Price Index For All Urban Consumers published by the Bureau of Labor Statistics of the Department of Labor.

(e) State Administration.

(1) In General. For the purpose of administering this section (including the coordination of activities under this part with, and providing technical assistance to, other programs that provide services to children with disabilities) a State may use not more than 20 percent of the maximum amount the State may reserve under subsection (d) for any fiscal year.

(2) Administration of Part C. Funds described in paragraph (1) may also be used for the administration of part C.

(f) Other State-Level Activities. Each State shall use any funds the State reserves under subsection (d) and does not use for administration under subsection (e) -

(1) **for support services** (including establishing and implementing **the mediation process** required by section 1415(e) of this title), which may benefit children with disabilities younger than 3 or older than 5 as long as those services also benefit children with disabilities aged 3 through 5;

(2) **for direct services** for children eligible for services under this section;

(3) for activities at the State and local levels to meet the performance goals established by the State under section 1412(a)(15) of this title;

(4) to supplement other funds used to develop and implement a **statewide coordinated services system designed to improve results** for children and families, including children with disabilities and their families, but not more than 1 percent of the amount received by the State under this section for a fiscal year;

(5) **to provide early intervention services** (which shall include an educational component that promotes school readiness and incorporates preliteracy, language, and numeracy skills) in accordance with part C to children with disabilities who are eligible for services under this section and who previously received services under part C until such children enter, or are eligible under State law to enter, kindergarten; or

(6) at the State's discretion, to continue service coordination or case management for families who receive services under part C.

(g) Subgrants to Local Educational Agencies.

(1) Subgrants Required. Each State that receives a grant under this section for any fiscal year shall distribute all of the grant funds that the State does not reserve under subsection (d) to local educational agencies in the State that have established their eligibility under section 1413 of this title, as follows:

(A) Base Payments. The State shall first award each local educational agency described in paragraph (1) the amount that agency would have received under this section for fiscal year 1997 if the State had distributed 75 percent of its grant for that year under section 1419(c)(3) of this title, as such section was then in effect.
(B) Allocation of Remaining Funds. After making allocations under subparagraph (A), the State shall -
　(i) allocate 85 percent of any remaining funds to those local educational agencies on the basis of the relative numbers of children enrolled in public and private elementary schools and secondary schools within the local educational agency's jurisdiction; and

(ii) allocate 15 percent of those remaining funds to those local educational agencies in accordance with their relative numbers of children living in poverty, as determined by the State educational agency.

(2) Reallocation of Funds. If a State educational agency determines that a local educational agency is adequately providing a free appropriate public education to all children with disabilities aged 3 through 5 residing in the area served by the local educational agency with State and local funds, the State educational agency may reallocate any portion of the funds under this section that are not needed by that local educational agency to provide a free appropriate public education to other local educational agencies in the State that are not adequately providing special education and related services to all children with disabilities aged 3 through 5 residing in the areas the other local educational agencies serve.

END OF PART B

APPENDIX A

SECTION 504 V. IDEA

You have learned that the "Purpose" is the most important section of any law because it describes the overall purpose of the law. If you have questions about a law, read the "Purpose" for answers to your questions.

Section 504 is a civil rights law that protects individuals from discrimination. The purpose of Section 504 of the Rehabilitation Act is "to empower individuals with disabilities to maximize employment, economic self-sufficiency, independence, and inclusion and integration into society…" (29 U.S.C. Chapter 16 Section 701(b)(1))

The Individuals with Disabilities Education Act provides educational rights and benefits for children with disabilities while also protecting these children from discrimination. The IDEA child has more rights and benefits, including the right to free appropriate public education, an IEP that is designed to meet the child's unique needs, and procedural safeguards that are not available to the Section 504 child.

Free Appropriate Public Education

The IDEA child has a right to a free appropriate public education (FAPE). Under IDEA, the child is entitled to an Individualized Educational Program (IEP) designed to meet the child's unique needs and from which the child receives educational benefit (Section 1414(d)).

The 504 child is not entitled to an individualized educational program (IEP) designed to meet the child's unique needs and from which the child receives educational benefit. The 504 child is entitled to a free appropriate public education that is defined as "the provision of regular or special education and related aids and services that … are designed to meet individual educational needs of persons with disabilities **as adequately as the needs of persons without disabilities are met…**" (34 C.F.R. § 104.33(b)(1))

The child may have a 504 Plan that describes accommodations and/or modifications that the school may provide. The law does not require the school to develop a written plan. The parent should request a written 504 Plan, not a verbal agreement to help the child.

Eligibility and Protections

If the child has a disability but the disability does not adversely affect educational performance, the child will not be eligible for special education and related services under the IDEA but may be eligible for protections under Section 504 of the Rehabilitation Act.

To be eligible for protections under Section 504, the child must have a physical or mental impairment that substantially limits at least one major life activity. Major life activities include walking, seeing, hearing, speaking, breathing, learning, reading, writing, performing math calculations, working, caring for oneself, and performing manual tasks. The key is whether the child has an "impairment" that "substantially limits … one or more … major life activities."

Accommodations and Modifications

Under Section 504, the child with a disability may receive accommodations and modifications that are not available to children who are **not disabled**. These accommodations and modifications are also available to children who receive special education and related services under IDEA.

The child who receives special education services under IDEA is automatically protected under Section 504. If the child has an IEP, the accommodations or modifications can be written into the IEP.

Procedural Safeguards

If a child does not receive special education services under IDEA, the child does not have the procedural protections that are available under IDEA. Section 504 does not require a meeting before a change in placement. Section 504 does not include clear requirements for "Prior Written Notice" (PWN). By contrast, IDEA includes an elaborate system of procedural safeguards designed to protect the child and parents. These safeguards include written notice before any change of placement and the right to an independent educational evaluation at public expense. Section 504 does not include these protections.

Section 504 and IDEA require school districts to conduct impartial hearings when parents disagree with identification, evaluation, or placement. Under IDEA, the parent has a right to a due process hearing to resolve a dispute. IDEA includes specific requirements about how due process hearings are to be conducted, by whom, and how decisions may be appealed. Under Section 504, the parent has an opportunity to participate and obtain representation by counsel, but the details are left to the discretion of the school district.

Discipline

Assume a Section 504 child misbehaves and the school determines that the child's misbehavior is not a manifestation of the disability. The Section 504 child can be suspended or expelled from school permanently. If the child receives special education services under an IEP under IDEA, the schools must provide the child with a free appropriate public education, even if the child is suspended or expelled from school.

ACCESS V. EDUCATIONAL BENEFIT

Let's change the facts to clarify the differences between these two laws. Assume your child has a physical disability and uses a wheelchair. Under Section 504, the school may not discriminate against your child because of the disability. The school must provide your child with **access** to an education, to and through the schoolhouse door. The school may have to make modifications to the school and provide other accommodations so your child has **access** to an education.

Assume your physically handicapped child also has neurological problems that adversely affect the child's ability to learn. If your child has a disability that adversely affects educational performance, the child is eligible for an IEP and an education that is designed to meet the child's unique needs and from which child receives educational benefit.

The Section 504 child has access to the same free appropriate public education that is available to children who are not disabled. Section 504 does not include any guarantee that a child will receive an education that provides educational benefit.

RESOURCE

Smith, Tom and James R. Patton. *Section 504 and Public Schools: A Practical Guide for Determining Eligibility, Developing Accommodation Plans, and Documenting Compliance.* Pro-Ed (1998)

END OF APPENDIX A

APPENDIX B

TUITION REIMBURSEMENT FOR PRIVATE PROGRAMS

The law about tuition reimbursement for parental placements in private programs did not change in IDEA 2004.

If the parent removes the child from a public school program and places the child into a private program, the parent may be reimbursed for the costs of the private program **if** a hearing officer or court determines that the public school did not offer a free, appropriate public education (FAPE) "in a timely manner." (Section 1412(a)(10)(C))

IDEA include many new requirements, timelines and procedures for due process hearings. If you are planning to request a due process hearing for tuition reimbursement, you need to be familiar with the federal statute and regulations and your state special education statute and regulations. You should also read the Rules of Adverse Assumptions. (Chapter 21, *Wrightslaw: From Emotions to Advocacy*)

Before taking steps to remove your child from a public school program, you must take specific steps if you hope to recover reimbursement:

At the most recent IEP meeting, before removing your child from the public school program -

- You must state your concerns

- You must state your intent to enroll your child in a private school at public expense

OR

Ten business days before you remove your child from the public school program, you must write a letter to the school that states:

- Your specific concerns, in detail, about the inadequacy of the school district's IEP and/or placement, your basis for rejecting the IEP, and why your child will be damaged if placed in the proposed program

- A statement of your intent to enroll your child in the private school at public expense.

We recommend that parents take both steps. Write out your statement of concerns and your intent to withdraw your child before the IEP meeting. At the meeting, read your statement aloud and give a copy of your statement to the IEP team. Remember: If it is not in writing, it was not said.

After the IEP meeting, write a thank you note to the IEP team in which you describe your concerns about the proposed IEP, and that you intend to enroll your child in the private program at public expense. (See the sample letters in *Wrightslaw: From Emotions to Advocacy*.)

RESOURCES

Johnson, Scott. "Reexamining Rowley: A New Focus in Special Education Law." *The Beacon: Journal of Special Education Law and Practice*, 2(2) 2003. *Available at* http://www.harborhouselaw.com/articles/rowley.reexamine.johnson.htm (visited on June 23, 2005)

Attorney Scott Johnson argues that the "some educational benefit" standard in *Rowley* no longer reflects the requirements of the Individuals with Disabilities Education Act. State standards and educational adequacy requirements provide requirements of FAPE; these standards exceed the "some educational benefit" benchmark. This requires a fundamental change in how courts, school districts, and parents view special education services.

Surviving Due Process: Stephen Jeffers v. School Board DVD /Video (ISBN: 1-892320-04-5) from Harbor House Law Press. *Surviving Due Process* takes you through a special education due process hearing, from initial preparations to testimony by the final witness. See exciting direct examination and dramatic cross-examination of witnesses, objections to hearsay and leading questions, arguments between counsel, and rulings by the hearing officer.

Wright, Pamela and Peter W. D. Wright. *Wrightslaw: From Emotions to Advocacy*. Hartfield VA: Harbor House Law Press, Inc. (2001) (877) LAW-IDEA; (877) 529-4332 (Toll Free)

END OF APPENDIX B

APPENDIX C

DISCREPANCY, RESPONSE TO INTERVENTION & LEARNING DISABILITIES

IDENTIFYING CHILDREN WITH SPECIFIC LEARNING DISABILITIES

Learning disabilities now account for more than half of all children enrolled in special education programs. The number of children identified with learning disabilities continues to grow at a fast pace. This has led experts in the field to question the current models for identifying children with learning disabilities.

Many experts in the field of learning disabilities believe that a majority of children identified with specific learning disabilities are "victims of poor teaching. The statement that many children identified as LD are actually "teaching disabled" is often accurate. Almost all children can learn to read if taught appropriately, but many do not get the help they need because teachers are not adequately prepared.[199]

The law about how to identify children with specific learning disabilities changed. IDEA 2004 says schools "shall **not** be required to take into consideration whether a child has a severe discrepancy between achievement and intellectual ability in oral expression, listening comprehension, written expression, basic reading skill, reading comprehension, mathematical calculation, or mathematical reasoning." (Section 1414(b))

Abandon Discrepancy Models

In the **Commentary and Explanation** on the proposed special education regulations, the Department of Education describes reasons why discrepancy models should be abandoned.[200]

> The IQ-discrepancy criterion is potentially harmful to students as it results in delaying intervention until the student's achievement is sufficiently low that the discrepancy is achieved. For most students, identification as having an SLE occurs at an age when the academic problems are difficult to remediate with the most intense remediation efforts (Torgesen, et. al., 2001)…the "wait to fail" model does not lead to "closing the achievement gap for most students placed in special education. Many students placed in special education as SLD show minimal gains in achievement and few actually leave special education (Donovon & Cross, 2002).

Adopt Response to Intervention Models

IDEA 2004 states, "In determining whether a child has a specific learning disability, a local educational agency may use a process that determines if the child responds to scientific, research-based intervention…" (Section 1414(b)(6)(B).

The Department of Education "strongly recommends" that schools use a response to intervention model that "use a process based on systematic assessment of the student's response to high quality, research-based general education instruction…that incorporate response to a research-based intervention…Identification models that

---

[199] Lyon, G. Reid and Jack M. Fletcher. Early Warning System. www.educationnext.org/20012/22.html (last visited on June 23, 2005)

[200] "Commentary and Explanation about the Proposed Regulations for IDEA 2004" published by the Department of Education is available at www.wrightslaw.com/idea/law.htm

incorporate response to intervention represent a shift in special education toward the goals of better achievement and behavioral outcomes for students identified with SLD…"[201]

DIAGNOSING LEARNING DISABILITIES

Psychologists often diagnose learning disabilities by exclusion. If the a child has a disability that adversely affects educational performance, and the child is not retarded, does not have a visual, hearing or motor disability, is not emotionally disturbed, and is not negatively affected by environmental, cultural or economic disadvantages, it is likely that the child has a learning disability.

According to the proposed federal regulations, States "may prohibit the use of a severe discrepancy between intellectual ability and achievement," and "must permit the use of a process that determines if the child respond to scientific, research-based intervention as part of the evaluation procedures," and "may permit the use of other alternative research-based procedures for determining whether a child has a specific learning disability…"[202]

RESOURCES

Discrepancy Models

Lyon, G. R., Fletcher, J. M., Shaywitz, S. E., Shaywitz, B. A., Torgesen, J. K., Wood, F. B., et al. (2001). ***Rethinking Learning Disabilities***. Washington, DC: Thomas Fordham Foundation. *Available at*
http://www.edexcellence.net/library/special_ed/index.html (Last visited on June 23, 2005)

These authorities describe their reasons for rejecting the IQ-achievement discrepancy models.. Discrepancy models delay classification until the child is in 3rd or 4th grade when academic achievement problems are more difficult to resolve. The IQ-achievement discrepancy is not related to decisions about intervention methods, goals, or results.

Horowitz, Sheldon H. ***The Discrepancy Formula-How the Aptitude-Achievement Formula Keeps Educators from Doing Their Jobs***. (adapted from Dr. Horowitz's presentation at the 49th Annual Conference of The International Dyslexia Association)
Available at www.ldonline.org/ld_indepth/assessment/horowitz_discrepancy_formula.html
(Last visited on June 23, 2005)

> The standard that opens the gates to remedial and support services in schools, the "discrepancy formula," has undermined the ability of teachers to provide timely and effective assistance for students with learning disabilities. It virtually requires that students "crash and burn" academically before they can gain access to special education services and it reinforces failure, ultimately making remediation much more difficult.

Pasternak, Robert. ***The Demise of IQ Testing for Children with Learning Disabilities***. A lecture by Dr. Pasternak, then Assistant Secretary, Office of Special Education and Rehabilitative Services, at the Annual Conference of the National Association of School Psychologists. *Available at*
http://www.nasponline.org/publications/cq307pasternack.html (Last visited on June 23, 2005)

Dr. Pasternak describes the "fallacies of the IQ-Achievement Discrepancy Model" and explains that this is not a valid way to identify individuals with LD and that eliminating IQ tests may shift the emphasis away from eligibility and toward the interventions children need.

---

[201] "Commentary and Explanation about the Proposed Regulations for IDEA 2004" published by the Department of Education *is available* at www.wrightslaw.com/idea/law.htm

[202] "IDEA 2004: Proposed Changes to the Code of Federal Regulations" published by the Department of Education *is available* at www.wrightslaw.com/idea/law.htm

Response to Intervention Models

Kovaleski, Joseph and David P. Prasse. ***Response to Instruction in the Identification of Learning Disabilities: A Guide for School Teams***," NASP Communiqué, Vol. 32, No. 4 (February 2004) *Available at*

www.nasponline.org/publications/cq325instruction.html (Last visited on June 23, 2005)

"Response to intervention appears to be a promising alternative to the traditional IQ-achievement discrepancy model for identifying students with learning disabilities while improving classroom instruction in general education."

National Research Center on Disabilities. ***Response to Intervention Models, Identify, Evaluate & Scale***
Available at www.nrcld.org/html/research/rti/RTIinfo.pdf Last visited on June 23, 2005.

Response to Intervention is an individual, comprehensive student-centered assessment and intervention concept, sometimes referred to as a problem-solving method. These models identify and address student difficulties with effective, efficient instruction that leads to improved achievement.

Websites

DIBELS—http://dibels.uoregon.edu/

National Reading Panel—www.nationalreadingpanel.org

Project ACHIEVE—www.projectachieve.info

END OF APPENDIX C

APPENDIX D

ROADMAP TO THE IEP

A roadmap to the IEP statute will come in handy if you need to find information quickly. IDEA 2004 changed the content of IEPs, transition, how IEPs may be amended without IEP meetings, how IEP team members may be excused.

Present Levels of Performance

The child's IEP must include "a statement of the child's present levels of academic achievement and functional performance . . ." For children who take alternate assessments, the IEP must include "a description of benchmarks or short-term objectives"

Annual Goals

Previously, IEPs were required to include a "statement of measurable annual goals, including benchmarks or short-term objectives." IDEA 2004 eliminated the requirements for "benchmarks and short-term objectives" and added language about "academic and functional goals." Now, the child's IEP must include "a statement of measurable annual goals, including academic and functional goals . . ."

Educational Progress

Previously, IEPs were required to include a statement about how the child's progress toward the annual goals would be measured and how the child's parents would "be regularly informed about their child's progress toward the annual goals." Now, the IEP must include "a description of how the child's progress toward meeting the annual goals . . . will be measured and when periodic reports on the progress the child is making toward meeting the annual goals (such as through the use of quarterly or other periodic reports, concurrent with the issuance of report cards) will be provided."

Special Education and Related Services

Congress added new language about research based instruction to IDEA 2004. The child's IEP must now include "a statement of the special education and related services and supplementary aids and services, based on peer-reviewed research to the extent practicable, to be provided to the child . . . and a statement of the program modifications or supports for school personnel that will be provided . . ."

Accommodations on High Stakes Tests

IDEA 2004 requires that "**All** children with disabilities are included in **all** general State and districtwide assessment programs . . . with appropriate accommodations . . ." States and school districts must develop guidelines for appropriate accommodations on state and district tests.

The child's IEP must include: "a statement of any individual appropriate accommodations that are necessary to measure the academic achievement and functional performance of the child on State and districtwide assessments . . ."

Alternate Assessments

If the IEP Team determines that the child shall take an alternate assessment on a particular State or districtwide assessment of student achievement, the team must include a statement about "why the child cannot participate in the regular assessment" and why "the particular alternate assessment selected is appropriate for the child . . ."

Alternate assessments must be aligned with the state's "challenging academic content standards and challenging student academic achievement standards. If the state has adopted alternate academic achievement standards, the achievement of children with disabilities must be measured against those standards

Transition

Congress changed some of the legal requirements for transition. Previously, the IEP had to include "a statement of transition services needs" (beginning at age 14) and "a statement of needed transition services for the child" (beginning at age 16). Now, the first IEP after the child is 16 (and updated annually) must now include:

appropriate measurable postsecondary goals based upon age appropriate transition assessments related to training, education, employment, and, where appropriate, independent living skills . . . and the transition services (including courses of study) needed to assist the child in reaching these goals.

Other Issues

In developing the child's IEP, the IEP team shall consider evaluation results, "academic, developmental, and functional needs of the child." (Section 1414(d)(3))

IEPs must be in effect at the beginning of the school year. (Section 1414(d)(2))

BOOKS

Bateman, Barbara and Cynthia Herr. ***Writing Measurable IEP Goals and Objectives***. Attainment Company, 2003.

Mager, Robert F. ***Making Instruction Work***. Atlanta: Center for Effective Performance, 1997.

Mager, Robert F. ***Goal Analysis***. Atlanta: Center for Effective Performance, 1997.

Mager, Robert F. ***Measuring Instructional Results***. Atlanta: Center for Effective Performance, 1997.

Mager, Robert F. ***Preparing Instructional Objectives***. Atlanta: Center for Effective Performance, 1997.

Twachtman-Cullen, Diane. ***How Well Does Your IEP Measure Up? Quality Indicators for Effective Service Delivery***. Starfish Specialty, 2003.

Wright, Pamela and Peter Wright. ***Wrightslaw: From Emotions to Advocacy***. Hartfield, VA: Harbor House Law Press, 2001. (Read Chapter 12, *SMART IEPs*)

END OF APPENDIX D

APPENDIX E
DUE PROCESS PROCEDURES AND TIMELINES

Many of the pre-trial procedures and timelines for due process hearings are new in IDEA 2004.

Due Process Complaint Notice

The party who requests a due process hearing must provide a detailed notice to the other party that includes identifying information about the child, the nature of the problem, facts, and proposed resolution. The party that requests the due process hearing may not have the hearing until they provide this notice.

The Due Process Complaint Notice must describe the nature of the problem, the facts, and the proposed resolution. (Section 1415(b)(7)(A)) A hearing is not permitted until after this Notice has been filed.

A Due Process Complaint Notice can be a letter to request a special education due process hearing that includes the required components. (Read Chapter 24, "Letter to the Stranger," in *Wrightslaw: From Emotions to Advocacy* to learn how to write persuasive letters that make readers want to help.)

Timelines

The requirements and timelines for the Due Process Complaint Notice and the Amended Complaint Notice are in Section 1415(c)(2).

If the school did not provide Prior Written Notice (PWN) to the parent previously, the school must send the notice within **10 days**.

After receiving the Due Process Complaint Notice, the other party must prepare and file a "response that specifically addresses the issues raised in the complaint" within **10 days**. (Section 1415(c)(2)(B)(ii))

If the notice is insufficient, the receiving party must complain to the Hearing Officer within **15 days**. (Section 1415(c)(2)(C))

The Hearing Officer must determine if the complaint is sufficient within **5 days**. (Section 1415(c)(2)(D)) If the hearing officer determines that the notice is not sufficient, the hearing officer may permit an amended complaint to be filed (Section 1415(c)(2)(E)(i)(2)) or may refuse to permit the Hearing to proceed. (Section 1415(b)(7)(B)) A party may amend the Due Process Complaint Notice only if the other party consents and is given the opportunity to resolve the dispute pursuant to a Resolution Session as described in Section 1415(f)(1)(B).

This requirement is similar to the "12(b)(6)" Motion to Dismiss proceeding in the Federal Rules of Civil Procedure (FRCP). When an amended notice is filed, the "time clock" resets.

Resolution Session

After the school district receives the parent's Due Process Complaint Notice, the district must convene a Resolution Session within **15 days**. (Section 1415(f)(1)(B))

The Resolution Session provides the parties with an opportunity to resolve their complaint before the due process hearing. The school district must send "the relevant member or members of the IEP team" who have knowledge about the facts in the parent's complaint and a school district representative who has decision-making authority (settlement authority).

The school board attorney may not attend the Resolution Session unless the parent is accompanied by an attorney. The parents and district may agree to waive the Resolution Session or use the mediation process.

If the school district has not resolved the complaint to the parents' satisfaction within **30 days** of receiving the complaint, the due process hearing can be held. (Section 1415(f)(1)(B)(ii))

Written Settlement Agreements

The requirements for legally binding written Settlement Agreements are new. (Section 1415(f)(1)(B)(iii)) Previously, when a party breached a settlement agreement, the other party had to enforce the agreement by filing suit under a breach of contract theory. Now either party can use the power of the federal courts to ensure that settlement agreements are honored.

Either party may void a settlement agreement within 3 business days. Note: The three-day rule does not apply to settlement agreements created in mediation.

DUE PROCESS PROCEDURES AND REQUIREMENTS

These new pre-trial procedural requirements are technical and appear cumbersome. The purpose of these requirements is to reduce litigation and cause disputes to resolve quickly, without expensive attorney fees.

A due process hearing request must be well-written and must include a clear description of the issues and desired resolution. The procedures in Section 1415 should cause the factual and legal issues to be clearly delineated. When the nature of the dispute, factual issues, and legal issue are clear, and the countdown clock to trial is moving quickly, the parties are forced to focus more on the facts and law, and less on the emotions that drive litigation. Reducing emotions increases the chances for a well-reasoned settlement.

Evaluations and Recommendations Must Be Disclosed Within 5 Business Days

IDEA 2004 requires that evaluations and recommendations be disclosed no less than **5 business days** before a due process hearing. (Section 1415(f)(2))

Most state statutes and regulations, and the standard of practice, requires that all exhibits (including evaluations and recommendations), exhibit lists, and witness lists, be disclosed at least 5 days prior to a hearing. Failure to comply with these requirements about disclosure often causes hearing officers to dismiss cases.

In addition to evaluations and other relevant documents specific to the child, the exhibit list should include research reports, learned treatises, journal articles, pertinent book chapters, and other documents that may be relevant to the case.

For a sample document list that can be used as an exhibit list, read Chapter 9, "The File: Do It Right!" in *Wrightslaw: From Emotions to Advocacy*.

To see courtroom dynamics in a special education due process hearing, watch the *Jeffers v. School Board* DVD video available from Wrightslaw.

2-Year Statute of Limitations

The two-year limit statute of limitations to present a complaint is new in IDEA 2004. If your state does not have a statute of limitations, you must request a due process hearing within two years. (Section 1415(b)(6)(B)) If a due process hearing may be on the horizon, you need to know the statute of limitations for your state —it may not be two years.

Because IDEA 2004 includes substantial new and different procedural requirements regarding pretrial matters for special education due process hearings, you should assume that your state is revising or will revise the state special education law and regulations. Contact your State Department of Education/State Education Agency (SEA) and request the present statute of limitations. Be sure to get this information in writing from the State. (Never rely on friends, listservs, or the Internet for legal advice.)

Appeal within 90 Days

The losing party must appeal to state or federal court within **90 days**. This 90 day timeline is new. States may provide different or **shorter timelines**. As with your state statute of limitations, you must learn your state's statute of limitations for filing appeals in Court. If it is longer than 90 days, you should assume that the longer timeline does not apply because IDEA requires an appeal within 90 days.

Substantive v. Procedural Issues

Issues of substance include determining whether a child has a disability that adversely affects educational performance (eligibility), whether a child has received FAPE (a free appropriate public education), or whether a child needs extended school year (ESY) services.

Procedural issues include delays in scheduling evaluations, delays in determining eligibility, delays in convening IEP meetings, and failure to include the appropriate personnel in IEP meetings. The facts of a case will determine whether the procedural breach rises to the level identified in Section 1415(f)(3)(E)(ii).

Subject-Matter of Hearing & Statute of Limitations

Be sure to read the subject-matter of the hearing (Section 1415(f)(3)(B)), additional reference to the new statute of limitations (Section 1415(f)(3)(C)) and the law about issues and claims about substantive matters v. violations of rules of procedure (i.e., notice requirements, timeliness, etc.) in Section 1415(f)(3)(E).

FEDERAL RULES OF CIVIL PROCEDURE (FRCP)

The pre-trial due process procedures in Section 1415 are similar to the Federal Rules of Civil Procedure (FRCP) that govern lawsuits filed in the U. S. District Courts. (The FRCP are available online at many different websites.)

In a civil suit, the complainant/petitioner/plaintiff prepares a pleading called a "Complaint." The Complaint identifies the parties, their relationship to the case, the factual issues, the legal basis for relief, and the desired relief. (See Rules 7, 8, and 10 of FRCP)

The recipient of the suit, i.e., the defendant/respondent, then must file a defensive pleading or answer, often called a Responsive Pleading. (FRCP 12) The Responsive Pleading may assert that even if all the facts are true and not in dispute, for legal or other reasons, the plaintiff does not have a case. This type of pleading is often referred to as a "12(b)(6)" Motion to Dismiss (FRCP 12(b)(6)) or a Rule 56 Motion for Summary Judgment. (FRCP 56)

If the Court grants this Motion, the case often ends. If the Court denies the Motion, the defendant will file an Answer that admits or denies the factual allegations and legal conclusions. If the defendant has additional issues that need judicial intervention, the defendant must file a mandatory counter-claim. Otherwise, these claims and issues may be waived forever. (FRCP 13)

Pursuant to Rule 11 of the FRCP, the signing and filing of pleadings in federal court is an affirmation and representation that the filing of the pleading is not for "any improper purpose, such as to harass or to cause unnecessary delay or needless increase in the cost of litigation…"

After the responsive pleadings have been filed and before the trial date, the attorneys often must file "Proposed Findings of Fact and Conclusions of Law" with the Court. After each side files their document, the Judge often requires the attorneys to meet and confer, face-to-face.

As part of the pre-trial proceedings, the attorneys must often jointly prepare a third document entitled "Agreed Upon Findings of Fact and Conclusions of Law." The agreed upon facts and conclusions of law remove these issues from litigation. The factual portion of litigation then focuses on the outstanding factual issues that remain. Legal issues are often resolved by subsequent briefs filed by the attorneys.

In federal court, timelines are calendar days. (See Rule 6 of the Federal Rules of Civil Procedure (FRCP 6)). IDEA 2004 includes statutes that provide timelines as "school days" or "business days." In those instances, the statute uses the phrase "school days" or "business days." In the subsection about due process procedures, the timelines are calendar days. If a due date falls on a Saturday, Sunday, or Federal Holiday, then the due date is the next business day. Missing a pre-trial filing deadline by even one day can have fatal consequences, causing the case to be dismissed or other onerous sanctions.

In federal court practice, pre-trial pleadings are usually frequent and extensive as each party attempts to frame the case around one or two key compelling issues. It is likely that special education litigation will move in this direction. While this may seem burdensome, it may cause factual and legal issues to be reduced to the most important issues. Pretrial work results in less court time, lowering expenses and fees for both parties.

LAY ADVOCATES

Parents have a right to be represented by an attorney in a due process hearing. Do parents have a right to be represented by a lay advocate? It depends.

According to the statute, "Any party to a hearing . . . shall be accorded . . . the right to be accompanied and advised by individuals with special knowledge or training with respect to the problems of children with disabilities..." (Section 1415(h)(1))

In most contested legal matters, the individual who represents a person before a judicial entity must be licensed to practice law in that state. The practice of law includes preparing a case for trial, filing exhibits, providing an opening statement, examining witnesses, and arguing or filing closing briefs.

The unauthorized practice of law is a criminal offense that can result in a fine and/or imprisonment. However, some states exempt individuals who have "special knowledge or training with respect to the problems of children with disabilities" in their state special education statute and state bar requirements. In these states, "lay advocates" can represent a child with a disability and the parent in a special education due process hearing.

Delaware ruled that a lay advocate cannot represent a parent in a special education due process hearing. Florida found that a lay advocate can represent a parent. The law on lay advocacy is evolving. Information about the Delaware and Florida cases and lay advocates is available on the Wrightslaw site.

Federal Judges do not permit lay advocates to represent parents and children with disabilities in the U. S. District Courts. The law about whether parents can represent their children is unsettled. Rulings in federal courts often vary from one Judge to another.

Usually, a parent who is not an attorney may represent themselves, pro se, in federal court on IDEA claims specific to the parent (i.e., requesting reimbursement for private school tuition). In general, a parent who is a licensed attorney and admitted to practice before the federal court, can represent themselves and their child. However, most courts deny attorney's fees to the parent attorney.

ATTORNEYS' FEES

Complaints about Excessive Attorneys' Fees

When Congress held meetings before reauthorizing IDEA, school districts complained that attorneys' fees for due process hearings were excessive. School districts did not disclose the fees they paid to their counsel.

In most cases, the school attorney fees are much higher than attorney fees incurred by parents. When parents seek reimbursement for attorneys' fees, they should use the Freedom of Information Act to request information about all fees charged, incurred, paid, and time expended by school district attorneys in preparing their case.

Attorneys' Fees from Parents and their Attorneys

Parents who prevail can recover attorneys fees from school districts. Under IDEA 2004, school districts may recover attorneys' fees from the parent or their attorney under specific, limited circumstances.

If the parent or parent's attorney files a complaint that is frivolous, unreasonable, or for an improper purpose (i.e., to harass, cause unnecessary delay, or needlessly increase the cost of litigation), the Court may award attorneys' fees to the school district.

This controversial new subsection includes law that is already effect in the Federal Rules of Civil Procedure (FRCP) and incorporates a ruling by the U. S. Supreme Court in *Christiansburg Garment Co. v. EEOC*, 434 U.S. 412 (1978).

In *Christiansburg Garment*, the U. S. Supreme Court denied an award of attorney's fees because the lawsuit was not meritless nor vexatious. The Court wrote that meritless is "groundless or without foundation." A court may award attorney's fees to a "prevailing defendant . . . upon a finding that the plaintiff's action was frivolous, unreasonable, or without foundation, even though not brought in subjective bad faith."

When Congress reauthorized IDEA, they added the caselaw of *Christiansburg Garment* and Rule 11 of the Federal Rules of Civil Procedure to this subsection about attorneys' fees.

SPECIAL EDUCATION LITIGATION: TRIAL PREPARATION

Pozner, Larry S, and Roger Dodd. *Cross-Examination: Science & Techniques.* Lexis Law (new edition Dec 2004

Weber, Mark. *Special Education Law and Litigation Treatise, 2ⁿᵈ Edition.* Horsham PA: LRP Publications, 2002.

END OF APPENDIX E

APPENDIX F

RESEARCH BASED INSTRUCTION AND READING

Most children with disabilities have severely deficient reading skills. Research has found a high relationship between poor reading skills, learning disabilities, and juvenile delinquency.

Sadly, schools often use reading programs that are not effective in teaching children with disabilities, English language learners, migratory children, Native American children, neglected children, delinquent children, and homeless children to read.

A primary focus of this law is the requirement that school districts and individual schools use effective, research-based reading remediation programs so all children are reading at grade level by the end of third grade.

No Child Left Behind authorizes funds:

> To provide assistance to State educational agencies and local educational agencies in establishing reading programs for students in kindergarten through grade 3 that are based on scientifically based reading research, to ensure that **every student can read at grade level or above not later than the end of grade 3.** (emphasis added) (20 U. S. C. § 6361)

The No Child Left Behind Act includes legal definitions of reading, reading instruction, and reading research.

Reading

Reading is defined as:

> "a complex system of deriving meaning from print that requires all of the following:
>
> skills and knowledge to understand how phonemes or speech sounds are connected to print,
>
> the ability to decode unfamiliar words,
>
> the ability to read fluently,
>
> sufficient background information and vocabulary to foster reading comprehension,
>
> the development of appropriate active strategies to construct meaning from print, and
>
> the development and maintenance of a motivation to read. (20 U. S. C. § 6368(5))

Essential Components of Reading Instruction

The NCLB statute defines the **essential components of reading instruction** as:

> explicit and systematic instruction in
>
> (A) phonemic awareness;
>
> (B) phonics;

(C) vocabulary development;

(D) reading fluency, including oral reading skills; and

(E) reading comprehension strategies. (20 U. S. C. § 6368(3))

No Child Left Behind defines **scientifically based reading research** as:

(A) applies rigorous, systematic, and objective procedures to obtain valid knowledge relevant to reading development, reading instruction, and reading difficulties; and

(B) includes research that

(i) employs systematic, empirical methods that draw on observation or experiment;

(ii) involves rigorous data analyses that are adequate to test the stated hypotheses and justify the general conclusions drawn;

(iii) relies on measurements or observational methods that provide valid data across evaluators and observers and across multiple measurements and observations; and

(iv) has been accepted by a peer-reviewed journal or approved by a panel of independent experts through a comparably rigorous, objective, and scientific review. (20 U. S. C. § 6368(6))

The more generic term, **scientifically based research**, appears seventy-nine times in the statute. The statute explains that "scientifically based research:"

(A) means research that involves the application of rigorous, systematic, and objective procedures to obtain reliable and valid knowledge relevant to education activities and programs; and

(B) includes research that

(i) employs systematic, empirical methods that draw on observation or experiment;

(ii) involves rigorous data analyses that are adequate to test the stated hypotheses and justify the general conclusions drawn;

(iii) relies on measurements or observational methods that provide reliable and valid data across evaluators and observers, across multiple measurements and observations, and across studies by the same or different investigators;

(iv) is evaluated using experimental or quasi-experimental designs in which individuals, entities, programs, or activities are assigned to different conditions and with appropriate controls to evaluate the effects of the condition of interest, with a preference for random-assignment experiments, or other designs to the extent that those designs contain within-condition or across-condition controls;

(v) ensures that experimental studies are presented in sufficient detail and clarity to allow for replication or, at a minimum, offer the opportunity to build systematically on their findings; and

(vi) has been accepted by a peer-reviewed journal or approved by a panel of independent experts through a comparably rigorous, objective, and scientific review. (20 U. S. C. § 7801(37))

Reading Assessments

No Child Left Behind describes three types of reading assessments: screeners, diagnostic assessments, and classroom-based instructional reading assessments.

A **screener** is a "brief procedure designed as a first step" to identify children "at high risk for delayed development or academic failure and in need of further diagnosis . . ."

A **diagnostic reading assessment** (i.e., the "further diagnosis" is based on research and is used for the purposes of:

identifying a child's specific areas of strengths and weaknesses so that the child has learned to read by the end of grade 3; determining any difficulties that a child may have in learning to read and the potential cause of such difficulties; and helping to determine possible reading intervention strategies and related special needs.

A **classroom based instructional reading assessment** consists of classroom-based observations of the child performing academic tasks. (20 U. S. C. § 6368(7))

If a school district receives Title I funds, the district is required to submit a plan to the state that describes assessments that will be used "to effectively identify students who may be at risk for reading failures or are having difficulty reading." The district's plan must describe how the district "will provide additional educational assistance to individual students assessed as needing help" to meet state academic standards. (20 U. S. C. § 6312(b))

RESOURCES

Hall, Susan and Louisa Moats. *Parenting a Struggling Reader.* Broadway. (2002)

Levine, Mel. *A Mind at a Time.* New York: Simon & Schuster (2003)

National Research Council. *Scientific Research in Education.* National Academy Press. (2005)

National Research Council. *Preventing Reading Difficulties in Young Children.* National Academy Press.

Shaywitz, Sally. *Overcoming Dyslexia: A New and Complete Science-Based Program for Reading Problems at Any Level.* New York: Knopf. (2003)

Database of evidence-based research on reading

Available at http://www.nifl.gov/partnershipforreading/explore/index.html (Last visited on June 23, 2005)

Research has identified instructional techniques that lead to observable, replicable, positive results as children work to become fluent, motivated readers. This searchable database is organized into seven categories related to the teaching of reading. (Sponsored by the Partnership for Reading, the National Institute for Literacy, National Institute of Child Health and Human Development, and the U.S. Department of Education)

END OF APPENDIX F

THIS PAGE FOR YOUR NOTES

GLOSSARY OF ACRONYMS, ABBREVIATIONS AND TERMS

The Individuals with Disabilities Education Act of 2004 incorporated definitions and terms from the No Child Left Behind statute and regulations, so the authors decided to include the definitions from No Child Left Behind. If you need to use a definition, be sure get the full definition from the No Child Left Behind Act.

Depending on where a term is located in the No Child Left Behind statute, a word may have more than one definition.

ACRONYMS AND ABBREVIATIONS

ADA	Americans with Disabilities Act
AYP	Adequate Yearly Progress
CSR	Class-size Reduction
EDGAR	Education Department General Administrative Regulations
ESEA	Elementary and Secondary Education Act of 1965
ESL	English as a Second Language
FY	Fiscal Year
HEA	Higher Education Act
IDEA	Individuals with Disabilities Education Act
IHE	Institution of Higher Education
LEA	Local Educational Agency (school district)
NCLB	No Child Left Behind, the Act that amended ESEA
OMB	Office of Management and Budget
RFP	Request for Proposal
SAHE	State Agency for Higher Education
SEA	State educational agency
Secretary	Secretary of Education, U.S. Department of Education
Department	The U.S. Department of Education

GLOSSARY OF TERMS

Accountability System. Each state sets academic standards for what students should know and learn. Student achievement is measured with tests and test results are reported to the public. (20 U. S. C. § 6311)

Achievement Gap. The difference between high- and low-performing children, especially the gaps between minority and non-minority students, and between disadvantaged children and their more advantaged peers. (20 U. S. C. § 6301)

Adequate Yearly Progress (AYP). Refers to annual improvement that states, school districts and schools must make each year, as measured by academic assessments, so that all public elementary and secondary schools have the same high academic standards. (20 U. S. C. § 6311)

Alaska Native Organization. A federally recognized tribe, consortium of tribes, nonprofit Native association, or organization that has expertise in educating Alaska Natives. (20 U. S. C. § 7546)

Alternative Certification. States are encouraged states to offer alternative methods of teacher certification so talented individuals are encouraged to teach subjects they know. (20 U. S. C. § 6613)

Arts and Sciences. An institution of higher education that offer majors in content areas that correspond to academic subjects taught; an academic subject or content area that is an academic major. (20 U. S. C. § 6602)

Assessment. Another word for "test." States are required to align their academic standards and academic assessments.

Average Daily Attendance. The number of days that students attend in one school year, divided by the number of school days. (20 U. S. C. § 7801)

Average Per-pupil Expenditure. Expenditures divided by the number of children who attend school daily. (20 U. S. C. § 7801)

Beginning Teacher. A public school teacher who has taught less than three full school years. (20 U. S. C. § 7801)

Bureau. Bureau of Indian Affairs of the Department of the Interior. (25 U. S. C. § 2021)

Charter School. Independent public schools that operate under public supervision but outside traditional public school systems. Charter schools are exempt from many state and local rules, do not charge tuition, have a performance contract that specifies how the charter school will measure student performance, and complies with federal civil rights and education laws. (20 U. S. C. § 7221i)

Child. A person within the age limits for which the State provides free public education. Note: Sections of NCLB define child differently. (20 U. S. C. § 7801)

Child with a Disability. A child with mental retardation, hearing impairments (including deafness), speech or language impairments, visual impairments (including blindness), emotional disturbance, orthopedic impairments, autism, traumatic brain injury, other health impairments, or specific learning disabilities; and who needs special education and related services. (20 U. S. C. § 1401(3(A))

Classroom-Based Instructional Reading Assessment. A reading assessment that relies on teacher observations. (20 U. S. C. § 6368)

Community Based Organization. A private nonprofit organization of demonstrated effectiveness, Indian tribe, or tribally sanctioned educational authority that represents a community or segments of a community and that provides educational or related services to individuals in the community. The term includes Native Hawaiian or Native American Pacific Islander native language educational organizations. (20 U. S. C. § 7011)

Community College. An institution of higher education as defined in section 101 of the Higher Education Act of 1965 that provides not less than a 2-year program that is acceptable for full credit toward a bachelor's degree; includes institutions that receive assistance under the Tribally Controlled College or University Assistance Act of 1978. (20 U. S. C. § 7011)

Comprehension. The ability to understand and gain meaning from reading. (20 U. S. C. § 6613)

Consolidated Local Application. An application submitted by a local educational agency pursuant to section 9305. (20 U. S. C. § 7801)

Consolidated Local Plan. A plan submitted by a local educational agency (school district) pursuant to section 9305. (20 U. S. C. § 7801)

Consolidated State Application. An application submitted by a State educational agency pursuant to section 9302. (20 U. S. C. § 7801)

Consolidated State Plan. A plan submitted by a State educational agency pursuant to section 9302. (20 U. S. C. § 7801)

Core Academic Subjects. English, reading or language arts, mathematics, science, foreign languages, civics and government, economics, arts, history, and geography. (20 U. S. C. § 7801)

Corrective Action. A Title I school that failed to meet its adequate yearly progress (AYP) goals after it was identified for school improvement for two consecutive years. In general, the school failed to meet its AYP goals for four consecutive years after it was identified for school improvement. (20 U. S. C. § 6316)

County. A division of a State used by the Secretary of Commerce in compiling and reporting data regarding counties. (20 U. S. C. § 7801)

Current Expenditures. Expenditures for free public education including administration, instruction, attendance and health services, transportation, plant operation and maintenance, and expenditures for food services and student body activities; does not include expenditures for community services, capital outlay, or debt service, or expenditures from funds received under title I and part A of title V. (20 U. S. C. § 7801)

Department. The Department of Education. (20 U. S. C. § 7801)

Diagnostic Reading Assessment. A valid, reliable assessment that is based on scientifically based reading research that is used to identify a child's areas of strengths and weaknesses so the child learns to read by the end of third grade. A diagnostic reading assessment determines difficulties a child has in learning to read, the cause of these difficulties, an d possible reading intervention strategies and related special needs. (20 U. S. C. § 6368)

Director. The Director of the Office of English Language Acquisition, Language Enhancement, and Academic Achievement for Limited English Proficient Students established by the Department of Education Organization Act. (20 U. S. C. § 7011)

Disaggregated Data. The practice of sorting test results into groups of students (i.e., economically disadvantaged, racial and ethnic minority groups, disabilities, or limited English fluency) to allow parents and teachers to see how each group is performing. (20 U. S. C. § 6311)

Distance Learning. Transmission of educational or instructional programming to geographically dispersed individuals and groups via telecommunications. (20 U. S. C. § 7801)

Distinguished Schools. Schools that make the greatest gains in closing the achievement gap or exceed adequate yearly progress serve as models for other schools and provide support to other schools. (20 U. S. C. § 6317)

Early Reading First. Federal grants to school districts and public or private organizations for early language, literacy, and pre-reading for preschool children, especially children for low-income families. (20 U. S. C. § 6371)

Educational Service Agency. A regional public multi-service agency authorized by State statute to develop, manage, and provide services or programs to local educational agencies. (20 U. S. C. § 7801)

Elementary School. A nonprofit day or residential school or public elementary charter school that provides elementary education. (20 U. S. C. § 7801)

Eligible Local Educational Agency. A local educational agency with a high number or percentage of students in kindergarten through third grade who are reading below grade level. (20 U. S. C. § 6362)

Eligible Partnership. An institution of higher education that prepares teachers and principals, a school of arts and sciences; and a high-need local educational agency. (20 U. S. C. § 6631)

Eligible Professional Development Provider. A provider of reading instruction that is based on scientifically based reading research. (20 U. S. C. § 6368)

Eligible Student/Child. For the purposes of public school choice, eligible students must attend Title I schools that are in need of improvement, in corrective action, or restructuring. Note: This differs from eligibility for supplemental educational services.

Essential Components of Reading Instruction. Explicit and systematic instruction in phonemic awareness, phonics, vocabulary development, reading fluency, oral reading skills, and reading comprehension strategies. (20 U.S.C. § 6368)

Exemplary Teacher. A highly qualified teacher who taught for at least five years in a public school, private school, or institution of higher education, is regarded as exemplary by administrators and other teachers, and helps others improve instructional strategies and skills. (20 U. S. C. § 7801)

Family Education Program. A language instruction program or alternative instruction program designed to help limited English proficient adults and youth become proficient in English; provides instruction on how parents and family can facilitate the educational achievement of children. (20 U. S. C. § 7011)

Family Literacy Services. Services that are sufficiently intense to enable a family to make sustainable changes; include specific activities. (20 U. S. C. § 7801)

Flexibility. A way to fund public education; gives states and school districts authority in how they use federal funds in exchange for accountability for results. (20 U. S. C. § 7315)

Fluency. The capacity to read text accurately and quickly. (20 U. S. C. § 6613)

Free Public Education. Elementary or secondary education provided at public expense, under public supervision and direction, and without charge; does not include education beyond grade 12. (20 U. S. C. § 7491)

Gifted and Talented. Students who are capable of high achievement in intellectual, creative, artistic, or leadership areas or academic fields and who need services or activities to develop these capabilities. (20 U. S. C. § 7801)

High-Need LEA. A school district that serves at least 10,000 children from families with incomes below the poverty line or at least 20 percent of the children from families with incomes below the poverty line, with a high percentage of teachers who are not highly qualified or a high percentage of teachers who are working with emergency, provisional, or temporary certificates or licenses. (20 U. S. C. § 6602)

Highly Qualified Teacher. New teachers and teachers in Title 1 programs who are certified by the state or pass the state teacher examination, have training in the subject area they teach, and hold a license to teach. Elementary school teachers must demonstrate knowledge of teaching math and reading. Middle and high school teachers must have majors in the subjects they teach or demonstrate knowledge of that subject. Teachers who were employed when NCLB was enacted must be highly certified by 2005. Teachers who are working under license or certification waivers are not highly qualified. (20 U. S. C. § 7801)

Highly Qualified Charter School Teacher. A charter school teacher who complies with state requirements about certification or licensure. (20 U. S. C. § 7801)

Highly Qualified Paraprofessional. A paraprofessional hired after NCLB was enacted must have a high school diploma or equivalent, complete two years of study at a college or university, have an associate's degree (minimum), or take a rigorous skills test. (20 U. S. C. § 6319)

Homeless Children and Youth. Children and youth who do not have a fixed, regular, nighttime residence. Includes children who live in motels, hotels, trailer parks, or campgrounds; children who live in emergency shelters; children who are abandoned or are waiting for foster care placement; children who live in cars, parks, public spaces, abandoned buildings, substandard housing, bus or train stations; and migratory children who are homeless. (20 U. S. C. § 11434a)

Immigrant Children and Youth. Individuals between the ages of 3 and 21 who were not born in the United States and have not attended school in a state for more than three full academic years. (20 U. S. C. § 7011)

Indian. A member of an Indian tribe or band, as membership is defined by the tribe or band; a descendant of an individual described above; an Eskimo, Aleut, or other Alaska Native. (20 U. S. C. § 7491)

Indian Tribe. An Indian tribe, band, nation, or other organized group or community, including a Native village as defined in the Alaska Native Claims Settlement Act, that is eligible for the special programs and services provided to Indians because of their status as Indians. (25 U. S. C. § 2511)

Institution of Higher Education. Meaning given to term in section 101(a) of the Higher Education Act of 1965. (20 U. S. C. § 7801)

Instructional Material. Instructional content provided to a student; includes print and audio-visual materials and electronic or digital materials (Title X, Sec. 1061)

Instructional Staff. Individuals who are responsible for teaching children to read; includes principals, teachers, library media specialists, teachers of academic subjects, and other individuals who are responsible for teaching children to read. (20 U. S. C. § 6368)

Language Instruction Educational Program. An instruction course to develop English proficiency for English-language learners; meets state academic content and student academic achievement standards; may use English and the child's native language to enable the child to attain English proficiency; is designed to enable all children to be proficient in English and a second language. (20 U. S. C. § 7011)

Limited English Proficient. An individual between the ages of 3 and 21 who attends an elementary school or secondary school, who was not born in the United States or whose native language is not English, who may be a Native American, Alaska Native, or a resident of the outlying areas, or a migratory child whose native language is not English. The individual's difficulties in speaking, reading, writing, or understanding English may not permit the individual to be proficient on state assessments. (20 U. S. C. § 7801)

Local Educational Agency (LEA). A board of education or public authority that has administrative control or direction of public schools and is recognized as an administrative agency for public schools. (20 U. S. C. § 7801)

Low-Performing School. An elementary school or secondary school that is identified as in need of improvement. (20 U. S. C. § 6631)

Mentoring. The process by which a responsible individual provides a positive role model for a child, forms a supportive relationship with the child, and provides academic help and exposure to new experiences and opportunities. (20 U. S. C. § 7801)

National Assessment of Educational Progress (NAEP). Assessments in reading, mathematics, science, writing, U.S. history, geography, civics, and the arts; is the only nationally representative, continuing assessment of what American students know and can do in various subjects. (20 U.S.C. § 9010)

Native American and Native American Language. These terms have the same meaning given those terms in section 103 of the Native American Languages Act of 1990. (20 U. S. C. § 7011)

Native Hawaiian. A citizen of the United States who is a descendant of the aboriginal people who occupied the area that now comprises the State of Hawaii as evidenced by genealogical records, Kupuna (elders) or Kamaaina (long-term community residents) verification, or certified birth records. (20 U. S. C. § 7117)

Native Hawaiian Community Based Organization. An organization composed primarily of Native Hawaiians from a specific community that assists in the social, cultural, and educational development of Native Hawaiians in that community. (20 U. S. C. § 7517)

Native Hawaiian Educational Organization. A private nonprofit organization that serves Native Hawaiians, has Native Hawaiians in policy-making positions, incorporates Native Hawaiian perspective, values, language, culture, and traditions, demonstrates expertise in the education of Native Hawaiian youth, and demonstrates expertise in research and program development. (20 U. S. C. § 7517)

Native Hawaiian Language. The Native American language indigenous to the original inhabitants of the State of Hawaii. (20 U. S. C. § 7517)

Native Hawaiian; Native American Pacific Islander Native Language Educational Organization. A nonprofit organization whose board and employees are fluent speakers of the Native American languages used in the organization's educational programs, and that has at least five years successful experience in providing educational services in traditional Native American languages. (20 U. S. C. § 7011)

Native Hawaiian Organization. A private nonprofit organization that serves the interests of Native Hawaiians, has Native Hawaiians in policy-making positions, and is recognized by the Governor of Hawaii for the purpose of planning, conducting, or administering programs for the benefit of Native Hawaiians. (20 U. S. C. § 7517)

Native Language. When used to refer to an individual who has limited English proficiency, refers to the language normally used by the individual, or by the parents of a child or youth. (20 U. S. C. § 7011)

Office of Hawaiian Affairs. The Office of Hawaiian Affairs established by the Constitution of the State of Hawaii. (20 U. S. C. § 7517)

Other Staff. Pupil services personnel, librarians, career guidance and counseling personnel, education aides, and other instructional and administrative personnel. (20 U. S. C. § 7801)

Glossary of Terms

Outlying Area. Includes the United States Virgin Islands, Guam, American Samoa, the Commonwealth of the Northern Mariana Islands, the freely associated states of the Republic of the Marshall Islands, the Federated States of Micronesia, and the Republic of Palau. (20 U. S. C. § 7801)

Out-of-Field Teacher. A teacher who teaches an academic subject or grade level for which the teacher is not highly qualified. (20 U. S. C. § 6602)

Paraprofessional. An individual employed in a public school who is supervised by a certified or licensed teacher; includes individuals who work in language instruction educational programs, special education, and migrant education. (20 U. S. C. § 7011)

Parent. A legal guardian or other person standing in loco parentis, a grandparent or stepparent with whom the child lives, or a person who is legally responsible for the welfare of the child. (20 U. S. C. § 7801)

Parental Involvement. Refers to participation of parents in regular, two-way, meaningful communication about learning and school activities; ensures that parents play an integral role in their child's learning, are encouraged to be actively involved in their child's education at school, are full partners in their child's education, are included in decision-making about their child's education. (20 U. S. C. § 7801)

Personal Information. Individually identifiable information; includes name, home or physical address, telephone number, or Social Security identification number. (Title X, Sec. 1061)

Phonemic Awareness. The ability to hear and identify individual sounds, or phonemes. (20 U. S. C. § 6368)

Phonics. The relationship between the letters of written language and the sounds of spoken language. (20 U. S. C. § 6368)

Poverty Line. Applies to a family of a particular size; defined the Office of Management and Budget and revised annually. (20 U. S. C. § 7801)

Principal. Includes an assistant principal. (20 U. S. C. § 6602)

Priority. The school district shall give priority to the lowest achieving children from low-income families for the purposes of public school choice. (20 U. S. C. § 6316)

Professional Development. Activities that improve teachers' knowledge of academic subjects, enable teachers to become highly qualified, give teachers and administrators' knowledge and skills so students meet high academic standards, and improve classroom management skills. Professional development is high quality, sustained, intensive, and classroom-focused, has a positive, lasting impact on classroom instruction and the teacher's performance in the classroom; does not include one-day or short-term workshops or conferences. (20 U. S. C. § 7801)

Proficient. Solid academic performance for the grade, demonstrates competence in subject matter. (20 U. S. C. § 6311)

Public School Choice. Students who attend schools identified as in need of improvement have the option to transfer to better performing public schools; districts will provide transportation to these students; priority will be given to low-income students. (20 U. S. C. § 6312)

Pupil Services Personnel. School counselors, school social workers, school psychologists, and other qualified professional personnel who provide assessment, diagnosis, counseling, educational, therapeutic, and other necessary services, including related services, as part of a comprehensive program to meet student needs. (20 U. S. C. § 7801)

Pupil Services. Services provided by pupil services personnel. (20 U. S. C. § 7801)

Reading. A complex system of deriving meaning from print that requires all of the following:
- The skills and knowledge to understand how phonemes, or speech sounds, are connected to print.
- The ability to decode unfamiliar words.
- The ability to read fluently.
- Sufficient background information and vocabulary to foster reading comprehension.
- The development of appropriate active strategies to construct meaning from print.
- The development and maintenance of a motivation to read. (20 U. S. C. § 6368)

Reading First. Grants to states and school districts to establish reading programs for students in kindergarten through grade 3 that are based on scientifically based reading research, to ensure that every student can read at grade level or above not later than the end of grade 3. (20 U. S. C. § 6361)

Restructuring. If, after one full school year of corrective action, a school fails to make adequate yearly progress, the local educational agency shall provide all students with the option to transfer to another public school, make supplemental educational services available to children who remain in the school, and carry out alternative governance arrangements for the school (i.e., replace all or most of the school staff, contract with a private management company to operate the school, turn over the school to the state). (20 U. S. C. § 6316)

School Improvement. A school that fails to make adequate yearly progress (AYP) for two consecutive years. (20 U. S. C. § 6316)

Schoolwide Program. A Title I program that upgrades the educational program of schools where at least 40 percent of children are from low-income families, or at least 40 percent of children enrolled in the school are from such families. (20 USC § 6314)

Scientifically Based Research. Refers to research that applies rigorous, systematic, and objective procedures to obtain reliable, valid knowledge about education activities and programs. Includes research that employs systematic, empirical methods that draw on observation or experiment, involves rigorous data analyses to test hypotheses and justify conclusions, relies on methods that provide reliable and valid data across evaluators and observers, and studies that are accepted by a peer-reviewed journal or approved by a panel of independent experts through rigorous, objective, and scientific review. (20 U. S. C. § 6368)

Screening Reading Assessment. An assessment that is valid, reliable, and based on scientifically based reading research; a **brief** procedure designed as a **first step** in identifying children who may be at high risk for delayed development or academic failure and **in need of further diagnosis** of their need for special services or additional reading instruction. (20 U. S. C. § 6368)

Secondary School. A nonprofit day or residential school, including a public secondary charter school, that provides secondary education, as determined by State law; does not include education beyond grade 12. (20 U. S. C. § 7801)

Secretary. The Secretary of Education. (20 U. S. C. § 7801)

State. The 50 States, the District of Columbia, the Commonwealth of Puerto Rico, and the outlying areas. (20 U. S. C. § 7801)

State Educational Agency (SEA). The agency responsible for State supervision of public elementary schools and secondary schools. (20 U. S. C. § 7801)

Supplemental Educational Services. Means tutoring and other supplemental academic enrichment services that are in addition to instruction provided during the school day and are high quality, research-based, and specifically designed to increase the academic achievement of eligible children on state academic assessments and attain proficiency in meeting the State's academic achievement standards. (20 U. S. C. § 6316)

Targeted Assistance Program. A Title I program that provides services to children who are identified as failing or most at-risk of failing to meet the state's academic achievement standards. (20 U. S. C. 6315)

Teacher Mentoring. Structured guidance and ongoing support for teachers, especially beginning teachers, to help teachers improve their teaching and develop instructional skills; may coaching, classroom observation, team teaching, and reduced teaching loads. (20 U. S. C. § 7801)

Technology. State-of- the-art technology products and services. (20 U. S. C. § 7801)

Title I. Authorizes programs to improve teaching and learning so all children have a fair, equal, and significant opportunity to obtain a high-quality education and reach, at a minimum, proficiency on challenging State academic achievement standards and state academic assessments. Title I reaches about 12.5 million students enrolled in public and private schools. ((20 U. S. C. § 6301)

Transferability. Allows states and school districts to transfer some funds they receive under Federal programs to other programs that effectively address their unique needs. (20 U. S. C. § 7305)

Unsafe School Choice Option. A student who attends a persistently dangerous public school, or has been the victim of a violent crime at school, is allowed to transfer to a safe public school. (20 U. S. C. § 7912)

Vocabulary. Words that students must know to read effectively. (20 U. S. C. § 6368)

BIBLIOGRAPHY

The authors wish to acknowledge and recommend the following references.

Bateman, Barbara and Cynthia Herr. *Writing Measurable IEP Goals and Objectives*. Attainment Company, 2003.

Fisher, Roger and William Ury. *Getting to Yes: Negotiating Agreement without Giving In*. New York: Penguin Books, 1991.

Fisher, Roger and Alan Sharp. *Getting It Done: How to Lead When You're Not in Charge*. New York: Harper Business, 1998.

Hall, Susan and Louisa Moats. *Parenting a Struggling Reader*. Broadway, 2002.

Hettleman, Kalman R. *The Road to Nowhere: The Illusion and Broken Promises of Special Education in the Baltimore City and Other Public School Systems*. (2004) *Available at* www.abell.org/publications/detail.asp?ID=92 (Last visited on June 23, 2005)

Johnson, Scott. *Reexamining Rowley: A New Focus in Special Education Law*. The Beacon: Journal of Special Education Law and Practice, Vol. 2, No. 2 (2003). *Available at* www.harborhouselaw.com/articles/rowley.reexamine.johnson.htm

Levine, Mel. *A Mind at a Time*. New York: Simon & Schuster, 2003.

Mager, Robert F. *Making Instruction Work*. Atlanta: Center for Effective Performance, 1997.

Mager, Robert F. *Goal Analysis*. Atlanta: Center for Effective Performance, 1997.

Mager, Robert F. *Measuring Instructional Results*. Atlanta: Center for Effective Performance, 1997.

Mager, Robert F. *Preparing Instructional Objectives*. Atlanta: Center for Effective P erformance, 1997.

National Research Council. *Scientific Research in Education*. National Academy Press. (2005)

National Research Council. *Preventing Reading Difficulties in Young Children*. National Academy Press.

Pozner, Larry S, and Roger Dodd. *Cross-Examination: Science & Techniques*. Lexis Law, 2004.

Bibliography

President's Commission on Excellence in Special Education. *A New Era: Revitalizing Special Education for Children and their Families*. (2002) *Available at*

www.ed.gov/inits/commissionsboards/whspecialeducation/index.html (Last visited on June 23, 2005)

Shaywitz, Sally. *Overcoming Dyslexia: A New and Complete Science-Based Program for Reading Problems at Any Level*. New York: Knopf, 2003.

Smith, Tom and James R. Patton. *Section 504 and Public Schools: A Practical Guide for Determining Eligibility, Developing Accommodation Plans, and Documenting Compliance*. Pro-Ed, 1998.

Spence, Gerry. *How to Argue and Win Every Time*. New York: St. Martin's Press, 1995.

Twachtman-Cullen, Diane. *How Well Does Your IEP Measure Up? Quality Indicators for Effective Service Delivery*. Starfish Specialty, 2003.

Ury, William. *Getting Past No: Negotiating Your Way from Confrontation to Cooperation*. New York: Bantam Books, 1991.

Weber, Mark. *Special Education Law and Litigation Treatise, 2nd Edition*. Horsham PA: LRP Publications, 2002.

FetaWeb.com

FetaWeb.com is the companion website to the FETA book

How the site is organized -

- Yellow Pages for Kids With Disabilities (Find Information & Support)
- Getting Started (Advocacy & Advocates, Master Plans, Project Manager)
- Advocacy 101 (Rules of Game, Obstacles to Success, Conflict, Crisis)
- Parents as Expert (The File, Learning about Disability, Tests & Measurements, IEP's)
- Special Education Laws (IDEA, Section 504 and ADA, FERPA)
- Tactics & Strategies (Assumptions, Image & Presentation, Letter Writing, Meetings)
- Free Resources "Help Section" (Directories, Appendices, Glossaries of Terms, Free Pubs and much more!)

Start your own FETA support group!

Your FETA group will help parents gain knowledge and skills to be effective advocates for their children. Instead of showing their emotions to school officials, parents can bring their problems to the group and receive guidance about how to handle specific problems.

Learn more from **FetaWeb.com**: http://www.fetaweb.com/feta.group.htm

What you will find on **FetaWeb.com** -

- Articles
- Checklists
- Sample Letters
- Charts
- Resources to supplement the book (FETA Owner's Manual)

Together the **Wrightslaw: From Emotions to Advocacy** book and **FetaWeb.com** will teach you effective advocacy skills. You will learn to recognize pitfalls and avoid mistakes that prevent parents from successfully advocating for their children.

FetaWeb.com! Open 24 Hours a Day, 365 Days a Year!
http://www.fetaweb.com

Special Education is Complicated and Confusing!

What does the law say about -

Evaluations and reevaluations? Test procedures? Eligibility?

Individualized Educational Programs (IEP's) and IEP teams?

IEP goals, objectives, benchmarks?

Placement? Inclusion? Least restrictive environment?

Discipline? Functional behavior assessments? Behavioral intervention plans? Interim alternative placements?

Parent rights and responsibilities? Notice?

Independent educational evaluations? Tuition reimbursement? Mediation? Due Process?

Get Answers to your Questions at Wrightslaw!

Advocacy Library
Articles, Columns & Tips
Advocacy Newsletter
News

Law Library
Statute & Regulations
Cases
Pleadings

Subscribe to The Special Ed Advocate Newsletter

A free weekly electronic newsletter about special education law and advocacy.

http://www.wrightslaw.com/subscribe.htm

Wrightslaw is Ranked #1 by Search Engines in education law, special education law, and special education advocacy.

In 2004:

1.4 million sessions

5.3 million page views

20.4 million hits

VISIT WRIGHTSLAW! OPEN 24 HOURS A DAY, 365 DAYS A YEAR!

http://www.wrightslaw.com